*and Drug*
*Addiction*

# CURRENT REVIEWS IN PSYCHIATRY

*Duncan Raistrick*
MB ChB MRCPsych MPhil
Consultant Psychiatrist, Leeds Addiction Unit

*Robin Davidson*
MSc MSc (Clin Psych)
Top Grade Clinical Psychologist,
Holywell Hospital, County Antrim

# *Alcoholism and Drug Addiction*

*Series Editors*
EUGENE S. PAYKEL AND H. GETHIN MORGAN

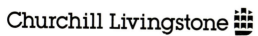
**Churchill Livingstone**
EDINBURGH LONDON MELBOURNE AND NEW YORK 1985

CHURCHILL LIVINGSTONE
Medical Division of Longman Group Limited

Distributed in the United States of America by Churchill
Livingstone Inc., 1560 Broadway, New York, N.Y. 10036,
and by associated companies, branches and representatives
throughout the world.

First published 1985

ISBN 0 443 03092 8

British Library Cataloguing in Publication Data
Raistrick, Duncan
    Alcoholism and drug addiction.——(Current reviews
    in psychiatry, ISSN 0266-5026)
    1. Alcoholism   2. Drug abuse
    I. Title   II. Davidson, Robin   III. Series
    362.2'9     HV5035

Library of Congress Cataloging in Publication Data
Raistrick, D. S.
    Alcoholism and drug addiction.
    (Current reviews in psychiatry,   ISSN 0266-5026)
    Includes index.
    1. Alcoholism.   2. Drug abuse.   I. Davidson,
Robin, M.Sc., M.Sc. (Clin. Psych), ABPS.
II. Title.   III. Series.   [DNLM: 1. Alcoholism.
2. Substance Dependence.   WM 270 R151a]
RC565.R26   1985     616.86'1       85-12782

Printed in Great Britain by
Butler & Tanner Ltd, Frome and London

# Foreword

This is a further volume in the series, Current Reviews in Psychiatry. The scope of psychiatry is wide and the expansion in the base of knowledge in recent years has been impressive. Texts on specific clinical topics need to be written by experts in the relevant field. It is difficult now to encompass psychiatry adequately in a single comprehensive textbook at postgraduate level, while at the same time keeping the edge of scientific advance. It is certainly not possible to do so in a single volume or with a single author.

Current Reviews in Psychiatry offers an alternative approach. Our aims as editors have been to select a single topic for each independent volume. Topics have been chosen for importance to informed postgraduates, including candidates for the MRCPsych, and equally for practising clinicians. Authors are actively engaged in practice, teaching and research in their fields. Each monograph aims to be an authoritative and up-to-date review of current practice and recent developments.

The busy clinician has to meet many time consuming demands; resolutions to allocate time in the library evaporate before other pressures. We believe that a series of succinct, balanced and topical reviews will be welcomed as an effective and easily readable way of presenting recent developments. Individually each book will stand alone; as a series we hope that they will provide manageable personal collections which can be returned to, as easily available reference sources, as the need arises.

LONDON                            EUGENE S. PAYKEL
BRISTOL                        H. GETHIN MORGAN
1985

# *Preface*

It is our hope that this book represents one step in the coming together often mooted by commentators in the addiction field. First, and most fundamentally, it is an attempt to highlight similarities between commonly misused substances in terms of pharmacology, treatment and prevention. The reasons for the separate approach by treatment agencies to drugs and alcohol can be traced to the different values placed on these two groups by society. The use of alcohol is deep-rooted in English culture and, further, alcohol is seen as a relatively safe drug, whereas 'hard' drugs have enjoyed only short periods in vogue before attracting widespread public condemnation and legal control because of their perceived dangerousness. The exception, of course, is cannabis which is widely seen as akin to alcohol as a recreational substance. The different moral and legal issues for practitioners dealing with alcohol and other drug problems are not dissimilar; artificial divisions are encouraged by concern for alcohol problems being given to the DHSS and drugs to the Home Office. In terms of types of user, mode of action, socio-cultural meaning, treatment approaches and many other important variables, common themes pervade and transcend all substance classification systems, not least the alcohol versus other drugs dichotomy.

Second, there is a coming together here of two traditionally competing disciplines, namely psychiatry and psychology. Much has been written, even more said, about multidisciplinary approaches and their special relevance to problems of substance misuse and yet, so frequently, at least in the authors' experience, we find services unable to overcome clannish, sometimes clownish, professionalism. Agreement on the structure of a multidisciplinary team raises many issues, not least political. The authors are not concerned in this text with debating the merits and relative status of any professions or group. We would argue that the existence of some clearly defined system of management is essential for any organisation to function well, but most crucial of all is that services should operate from some resource centre where enthusiasm and energy will be generated and where dominant wisdoms are challenged, developed and, on occasions, attenuated.

Third, there is a possibility of bringing together treatment settings for substance misuse. The authors do not suggest that this is invariably an appropriate step; the size and scope of work of any unit is going to be determined, ideology apart, by the resource available, which in turn is a function of the population being served. In the authors' view, bringing together the treatment of different substance misuse problems in one place brings no reduction in therapist requirements, perhaps the opposite, but there will be savings in non-staff costs and the requirements for support staff. In the authors' experience, mixing alcohol dependent individuals with other drug misusers is generally stimulating both for therapy purposes and for staff interest; there are, of course, problems, but in our view they are no greater than dealing with these people as if their difficulties were quite unique. Whatever the chosen range of activity on any unit, an awareness of the possibilities for 'substance substitution' and spurious satisfaction with outcome figures must be borne in mind.

Finally, we would like to acknowledge the help and support of colleagues, especially the staff of the Leeds Addiction Unit, in shaping our thoughts on some of the issues discussed in this book and facilitating our efforts at committing them to paper. Particular thanks are due to Gillian Tober, who kindly read through earlier manuscripts and made constructive comments, many of which have been incorporated into our final draft. Thanks are also due to Simon Polley, for preparing the index, and to Cathy Jenkin, Jackie Stainer and Jane Coleman for their careful secretarial work. Cathy Jenkin also assisted with the indexing.

Leeds                                          Duncan Raistrick
Antrim                                         Robin Davidson
1985

# Contents

# 1
# *Introduction*

The use of drugs which affect mood and cognition has been a feature of human life in numerous social contexts throughout history and there have inevitably been people whose pattern of use was at odds with contemporary norms and customs. Such individuals have always been at risk of incurring psychological, social and physical harm as a result of misusing psychoactive substances. The prevalence of drug use seems to ebb and flow in the face of social acceptability and availability. While alcohol intake for instance rose during the 1970s it never reached the level of the 19th century. Heroin use increased in the 1960s, levelled out in the 1970s and has begun to increase in the 1980s. Smoking has recently been decreasing in men but increasing amongst women. Generally however, the past 30 years have seen an increase in the prevalence of psychoactive drug consumption. Description of the aetiology, assessment, management and prevention of drug misuse and its consequent problems is complicated by the almost endless permutations generated by the environment/person/drug interaction. Each individual has a different personal and social history making explanations (whether they be in the language of sociology, psychology, physiology or neurology) extensive and interactive. It is axiomatic to say that there is no simple account of the causes and consequences of drug misuse, a theme which will be returned to often in this text.

With increasing awareness of the importance of individual differences there is a current trend away from the imposition of somewhat arbitrary distinctions when considering the various classes of drug. The use of socially acceptable recreational drugs like alcohol or nicotine is dissimilar in some respects from the use of controlled drugs especially when viewed from a sociological

1

perspective and it is important not to lose sight of this. Nevertheless commonalities do exist and there has been considerable cross-fertilisation of ideas between drug and alcohol studies as a result of a more integrated approach. There is now greater concentration on the process of change into and out of addiction and a renewed emphasis on differences in personal histories rather than differences between drugs. As a consequence what Saunders (1983) has called pan-substance study need not lead to broad generalisation and overinclusive research. Miller (1980) has observed the growing trend for addiction behaviours to be seen as one area of study and the W.H.O. (1981) are searching for a common nomenclature and classification. Some overlap occurs between all psychoactive substances liable to be misused in assessment and evaluation, in the theoretical variables employed to explain initiation and maintenance of drinking and drug related behaviour, in clinical phenomena such as relapse and degree of dependence and in methods of treatment.

This text is an attempt to provide an integrative account of alcohol and drug dependence although alcohol and other drugs will be considered separately when appropriate.

Throughout this book the word drug when used in the collective sense will refer to all psychoactive substances, including alcohol, which are likely to be self administered. The present chapter will summarise current views on terminology, dependence and the aetiological factors commonly associated with the development of dependence. First, however, a brief historical note may help place present thinking in perspective.

## Historical perspectives

Towards the end of the 19th century there existed strong organisational links between medical specialists in inebriety, morphinomania and the temperance movement (Berridge & Edwards 1981). The word inebriety covered both alcoholism and drug addiction and so the rediscovery of these links is not something which can be presented *de novo*. This was a time of increasing medicalisation of a variety of problems which had previously been conceptualised in moral or social terms. The medicalisation of alcoholism and drug addiction was part of this process (Scull 1979) although even after the turn of the century the medical literature was still characterised by a strong moral emphasis. Collins (1915) for example described alcoholism and drug addiction as 'examples of the surrender of self control in favour of self indulgence'. The drug and alcohol user was then, and has been since, the subject of different yet overlapping types of regulation, particularly moral, social, legal and medical. For the interested reader there are a number of detailed recent reviews of historical developments in the conceptualisation and regulation of drug and alcohol misuse (Berridge 1984, Levine 1984, Smart 1984). One aspect of this development which is worth considering in some more detail and which can help place current approaches in perspective is the divergence in thinking on alcohol from other psychoactive drugs during the first half of the 20th century. The popular, and indeed scientific view of alcohol during this time seemed to follow a more circuitous path than that of other drugs.

By the end of the 19th century there were numerous temperance groups in Britain and America with the popular view being that alcohol was a dangerous addictive drug much like any other. Anyone given sufficient intake could become an habitual drunkard. The temperance movement recommended abstinence for all and the alcohol misuser was regarded as morally weak willed. By the mid 20th century, public attitude to alcohol misuse had changed. A W.H.O. Expert Committee (1952) considered alcoholism separately and defined it differently from other forms of drug addiction. A variety of influences contributed to this including (i) the experience of prohibition in the U.S.A. (ii) the development of Alcoholics Anonymous (A.A.) and (iii) the work of arguably the most influential alcohologist of all, E. M. Jellinek. During prohibition the hoped for decrease in alcohol related problems and crime did not materialise. The predictions of the temperance movement were seen to be untenable and the U.S. population moved away from the view that alcohol itself was inherently evil or that drinkers were in some way morally weak. The preferred view was that there was nothing wrong either with alcohol per se or most people who drank it (Shaw 1982). The doctrine of A.A. was part of this *zeitgeist*. A.A. was one of a number of self help groups which arose after the repeal of prohibition as part of the post Depression climate of increased concern for human welfare. Their argument was that only a few *allergic* individuals would suffer from the illness of alcoholism and that addiction was a result of a biological predisposition of the user rather than a property of the drug. Alcoholism was said not to be caused by the drug itself but by a response to alcohol among a few vulnerable people. Conversely other psychoactive drugs were popularly regarded as inherently addictive and any individual, given sufficient consumption, could become dependent. The work of Jellinek (1952) was cited by A.A. in support of what has since been termed the disease model of alcoholism. He postulated five species of alcoholism namely:

Alpha: a psychological dependence
Beta: heavy drinking resulting in physical damage
Epsilon: episodic heavy drinking
Gamma: physical dependence accompanied by loss of control
Delta: complete inability to abstain from alcohol for even short periods of time.

It was the latter two species which were regarded as the most common and which were essentially the disease varieties. Although he specified five species Jellinek argued that there could well be very many more and was in a sense predicting the view that was to become more fashionable years later, that there existed a continuum of alcohol dependence ranging from mild to severe. Jellinek also suggested that loss of control did not invariably occur when the alcoholic ingested some alcohol and he emphasised the importance of learning in the acquisition of alcoholism. His ideas therefore, although incorporated by A.A. did not in fact fully support their position.

The suspicion of the temperance movement ideal arising from the aversive experience of prohibition, the pressure of business interests, the development of A.A. and the apparent medicalisation of their view were influential in establishing the disease model of alcoholism. The evidence for this was however more anecdotal than scientific. The main implication was that loss of control, as demonstrated by an irresistible craving for alcohol when some drink had been imbibed, would normally result in continued drinking to the point of complete intoxication among the alcoholic population. Total abstinence for this group was regarded as the only viable treatment goal. The second implication was that once alcoholism had been diagnosed the individual would remain alcoholic despite even years of abstinence.

Since the early 1960s there have been a number of important pieces of research which have questioned these assumptions and heralded a change in the scientific, if not the popular, view of alcoholism. Davies (1962) reported a long term follow up assessment of diagnosed alcoholics which revealed that some had taken up normal drinking, a finding which has been replicated in numerous subsequent surveys (Pattison et al 1977, Polich et al 1981). Longitudinal studies have also demonstrated that people can move in and out of troubled drinking as a response to environmental changes (Clark 1976, Saunders & Kershaw 1979). Furthermore it is increasingly clear that per capita consumption is the most powerful indicator of the prevalence of alcoholism. It is the overall amount drunk by any group which determines the number of alcoholics in the group rather than a predisposition among a particular subgroup (see Chapter 6). Population surveys of drinking practices have confirmed that there is no discreet group of alcoholics but that the distribution is continuous and unimodal (Delint 1976). In the face of such evidence the traditional disease concept of alcoholism has lost credibility over the past 20 years and alcohol is now regarded as having similar properties to all psychoactive drugs capable of misuse. The view that consideration of specific forms of addiction based on the substance of abuse is too narrow (Advisory Council on the Misuse of Drugs 1982) is a salutary reminder that contemporary debate often reflects ideas which have gone before.

## Terminology

In order to conform with current descriptive terminology the material for this account has in the main been drawn from the W.H.O. Memorandum on Nomenclature and Classification of drug and alcohol related problems (1981) as summarised by Edwards et al (1982) and the work of Jaffe (1980) in the Pharmacological Basis of Therapeutics.

## Types of behaviour

The description of behaviour which has been conceptualised as a social problem is complicated by the fact that the same behaviour can be defined differently according to the historical moment and the culture in which it occurs. What is considered deviant in one place or time may on other occasions be seen as socially quite appropriate and there are variations too according to the psychoactive substance used. Occasional intoxication as a result of alcohol drinking for example is socially acceptable in Western countries while occasional use of self administered opioids is not. Alcohol was positively regarded by the population in the 17th and 18th centuries but in the 19th century was seen as a toxic and dangerous substance (Levine 1984). Defining behaviour as illegal is also different from the process of defining behaviour as abnormal in medical or social terms although there is some historical overlap in the development of penal and medical approaches to drug regulation.

### Non medical drug use

This is a collective description of a range of behaviours from occasional use of nicotine to regular use of heroin. It covers *experimental* use as a result of simple curiosity, *recreational use* in which relatively small quantities are used occasionally, *functional use* when certain drug effects are sought as a coping strategy and *compulsive use* when the drug is used in a regular and inflexible way despite adverse consequences. Non medical use describes almost all self administration of drugs and as such is too general to be descriptively useful.

### Drug abuse

This has been defined by a W.H.O. Expert Committee (1969) as 'persistent or sporadic excessive drug use inconsistent with or unrelated to acceptable medical practice'. It is unclear from this definition what constitutes excessive and the term can be employed in a pejorative sense to denote self administration of drugs in a way which does not correspond to the culturally approved medical and social pattern of the time. Furthermore alcohol for instance is not normally used in medical practice therefore in terms of the above definition occasional intoxication would be regarded as abuse. Despite its lack of clarity drug abuse remains a common description of usage somewhere between experimental and compulsive and can apply to behaviours ranging from regular smoking to an accidental barbiturate overdose. In order to clarify the issue the W.H.O. Memorandum suggests that drug abuse can be broken down into four types of use which may well overlap at times.

(i) Unsanctioned use: this refers to the use of a drug which is disapproved of by society.
(ii) Hazardous use: the use of a drug that will probably lead to harmful consequences for the user.

(iii) Dysfunctional use: the use of a drug that is leading to impaired psychological or social functioning of the user.

(iv) Harmful use: use of a drug that is known to have caused tissue damage or mental illness in the particular user.

**Drug misuse**

This term is often used as synonymous with drug abuse although it includes the taking of legitimately prescribed drugs in an unorthodox way, and is also less judgemental than the word *abuse*. There is arguably a need for a shorthand term which despite inevitable limitations takes into account any combination of Hazardous, Dysfunctional and Harmful use. Drug misuse will be employed as such a term in this text and it has the added advantage of being consistent with current legal nomenclature as used in the Misuse of Drugs Act (1971).

## Types of people

The taxonomical approach of categorising individuals according to particular observed behaviour and then going beyond this by assuming an underlying pathology which is amenable to some form of solution has given rise to confusion between diagnosis and classification. Behaviour which is observed and categorised can lead to qualitative distinctions between people who display some of the behaviour and others who do not. This has been a particular problem in the area of drug and alcohol use.

### Alcoholic

The alcoholic is commonly regarded by the drinking population as someone different from themselves in a qualitative sense, mainly on the basis of stereotyped drinking behaviour. Because of this taxonomical anomaly the term has fallen into disfavour in scientific circles although it remains common in popular literature. The implication is that the individual has the condition of *alcoholism*.

In the present text the term alcoholic is used sparingly as a convenient shorthand description of the individual who is moderately or severely dependent on alcohol. The concept of alcoholism has been superseded by *alcohol dependence* which is generally regarded as continuous within the drinking population and as purely descriptive without any implication of underlying pathology. Alcoholism has been used in so many ways that its meaning has become ambiguous and uncertain, although it can still be used in a general and broad sense to describe psychosocial or physical damage as a result of chronic drinking (Edwards 1982).

## Problem drinker

This term has often been employed as a euphemism for those who dislike the implications of the word alcoholic. The term can be used however to describe the individual who behaves in a manner harmful to himself or others as a result of alcohol but whose consumption need not necessarily be excessive. When used in this sense it preserves the distinction between dependence, intake and harm.

## Heavy drinker

This term has been defined as someone who drinks more than the currently accepted safe limit. However, what is regarded as heavy drinking does vary across social contexts and national boundaries. The same individual may be regarded as a light drinker by his catering industry colleagues but a heavy drinker by his fellow church members. Because of the ambiguities inherent in the terms alcoholic, problem or heavy drinker, it is best to use them carefully and only when specifically defined.

## Drug addict

This does not seem to have suffered the same fate as has alcoholic and although it is possible to describe all types of drug users or patterns of use without recourse to the term addict or addiction, they are widely used in the legal and scientific literature. An addict can be defined as someone who exhibits a behavioural pattern of use characterised by overwhelming involvement with the use of a drug, the securing of supply and a high tendency to relapse after withdrawal (Jaffe 1980). Within this definition an addict would be considered as someone who is markedly drug dependent according to current W.H.O. guidelines.

**Problem drug taker**

This term is becoming a fashionable one to describe people who encounter psychological, physical, social and/or legal problems as a result of acute intoxication, excessive consumption or dependence on psychotropic drugs. This definition however excludes those who may be dependent yet problem free, for instance people on regular maintenance prescriptions who may not have experienced problems for many years.

**A drug user**

In the present context, a drug user can be regarded as someone who is involved in the non-medical use of drugs but is not an addict or problem drug-taker according to the above definitions.

## Types of drug

Psychoactive drugs are those which alter mood, cognition and/or behaviour. (See Chapter 2.) Some such drugs notably antidepressants have less reinforcement potential than others and so are less likely to be self administered. The major groups will be summarised here and although the drugs within each group have much in common there are differences in incidence, subjective effect and related behaviour.

### The opioids

These are substances with a morphine-like action and include opium derivatives, or opiates, like heroin, morphine, and codeine. Opium itself is the dried 'milk' of the poppy plant. The group also includes synthetic morphine-like substances common examples being pethidine, methadone and dipipanone. Small doses produce an effect similar to that of the C.N.S. depressants although there is less interference with motor and intellectual processes.

### C.N.S. depressants

This type covers a range of widely used substances, notably alcohol, barbiturates, the cannaboids, the benzodiazepines, and other related sedatives or anxiolytics like glutethimide and methaqualone. Short acting barbiturates and benzodiazepines are more typically preferred by users to their long acting counterparts. The barbiturates are marketed under a wide variety of trade names the most commonly misused being Seconal, Amytal, Tuinal and Nembutal and are particularly dangerous when taken in overdose. Cannabis is derived from the Cannabis Sativa plant whose main psychoactive ingredients are the tetra-cannabinols which are concentrated in the resin found mainly in the flowering tops of the plant. Herbal cannabis comes from the dried leaves or flowers of the plant and contains less of the active substance. Low doses of C.N.S. depressants will make the user feel relaxed and sociable with mild impairment of intellectual functioning and concentration. The effects vary considerably according to the situation and mood of the user.

**C.N.S. stimulants**

In small doses these drugs produce an increased sense of alertness and energy, elevated mood and decreased appetite. The group includes amphetamines, cocaine, caffeine and related drugs. The three forms of amphetamine are amphetamine sulphate, dexamphetamine and methylamphetamine and there are several amphetamine-like preparations such as methylphenidate (Ritalin) and phenmetrazine (Preludin). Cocaine is a white powder derived from the leaves of the Andean coca shrub and although it has a completely different social and legal background to the amphetamine-like drugs, users often find the effects of the two virtually indistinguishable.

**The hallucinogens**

This is a rather misleading description of this group of drugs as the production of hallucinations is only one aspect of their general pharmacological effect and several other classes of drug can also produce hallucinations or illusions accompanied by alteration of mood and thought. What distinguishes this class is their capacity to *reliably* induce altered perception, thought and feeling. Lysergic acid diethylamide (L.S.D.) and mescaline are common examples. The use of so called 'magic mushrooms', whose active ingredient is psilocybin has recently developed in Western countries as an organic alternative to L.S.D.

The volatile solvents can produce effects similar to C.N.S.

depressants, anaesthetics and hallucinogens when their vapour is inhaled. These are carbon based compounds, the use of which is historically particularly subject to the vicissitudes of fashion. The 1970s saw a dramatic increase in the prevalence of *glue sniffing* among young people. This is a generic term covering the use of preparations with hydrocarbon constituents which can have applications not only as solvents in glue, but also in products like nail polish and propellant gases in aerosols or fuel. Chloroform, trichlorethylene and other volatile anaesthetics have also been misused by particularly at risk occupational groups.

## Types of neuroadaptive effect

Neuroadaption has been suggested (Edwards et al 1982) as a term which refers to neuronal changes associated with tolerance and withdrawal effects. The word was introduced into drug parlance in part to circumvent the confusion surrounding the notion of physical dependence.

### Tolerance

Tolerance includes, initial tolerance: 'the sensitivity to a drug of an individual not previously exposed to it' or as it is more normally used, acquired tolerance: 'decreased responsiveness to a drug which has been previously administered'. In the latter sense as tolerance develops increasingly larger amounts of the substance are required to produce the equivalent effect although tolerance to different effects of the drug does not necessarily develop at the same rate. The relationship between pharmacological and psychological factors in the development of tolerance is unclear. For example it will develop more quickly if drug administration occurs in the same environment. It also develops more rapidly for behaviours impaired by the drug but which are important to the individual i.e. tolerance develops more quickly if the effect of the drug incurs some behavioural cost. This suggests that there may be a learning component in its acquisition. Repeated exposure to the cycle of drug administration, withdrawal effects and abstinence tends to accelerate re-acquisition of tolerance. A number of neurophysiological and biochemical explanations of acquired tolerance have been proposed and the body of knowledge is growing rapidly. There may well be several types of neurochemical mechanism underlying tolerance acquisition which could be operating independently or concurrently. Cross tolerance indicates reduced sensitivity to one substance which follows administration of others.

## A withdrawal effect

This is the reaction to sudden absence or reduction of a drug to which the body has become adapted and which can be attenuated by further administration of the drug. The effect is normally opposite to that induced by the drug. Thus amphetamines which can suppress appetite or alleviate fatigue produce hyperphagia and lack of energy on withdrawal. Anxiety, restlessness and decreased seizure threshold can follow withdrawal of C.N.S. depressants and opioid withdrawal symptoms include pupil dilation, restlessness, insomnia and hyperexcitability of spinal reflexes. The time required to produce a withdrawal syndrome depends on the nature of the drug and rate of intake. What constitutes withdrawal and how it is defined also depends to some extent on available technology. It has been demonstrated that by using the opioid antagonist naloxone, a single dose of morphine can produce some clinically significant signs of withdrawal. EEG recordings have shown a sleep rebound effect when a short acting sedative has been discontinued after only a few days use (Kales et al 1978). It is possible therefore that in the case of opioids and C.N.S. depressants particularly, but arguably with all psychoactive substances, that the adaptional processes underlying withdrawal effects on discontinuation can begin with the first dose. Acute withdrawal symptoms generally clear after a number of days abstinence although there is evidence of a longer opioid abstinence syndrome which incorporates psychological and physical symptoms and which can persist for weeks rather than days. Withdrawal symptoms, like tolerance, have a psychological component in that they can be invoked by environmental stimuli after the drug has not been used for some time. Ex-smokers or drinkers often report the subjective experience of minimal withdrawal effects long after they have given up and this has been described as sub-clinical conditioned withdrawal (Wikler 1973).

## Physical dependence

This has traditionally been regarded as an altered physiological state necessitating continued use of the drug to attenuate the withdrawal syndrome. However, the presence of withdrawal symptoms does not invariably produce a subjective desire or craving for continued use. Physical dependence is only one of many variables which contribute to continued drug seeking behaviour. An oft quoted example is the administration of morphine for pain relief when even severe withdrawal effects do not normally lead to a desire for further use. Physical dependence is in this case a misnomer as dependence can only be said to exist if the individual wishes to continue with the drug. Medical patients, even those who self-administer opioids, will typically discontinue drug use when the medical condition has been relieved. Drug taking behaviour is influenced by a range of antecedent cues some of which are psychosocial and others a result of neuroadaptive processes. The distinction between physical and psychological dependence has been to some extent replaced by the view of dependence as a clustering of cognitive, behavioural and physiological events. As outlined in the next section evidence of withdrawal or tolerance effects need not necessarily be the most important criteria in the assessment and description of drug dependence.

## Drug dependence

### A model of drug use

A model is a simple heuristic device more important in the journey of discovery than in justification. Unlike a theory it can even contain assumptions which are false but nevertheless retain its usefulness. The question is not which model is correct but rather, given the present state of knowledge, which gives the best account of the situation. A few decades ago in the light of contemporary knowledge the disease model was appropriate and generated some good management and preventative strategies. Today a more broadly based psychosocial model seems best to explain the initiation and maintenance of drug seeking behaviour. Such a model has been produced by the W.H.O. (1981) and will be outlined below (Fig. 1.1.). It is possible that in the future with increased biochemical sophistication and technological advances a modified disease model will once again become a relevant analogue.

Figure 1.1 is a diagrammatic representation of a model of drug using behaviour which can vary along a range of dimensions including amount consumed, frequency of use, route of

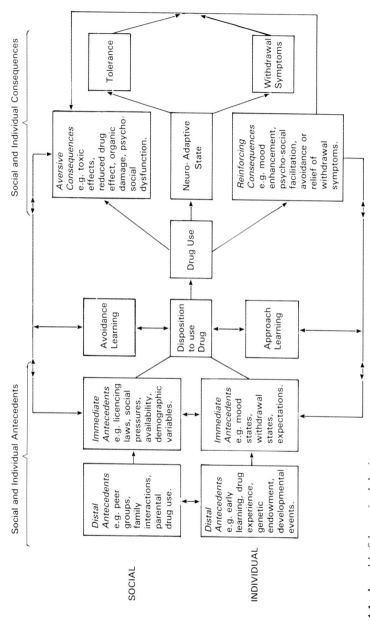

**Fig. 1.1**  A model of drug using behaviour

administration and longer term patterns of use. The observed behaviour, however it is defined, is influenced by cue complexes and actual or expected consequences. Thus particular antecedent cues and reinforcing consequences are seen as initiating and maintaining drug seeking behaviour. The authors have also included what they call distal antecedents to take account of longer term influences on the genesis of drug misuse including early familial background, particular life events, genetic endowment and peer group pressure.

This model demonstrates that causes and effects of drug misuse are multiple and interactive. Other current behavioural approaches do tend to embrace a broader social learning perspective (Miller 1983, Hodgson & Stockwell 1983, Marlatt 1978), emphasising the contribution of individual cognitions to overt behaviour. Expectations, attributions and the outcome of self-evaluation as well as observed cues and consequences can substantially influence drug seeking behaviour.

It is clear however that the majority of commentators accept that the traditional disease model has been superceded by one which articulates the interaction between the individual, environment and drug. Assessment of dependence could be located within this model at a number of stages. One such assessment could be based on the number and nature of antecedent cues which trigger drug use. The number of cues which elicit the behaviour will increase as a result of generalisation and the more dependent user will be more likely to experience the cognitive and physiological cues linked to withdrawal effects (Stockwell et al 1982). Thus appropriate weighting of the antecedents which influence an individual's drug intake could generate a measure of dependence. Degree of dependence could also be said to vary according to the nature of the reinforcing consequences. The mildly dependent user for example, may be more responsive to social approval than the isolated severely dependent person.

It is probably more useful however, as the authors of the W.H.O. Memorandum suggest, to view dependence as part of the whole system thus taking into account the interaction between the psychological and physiological state of the individual in the general context of his environment. The alcohol and drug dependence syndromes are a number of behavioural, physiological and subjective markers which are predicted in part by this model and partly arise from clinical impression. These markers are no more than a concurrence of a set of phenomena which tend to vary and which allow for quantitative assessment of degree of dependence but assume nothing about any underlying pathological process.

## Alcohol dependence syndrome

The outline of alcohol dependence syndrome was provided by the W.H.O. Expert Committee (1977). These ideas were provisionally described by Edwards and Gross (1976) and summarised by Edwards (1977). The notion of alcohol dependence syndrome is arguably the most important and influential development in the field since Jellinek's work (Jellinek 1952, 1960). It is appropriate here to consider alcohol dependence syndrome in some detail for three main reasons. First, it has been around long enough to stimulate considerable informed debate and not a little controversy (Shaw 1982, Heather & Robertson 1983, Chick 1980). Second, as a result of the W.H.O. deliberations the term *alcoholism* has been dropped from the International Classification of Diseases (I.C.D.) and replaced by *alcohol dependence syndrome*. Third, it has given rise to the description of a more broadly based drug dependence syndrome although Edwards et al (1982) comment that it is as yet premature to consider the more general ideas on the classification of drug dependence and drug-related problems for inclusion in the I.C.D.

The word syndrome means a cluster of observations which are seen to covary and it is stressed that each element of the syndrome need not always be present. Alcohol dependence syndrome is described as consisting of seven core elements.

### (i) Narrowing of drinking repertoire

As the individual becomes increasingly dependent he tends to demonstrate less and less variation in his drinking habits. Weekend drinking for example can begin to look like weekday drinking.

### (ii) Salience of drink seeking behaviour

This is an assessment of the degree of importance placed on drinking behaviour at the expense of other erstwhile valued activities such as work and family responsibilities. Other activities tend to become neglected as drinking takes their place.

**(iii) Increased tolerance to alcohol**

Acquired tolerance is seen as an indicator of increasing dependence.

**(iv) Repeated withdrawal symptoms**

The more regularly or heavily drink is consumed the more intrusive withdrawal symptoms become. Although typically these are experienced on waking the dependent individual may experience sub-acute withdrawal symptoms most of the time. The most useful for assessing dependence are more common signs like tremor and sweating. More dramatic effects like the D.T.s or withdrawal seizures are less important in this context as they are relatively rare.

**(v) Relief drinking**

Withdrawal effects can trigger further drinking to relieve them. This normally occurs in the morning and within about half an hour the unpleasant symptoms are considerably relieved. As repeated withdrawal signs indicate increased dependence so it is argued does repeated relief drinking.

**(vi) Subjective awareness of a compulsion to drink**

As dependence develops the individual is said to think more consistently and intensively about drink and drinking. This is to some extent akin to the idea of 'impairment of control'. It is however expressed in cognitive rather than behavioural terms as it has not the flavour of inevitability inherent in the traditional view of 'loss of control'.

**(vii) Reinstatement after abstinence**

Despite periods of even protracted abstinence the dependent individual is said to be more likely to reinstate his old pattern of drinking and rapidly regain his previous level of tolerance. It has been commented (Edwards & Gross 1976) that a syndrome which has taken years to develop can be completely reinstated in as little as three days.

The syndrome consisting of these seven elements is described as a psychophysiological disorder. The presentation of dependence is a result of psychological and physiological influences and is in fact a complex interaction of both. This does not allow therefore for dependence to be described in either psychological or physical terms but is an attempt to assess a motivational system involving components at various levels of reality. In earlier descriptions of the syndrome the authors tended to emphasise the physiological changes namely withdrawal effects and tolerance and the leading symptom was said to be 'impaired control over alcohol intake'. More recently the authors have argued in discussions of drug dependence syndrome that evidence of neuroadaption should not be considered most important and that each of the components should be extensively researched in order to assign a relative weight to each. The syndrome also makes a quantitative rather than qualitative distinction between individual drinkers. There is continuous variation within all the elements and so dependence is not an all-or-none classification but rather a continuum ranging from mild to severe with mild dependence on alcohol being a statistically normal condition.

An important distinction is drawn between alcohol dependence and alcohol related disability. Traditional definitions of alcoholism have often confused dependence and damage and it is emphasised that not all drinkers showing alcohol related damage are necessarily quite dependent. It is, on the other hand, possible for an individual to be markedly dependent and yet not have observable problems. Take for example a publican who begins drinking early in the morning, ostensibly to taste the beer and continues throughout the day till closing time. His drink is bought for him by the customers, he lives on the premises, he never gets very intoxicated, his wife works alongside him and he may not yet have encountered ill health. Under these circumstances he will not have experienced marital, financial, vocational, legal or physical harm and yet possibly be severely alcohol dependent. Conversely acute pancreatitis could cause death after a one off drinking binge in someone who is at worst only mildly dependent. Thus medical and social concern in alcohol treatment and prevention should not be restricted to those who are deemed to be markedly dependent and alcohol related harm should be assessed in its own right.

The alcohol dependence syndrome has been criticized on a number of counts. Shaw (1982) suggests that it is little more than a reaffirmation of the traditional disease model designed to give more credence to the medical practitioner in the field despite repeated emphasis that the syndrome subsumes behavioural and cognitive as well as physiological phenomena. A similar but more substantive criticism has been levelled by Heather and Robertson (1983), who point out that if dependence is continuous within the entire population then it is illogical to describe a specific syndrome no matter how plastic it is declared to be. This they say inevitably indicates an abnormal kind of dependence and object to the assertion that some biological antecedents have been described as abnormal (Edwards & Gross 1976). They say that a disease entity is 'simultaneously being rejected and objectified'. While this qualitative/quantitative argument has some validity, several authors (Madden 1979, Raistrick et al 1983) have suggested that it can to an extent be circumvented by omission of the word syndrome which has unfortunate semantic connotations. A further criticism (Shaw 1979) is that while the psychobiological markers can be empirically justified, the evidence for an altered behavioural or cognitive state remains more tenuous. Small, well controlled descriptive studies, or single case work would add some substance to these clinical observations, particularly in relation to the narrowing of drinking repertoire and salience of drink seeking behaviour. There is also some factor analytic evidence suggesting that the syndrome may not be unidimensional (Chick 1980) although this has not yet been fully replicated. Essentially however the description of alcohol dependence syndrome has provided a framework for debate and research and has been a significant move forward from the more sterile traditional view of alcoholism.

## Drug dependence syndrome

The formulation of alcohol dependence has led to the more general description of drug dependence syndrome and classification of drug related disabilities (W.H.O. Memorandum 1981, Edwards et al 1982). The word drug in this context covers all psychoactive substances which are likely to be self administered including alcohol. The proposed dimensions which identify the syndrome are similar to those already described for alcohol, and include the following.

(i) A subjective awareness of a compulsion to use a drug or drugs usually during attempts to stop or moderate drug use.
(ii) A desire to stop drug use in the face of continued use.
(iii) A relatively stereotyped drug taking habit and a narrowing of repertoire of drug seeking behaviour.

(iv) Evidence of neuroadaption.

(v) Use of the drug to relieve or avoid withdrawal symptoms.

(vi) The salience of drug seeking behaviour over other priorities.

(vii) Rapid reinstatement of the syndrome after a period of abstinence.

The syndrome is described as not being all-or-none but existing in varying degrees. It is seen as separate from more general drug related disability and has cognitive, psychological and physiological components. The syndrome is a clustering of phenomena and all the elements need not be present. The authors suggest that our state of knowledge is such that we cannot weigh or prioritise the syndrome components. They do however go on to define drug dependence as 'a syndrome manifested by a behavioural pattern in which the use of a given psychoactive drug is given a much higher priority than other behaviours which once had a higher value'. This definition would seem to suggest that salience of drug seeking behaviour is now regarded as a leading component and they emphasise that evidence of neuroadaption, while an important criterion, is not sufficient to define drug taking behaviour as dependent.

There are factors which complicate an all embracing description of drug dependence and drug related disability. Inevitably different drugs have different patterns of use and route of administration. Social context varies as do neuroadaptive effects and the prevalence of multi-drug use is increasing. The general description of drug dependence syndrome should be regarded as a heuristic aid to understanding and it is possible that a series of dependence syndromes will be described, one for each class of drug.

Finally, for a complete description of any individual's drug use there should be: (i) a statement of degree of dependence; (ii) an assessment of the nature and extent of harm incurred through drug misuse; (iii) a description of the personal and environmental factors which influence and colour the presentation of dependence and harm.

## Causal influences

Each individual who misuses drugs arrives at that point via an idiosyncratic pathway. The route into addiction involves a process of change with many different influences operating at different points during the process. Some of the longer term individual and social influences referred to above as distal antecedents will be summarised in this section. Individual influences can include constitutional factors and psychological characteristics while the environment takes in familial, peer, community and cultural influences surrounding the individual. Any such distinction is necessarily arbitrary and many different factors can interact to shape an addiction career. It is also important to distinguish those factors which are a cause of drug misuse and those which are correlates.

## Individuals

### Personality

There has been much, perhaps too much, investigation into the so called alcoholic or addictive personality. The search has been for a constellation of personality traits which predispose individuals to drug misuse based on differences in formal self-report personality testing (Nerviano & Gross 1983, Gossop & Eysenck 1980). The major problem with such research lies in the evaluation of which personality anomalies predate drug misuse and which result from it. This search has been unrewarding and most workers now agree that anyone given a particular set of circumstances can become dependent irrespective of personality attributes.

Hofman (1983) argues that the search for an addictive personality is an oversimplification which leads to the use of stereotypes and thus limits rather than increases our understanding of the individual. Rather than isolating personality types or constellations of converging traits, it has been suggested that some specific personality traits occur more frequently in the drug using population. This is however complicated by the fact that the analyst, behavioural psychologist and psychiatrist formulate personality in rather different terms although psychometricians seem to be holding sway at present. Variables which have been associated with drug misuse include anxiety, depression, emotional dependence, non conformity, emotional instability, hypochondriasis, defensiveness, rebelliousness, hostility and locus of control.

The list of traits isolated in a variety of studies as predisposing the individual to alcohol and drug misuse is almost endless. The literature has recently been critically reviewed (Murray et al 1984) and these authors conclude that personality traits are not of much aetiological importance. Description of global differences between drug misusers and others either in terms of personality types or specific traits is less clinically meaningful than thorough assessment of how drug use is functional in the relief of an individual's own intra-personal difficulties.

**Genetics**

The inheritance of alcohol dependence has generated renewed interest over recent years and has been reviewed elsewhere (Cloninger et al 1984, Schuckit 1980). The genetic contribution to dependence on other drugs has received somewhat less attention (Plant 1980, Madden 1979). Data has been derived from animal work, family surveys (Bohman 1978), twin studies (Hrubeck & Omenn 1981), adoption studies (Cloninger et al 1981), genetic markers such as colour blindness and blood groups (Swinson & Madden 1973), and genetic differences in neurophysiological parameters (Propping et al 1981). There are a number of specific difficulties with much research on the genetics of dependence, notably subject numbers, prenatal drug effects and maternal life style. Although much of the evidence is conflicting, it is suggestive that genetic factors, whether the mode of transmission be general or specific, cannot be discounted as part of the aetiological picture of alcohol dependence.

The evidence for other drug dependence is more tenuous. The interpretation of, and importance attached to, such data does however vary from author to author and explanations of some discrepancies in the findings have been reviewed by Gurling et al (1981).

**Learning**

As outlined above, an individual's drug taking behaviour can be understood in terms of his past history of reinforcement. The differential effect of early learning as opposed to constitutional influences is difficult to unravel. Most commentators would agree with Edwards (1982) however that 'parental example is generally more important than parental genes'. Social learning theorists (Hodgson & Stockwell 1983, Hodgson 1984) argue that addictive behaviour is a learned habit acquired through a number of psychological determinants of behaviour, namely antecedents (classical conditioning), consequences (operant conditioning) and mediational influences (cognitions). Numerous social and environmental influences, some of which will be reviewed below, promote the learning of alcohol and drug intake. It must be emphasised that in the main social learning approaches concentrate more on the maintenance rather than genesis and initiation of drug using behaviour; what Cappell (1977) calls a *strategy* rather than an *aetiology* approach.

## Environment

### Family

Patterns of parental drug use and other aspects of parental environment have been linked to prevalence of drug use among their children (Bradshaw 1983, Gorsuch & Butler 1976). The difficulties however in identifying and distinguishing predictors and correlates as well as assessing the strength and direction of familial effects have been discussed elsewhere (Kandel 1978). Most of the work in this area generates data from self-report of children. Vogt (1980) comments that when information is collected from parents on their own behaviour and that of their children the relationship is less clear. He suggests that the important variable is the child's perception of his parents drug using behaviour rather than their actual pattern of use. Pandina & Schuele (1983) have also demonstrated that the relationship between perceived parental environment and what they call *substance use involvement,* is complex. Plant (1980) suggests that it is wrong to assume that drug use is associated with various types of family disruption, particularly early separation from parents although he does report that many drug users in treatment have severely disturbed parents.

Reviews of alcohol surveys of parents and offspring have revealed a general trend towards higher alcohol intake among children of heavy drinking parents (Orford & Harwin 1982). This is true for many other social habits and the trend may mask a variety of parental drinking patterns and a wide variation in effect from child to child. O'Connor (1978) has shown that parental attitude to alcohol rather than behaviour or general family relationships is the main predisposing factor. Like Vogt she suggests that too often information has been gathered from self-report of children rather than simultaneous study of the family unit. O'Connor comments that it is the perception of parental attitudes by children and the influence of pressure from peers which are the two single most important factors regulating future alcohol intake. Despite methodological shortcomings and difficulties of interpretation most authors would agree on the need to understand drug and alcohol use within a family context. There can be little doubt that the child's perception of early familial environment can have a profound impact in the shaping of some addiction careers.

**Peers**

Drug consumption has been described (Schlaadt & Shannon 1982) as constituting on occasions a 'group entry requirement'. The socialisation process of the group can shape and direct a wide variety of behaviour and as the influence of parents wanes that of peer group increases. Madden (1979) lists a number of symbolic aspects of taking alcohol and other drugs including an indication of unity within the group, acceptance within the group and membership of a particular social or occupational class. Deviant or rebellious sub groups can also adopt an unconventional psychoactive substance use pattern as the norm. Plant (1975) in the participant study of drug use in Cheltenham confirmed that drug taking could be regarded as an overt token of commitment to a particular life style. He comments (Plant 1980) that strong social support of peers is needed to convert individuals to the view that certain drug taking is safe, accepted by the group and even prestigious. This process of redefinition will almost invariably run contrary to the establishment view although such a change will be optimised if the individual views his peers as a credible and acceptable reference group. Such a group can direct, at least in part, the individual's self esteem, orientation and view of the world and this direction can include the use of psychoactive drugs especially in those people with strong affiliative needs.

**Sociocultural influences**

The knowledge, beliefs and attitudes which an individual acquires as a member of a society as well as the norms and rules regulating social groups and social relationships can influence his drug taking behaviour. It has been demonstrated that while Jewish and Chinese

Americans have a low incidence of alcoholism, the prevalence rate among the Irish American community is high. Madden (1979) comments that there is strong disapproval of drunkenness in the Jewish and Chinese communities. It has been noted (Malyon 1983) that despite the increase in heroin use in the U.K. during 1981/1982 there was a significant lack of involvement among young West Indians. This was almost certainly due to the well established cultural and spiritual belief that while cannabis is an acceptable and safe intoxicant, heroin is harmful and evil. As would be expected there is a higher incidence of cannabis use in this group. While social controls do offer protection against excessive drug use this will decrease as the individual moves away from their restraining influence or during times of rapid sociocultural change. Leading on from *acceptability* the sociocultural influence on *availability* is perhaps the most critical factor of all and there is little doubt that availability of a drug regulates its consumption. Westermeyer (1981) reviewed several surveys which clearly indicated that opium producing countries such as Pakistan and Thailand, where it is openly available, have a high prevalence rate of addiction. The availability of heroin also contributed to high intake by American servicemen in Vietnam, the vast majority of whom stopped using heroin on their return to the U.S.A. (Robins 1975). The influence of availability of alcohol on consumption is more fully discussed in Chapter 6. In summary, when considering interpersonal factors in the development of drug using behaviour it is important to take into account the interaction of parental, peer and sociocultural influences.

## Towards the future

A characteristic of the addictions literature as demonstrated by the above review is that there can be no simple account of the aetiology, process and treatment of psychoactive substance misuse. Workers from several backgrounds can make a valuable contribution to the knowledge base. Different levels of explanation ranging from the biochemical to the sociological can well account for aspects of drug using behaviour. All too often in the past there has been much sterile debate conducted at the level of interdisciplinary rivalry with workers emphasising the importance of sociological, psychological or biological factors according to their own disciplines' conceptual framework. This has led to what

Miller (1980) termed *aetiological chauvinism*. This has fortunately been changing in recent years with the realisation that any comprehensive account of drug misuse must be multifactorial and incorporate evidence from many traditionally separate subject fields. An increased understanding of the role of endorphins does not negate the aetiological importance of cultural factors or awareness of genetic modes of transmission the effect of cognitive processes. Workers from any particular background should pay more than token attention to what is going on within other disciplines. As Fazey (1977) suggests, there is a continuing need to integrate *vertically* in a field where a number of levels of explanation have a part to play. Drug misuse can only be understood by convergence, rather than divergence, of different perspectives on reality.

Likewise there is a need for a more *longitudinal* view of drug misuse. Study of the effect of one variable at one point in time may mask the continuing dynamic relationship between user, drug and environment. The move into or out of addiction is a process rather than an isolated event. Various inter- and intra-personal influences will operate at different points in this process. What is important is a clearer understanding of the development and nature of the process (Prochaska & DeClemente 1982, Edwards & Busch 1981). Individual case studies which concentrate for example on naturally occurring determinants of change can be just as useful as large group studies comparing the efficacy of particular types of treatment.

The *width* of the field of study is also increasing with more cross fertilisation between work in all classes of psychoactive substances which have the potential for misuse. While the old 'rush to combine alcoholism and drug misuse' criticism (Pittman 1967) has been noted, there is a real need for multidisciplinary research which is not limited to any particular class of drug. Cross cultural studies have demonstrated that legal and social effects can be as important as the direct physiological effects in determining the use of any psychoactive substance. Different drugs can be misused for similar reasons while on the other hand the same drug can be misused for a variety of reasons. Specialists need not work in isolation with increased recognition of commonalities among the addictive behaviours. Not only should there be integration between specialists in different areas of addiction but also increased cooperation among clinicians, researchers and policy makers if legal and social regulation of drug misuse is to be effective.

REFERENCES

Advisory Council on the Misuse of Drugs Report 1982 Treatment and Rehabilitation. HMSO, London
Berridge V 1984 Drugs and social policy: the establishment of drug control in Britain 1900/30. British Journal of Addiction 79: 17-29
Berridge V, Edwards G 1981 Opium and the people. Allen Lane, London
Bohman M 1978 Some genetic aspects of alcoholism and criminality: a population of adoptees. Archives of General Psychiatry 35: 269-276
Bradshaw J 1983 Drug misuse in Ireland 1982/83. The Medical Social Research Board, Dublin
Cappell H 1977 Behavioural analysis of alcoholism. In: Edwards G, Grant M (eds) Alcoholism: new knowledge and responses. Croom Helm, London, Ch 6
Chick J 1980 Is there an undimensional alcohol syndrome? British Journal of Addiction. 75: 265-280
Clark W B 1976 Loss of control, heavy drinking and drinking problems in a longitudinal study. Journal of Studies on Alcohol 37: 1256-1290
Cloninger C R, Bohman M, Sigvardsson S 1981. Inheritance of alcohol abuse: cross-fostering analysis of adopted men. Archives of General Psychiatry 38: 861-869
Cloninger C R, Knorring A L, Sigvardsson S, Bohman M 1984. Gene-environment interaction in the familial relationship of alcoholism, depression and anti-social personality. In: Edwards G, Littleton J (eds) Pharmacological treatments for alcoholism. Croom Helm, London, Methuen, New York, Ch 23
Collins W 1915 The ethics and law of drug and alcohol addiction. British Journal of Inebriety. 13: 131-154
Davies D L 1962 Normal drinking and recovered alcohol addicts. Quarterly Journal of Studies on Alcohol 23: 94-104
Delint J E E 1976 Epidemiological aspects of alcoholism. International Journal of Mental Health 5: 19-51
Edwards G 1977 The alcohol dependence syndrome: usefulness of an idea. In: Edwards G, Grant M (eds) Alcoholism: new knowledge and new responses, Croom Helm, London, Ch 9
Edwards G 1982 The treatment of drinking problems — a guide for the helping professions. Grant McIntyre, Bath
Edwards G, Arif A, Hodgson R 1982 Nomenclature and classification of drug- and alcohol-related problems: a shortened version of a WHO memorandum. British Journal of Addiction 77: 3-20
Edwards G, Busch C 1981 The partnership between research and policy. In: Edwards G, Busch C (eds) Drug problems in Britain: a review of ten years. Academic Press, London, Ch 11
Edwards G, Gross M M 1976 Alcohol dependence: provisional description of a clinical syndrome. British Medical Journal 1: 1058-1061
Fazey C 1977 On the need to reconcile the aetiologies of drug abuse. In: Madden J S, Walker R, Kenyon W H (eds) Alcoholism and drug dependence, a multidisciplinary approach. Plenum Press, New York
Gorsuch R L, Butler M C 1976 Initial drug abuse; a review of predisposing social psychological factors. Psychological Bulletin 83: 120-137
Gossop M R, Eysenck S B G 1980 A further investigation into the personality of drug addicts in treatment. British Journal of Addiction 75: 305-311
Gurling W M, Clifford C A, Murray R M 1981 Genetic contributions to alcohol dependence and its effect on brain function. In: Gedder L, Parisi P, Nance W E (eds) Alan Liss, New York
Heather N, Robertson I 1981 Controlled drinking. Methuen, New York
Heather N, Robertson I 1983 Controlled drinking, 2nd edn, Methuen, New York

28    *Alcoholism and drug addiction*

Hodgson R J 1984 Craving and priming. In: Edwards G, Littleton J (eds) Pharmacological treatments for alcoholism. Croom Helm, London, Methuen, New York

Hodgson R J, Stockwell T R 1983 The theoretical and empirical basis of the alcohol dependence model: a social learning perspective. In: Heather N, Robertson I, Davies P (eds) Alcohol misuse: three crucial questions. Junction Books, London

Hofman F G 1983 A handbook on drug and alcohol abuse, 2nd edn, Oxford University Press, Oxford

Hrubec Z, Omenn G S 1981 Evidence of genetic predisposition to alcoholic cirrhosis and psychosis. Alcoholism 5: 207–215

Jaffe J H 1980 Drug addiction and drug abuse. In: Gilman A G, Goodman L S, Gilman A (eds). The pharmacological basis of therapeutics. MacMillan Publishing Co, Toronto

Jellinek E M 1952 Phases of alcohol addiction. Quarterly Journal of Studies on Alcohol 13: 673–684

Jellinek E M 1960 The disease concept of alcoholism. Hillhouse Press, Newhaven

Kales A, Scharf M B, Kales J D 1978 Rebound insomnia: a new clinical syndrome. Science 201: 1039–1041

Kandel D B 1978 Convergences in prospective longitudinal surveys of drug use in normal populations. In: Kandel D B (ed) Longitudinal research on drug use; empirical findings and methodological issues. Hemisphere, New York

Levine H G 1984 The alcohol problem in America; from temperance to alcoholism. The British Journal of Addiction 79: 109–119

Madden J S 1979 A guide to alcohol and drug dependence. Wright, Bristol

Madden J S 1979 Commentary on Shaw. British Journal of Addiction 74: 349–352

Malyon T 1983 A nation drugged. The Health Services. Times Newspapers, London, p 10–11

Marlatt G A 1978 Craving for alcohol, loss of control and relapse: a cognitive-behavioural analysis. In: Nathan P, Marlatt G A, Lodberg T (eds) Alcoholism: new directions in behavioural research and treatment. Plenum Press, New York

Miller W R 1980 The addictive behaviours. In: Miller W R (ed) The addictive behaviours. Pergamon Press, Oxford, Ch 1

Miller W R 1983 Motivational interviewing with problem drinkers. Behavioural psychotherapy 11: 147–172

Murray R M, Gurling H M D, Bernadt M, Ewusi-Mensah I, Saunders J D, Clifford C A 1984 Do personality and psychiatric disorders predispose to alcoholism? In: Edwards G, Littleton J (eds) Pharmacological treatments for alcoholism. Croom Helm, London, Methuen, New York, Ch 24

Nerviano V J, Gross H W 1983 Personality types of alcoholics on objective inventories: a review. Journal of Studies on Alcohol 44: 837–851

O'Connor J 1978 Young drinkers. Tavistock, London

Orford J, Harwin J 1982 Overview: problems in establishing a family perspective. In: Orford J, Harwin J (eds) Alcohol and the family. Billing & Son Ltd, Guildford, Ch 13

Pandina R J, Schuele J A 1983 Psychosocial correlates of alcohol and drug use of adolescent students and adolescents in treatment. Journal of Studies on Alcohol 44: 950–973

Pattison E N, Sobell M B, Sobell L C 1977 Emerging concepts of alcohol dependence. Springer, New York

Pittman D 1967 The Rush to combine. British Journal of Addiction 62: 337

Plant M A 1975 Drug-takers in an English town. Tavistock, London

Plant M A 1980 Drug taking and prevention: the implications of research for social policy. British Journal of Addiction 75: 245–254

Polich J M, Armor D J, Braiker H B 1981 The course of alcoholism: four years after treatment. Wiley Interscience, New York

Prochaska J O, Di Clemente C C 1982 Transtheoretical therapy toward a more integrated model of change. Psychotherapy: Theory, research and Practice: 19: 276–288

Propping P, Kruger J, Mark N 1981 Genetic predisposition to alcoholism. An EEG study in alcoholics and relatives. Human Genetics 59: 51–59

Raistrick D S, Dunbar G, Davidson R J 1983 Development of a questionnaire to measure alcohol dependence. British Journal of Addiction 78: 89–95

Robins L N 1975 Veterans drug use three years after Vietnam. Department of Psychiatry mimeograph, Washington University

Saunders W M 1982 Prevention. In: Plant M A (ed) Drinking and problem drinking. Junction Books, London, Ch 7

Saunders W M 1983 Alcohol studies and those other addictions: a need for cognizance but not combination. New directions in the study of alcohol 6, p 57–60

Saunders W M, Kershaw P W 1979 Spontaneous remission from alcoholism — a community study. British Journal of Addiction 74: 251–265

Schlaadt R, Shannon D 1982 Drugs of choice: current perspectives on drug use. Prentice-Hall, New Jersey

Schuckit M A 1980 Charting what has changed. In: Edwards G, Grant M (eds) Alcoholism treatment in transition. Croom Helm, London, Ch 4

Scull A 1979 Museums of madness. Allen Lane, London

Shaw S A 1979 Critique of the concept of alcohol dependence syndrome. British Journal of Addiction 74: 339–348

Shaw S A 1982 What is problem drinking? In: Plant M A (ed) Drinking and problem drinking. Junction Books, London, Ch 1

Smart C 1984 Social policy and drug addiction: a critical study of policy development. British Journal of Addiction 79: 31–39

Sobell M B, Schaeffer H H, Mills K C 1972 Differences in baseline drinking behaviour between alcoholic and normal drinkers. Behaviour Research and Therapy 10: 257–267

Stockwell T, Hodgson R J, Rankin H 1982 Alcohol dependence, beliefs and the priming effect. Behaviour Research and Therapy 20: 513–522

Swinson R P, Madden J S 1973 A B O blood groups and A B H substance secretion in alcoholics. Quarterly Journal of Studies on Alcohol 34: 64–70

Vogt I 1980 Mother-child interaction and patterns of drug consumption. In: Madden J S, Walker R, Kenyon W H (eds) Aspects of alcohol and drug dependence. Pitman, Bath

Westermeyer J 1981 Opium availability and the prevalence of addiction in Asia. British Journal of Addiction 76: 85–90

WHO 1952 Expert committee on mental health, alcoholism sub-committee. Technical Report Series, No 48, Geneva

WHO 1969 Expert committee on drug dependence. Technical Report Series, No 407, Geneva

WHO 1977 Alcohol-related disabilities. Offset Publication No 32, Geneva

WHO Memorandum 1981. Bulletin of the World Health Organisation 59: 225–242

Wikler A 1973 Dynamics of drug dependence: implications of a conditioning theory for research and treatment. In: Fischer S, Freedman A M (eds) Opiate Addiction: origin and treatment. Wiley, New York

# 2
# *Drug effects and physical harm*

An obviously essential part of understanding problems of substance misuse is to understand the nature of the substances themselves and how they are used. The rich symbolism and ritual involved in the use of both licit and illicit substances and the psychological consequences of this behaviour are constantly present for all to analyse. The equal richness of material at a biochemical level may only be accessible to basic scientists but should not be neglected by practitioners; there is a crucial need for pharmacologists and biochemists to present their work in a clinical context as much as clinicians need to see their cases at a biochemical level.

This chapter will first consider some general aspects of drug effects and then move on to a catalogued discussion of commonly misused drugs under the following headings:

    i) absorption, metabolism;
    ii) mode of action;
    iii) effects of intoxication;
    iv) withdrawal states;
    v) medical complications.

The range of subheadings is very varied and reflects both the true scope of data and the fact that some drugs have been far more extensively researched than others.

## General factors determining the drug effect
### Pharmacokinetics
Major differences in the effect of compounds belonging to the same group of drugs are created by manipulating the

30

pharmacokinetic properties rather than altering the specific site of action and, similarly, the effects of any single compound vary considerably depending on how it is taken. Mayer et al (1980) discuss pharmacokinetic principles in some detail and Luscombe (1984) has made a very useful review with reference to benzodiazepines. All drugs are subject to a three phased life span in the body (Fig. 2.1) namely absorption, distribution and elimination, and the duration of each phase plays a critical role in determining the overall drug effect.

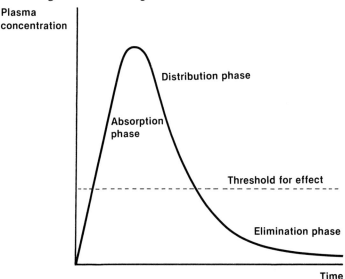

**Plasma concentration**

Distribution phase

Absorption phase

Threshold for effect

Elimination phase

Time

**Fig. 2.1** Pharmacokinetic profile of a drug

The rate at which a psychoactive substance is available to the central nervous system is a factor in the 'buzz', 'high' or 'rush' generated by that substance and therefore a determinant of its addictive properties; clearly an important variable here is route of administration. However, there are significant differences between drugs with a similar mode of action taken by the same route; for example, the benzodiazepine *flunitrazepam* and the opiate *diamorphine* are preferred by addicts to drugs of the same class that are available more slowly, such as the benzodiazepine *oxazepam* or opiate *morphine*.

Following absorption a drug is redistributed throughout the body. The tissue volume into which the drug is redistributed and the affinity of tissues, determined by membrane permeability, lipid solubility and binding to other molecules, will determine how long a single dose of a drug remains centrally active. *Cannabis*, for example, is lipophillic and rapidly dispersed into fatty tissue, whereas alcohol remains in the water soluble compartment of the body.

Elimination may occur by metabolism of a drug to inert breakdown products or active metabolite, and by excretion of the drug unchanged. The elimination phase is usually estimated in terms of half-life ($t\frac{1}{2}$), which is simply the time taken for the concentration of a drug in blood or plasma to fall to half of its original value.

Drugs with a relatively long half-life for their class, such as *chlordiazepoxide, methadone and phenobarbitone*, are particularly suitable for covering the withdrawal of cross-tolerant substances since the gradual reduction of plasma levels minimises the severity of withdrawal symptoms. Caution must be exercised when prescribing drugs with a long half-life to avoid accumulation and toxic plasma concentrations.

## Plasticity

The precise character of any drug will vary, sometimes strikingly, from person to person and for any individual from one occasion to another. Edwards (1974) has described the concept of *pathoplasticity* which refers to the extent that the drug effects can be shaped by external influences; *pathoplasticity* is conceived as varying in degree along a continuum. A drug such as alcohol is somewhere around the middle of this continuum indicating that there are aspects of alcohol intoxication which are fairly constant but other features that depend on the circumstances at the time of drinking. For example drinking because of loneliness is likely to worsen feelings of unhappiness, whereas drinking exactly the same amount of alcohol at a party is likely to facilitate enjoyment. Hallucinogens are highly pathoplastic drugs, which is to say that their effects are very susceptible to outside influences and hence the danger of a 'bad trip' if these drugs are used in unfamiliar or some way threatening circumstances. Stimulants and opioids fall at the opposite end of the spectrum and their use results in very predictable effects no matter the prevailing situation. It is interesting to note an inverse relationship between *pathoplasticity* and *dependence forming potential*.

In a condition of drug-induced arousal or disinhibition, cognitive set will be the critical determinant of the mental state that develops and clearly a positive set is of greater importance the more pathoplastic the drug that is taken. Cognitive set is an obscure and changing entity embracing cognition of the values of society, subcultures within society and beliefs and expectations learned from personal experience. A list of other non-pharmacological factors that have been suggested as influencing drug effects would be extensive and for the most part lacking in supportive evidence. It is the case however, that cognitive set alone cannot account for all the variability of drug effects and observers should always consider the possible contributions of nutritional status, physical health, tolerance and recent drug use, idiosyncrasy and predisposition to psychiatric illness.

## Tolerance and withdrawal

Tolerance and withdrawal are central tenets in most models of alcohol or other drug dependence and the terms are defined and discussed in general form in Chapter 1; in addition to the neuroadaptive and psychological mechanisms of tolerance, enzyme induction may contribute a significant *metabolic tolerance* to the composite picture.

The biochemical relationship between neuroadaptive tolerance and withdrawal has tentatively been unravelled for selected substances and will be discussed for each group of drugs where relevant. Only so called 'physical' withdrawal states are outlined in this chapter; 'psychiatric' disorder precipitated by withdrawal is dealt with in Chapter 3. It is emphasised that the division into 'physical' and 'psychiatric' withdrawal states is quite artificial and based on a separateness of clinical presentation not putative aetiology.

## Adulterants, contaminants and additives

Many serious medical problems arising from the misuse of drugs are caused by agents other than the active substance. Few drugs are taken in pure form and it is usual to make up bulk by mixing drug and filler; illegal drugs are said to have been 'cut' when added to in this way. Unlike preparations from the pharmaceutical industry, no regulations guarantee the nature of filler used for 'street' sales so that users are uncertain about the dose of drug that they are taking and uncertain whether cheap, psychoactive adulterant drugs with their own unwanted effect are included in the filler.

## Complications of injecting

Intravenous use of any drug requires caution to guard against an overdose or idiosyncratic reaction but the two most common problems for drug addicts are injection of infected or irritant material.


**Irritants**

The scarcity on the 'street' of products prepared for i.v. administration necessitates that addicts crush and dissolve tablets or powders for injection. Barbiturate tablets make a solution of high pH which is extremely irritant and the talc filler used in some tablets, notably DF118 and Diconal, is similarly hazardous. Accidently injected into tissues because the vein has been missed, complications such as sterile abscess formation, ulcers, lymphoedema and muscle ischaemia ocur. When injected into blood vessels thrombophlebitis and occlusion of superficial veins is common; accidental injection to an artery, usually the femoral can cause spasm and gangrene requiring amputation (Ghodse 1981). There have been several reports of Diconal causing arterial spasm, particularly mesenteric, even when injected into a vein.


**Infectious material**

Use of unsterile technique, dirty syringes and needles and unsterile water, sometimes taken from toilets, can cause infected abscesses at the injection site or septicaemia.

The habit of sharing syringes allows for the rapid spread of hepatitis B virus among addicts. The virus has an incubation period of 3–5 months. A general malaise with joint pains is usually, though by no means always, followed by the appearance of jaundice. Recovery is usually uneventful with a mortality rate of about 1 per cent and some 5 per cent progressing to a carrier state. Current hepatitis B infection is indicated by the presence of the surface antigen HBsAg (formerly known as Australia Antigen) and post infection and immunity by detection of the antibody anti-HBs. Especially high infectivity is found when tests for the e-antigen, HBeAg, or core antigen HBcAg are positive. Patients suffering from acute hepatitis B infection can be managed at home and require only rest and supportive measures; most deaths occur from fulminating hepatic failure and this complication must be watched for. During HBsAg positive stage, infection can be transmitted by sexual intercourse and by sharing razors, toothbrushes or anything that may be contaminated by blood; all patients should be warned of these risks and carriers must also be told never to give blood. Simple precautions such as wearing plastic gloves and marking all samples 'Biohazard' should be taken when handling blood or body fluids from addicts especially if they are known to be HBsAg positive. At risk staff should be offered innoculation against hepatitis B virus (Tedder 1980).

Non-A non-B hepatitis is a diagnosis of exclusion and is really an umbrella term for any viral hepatitis that is negative for A or B antigens. The agents concerned seem to be similar, as judged by symptomatology and course of illness, to hepatitis B virus.

Acquired Immune Deficiency Syndrome (AIDS) is probably caused by a virus, similar to hepatitis B virus, which can be transmitted sexually, parenterally and perinatally. The eventual mortality rate is virtually 100 per cent but the infectivity of the virus is low and the use of similar precautions to those for hepatitis B will eliminate the risks from handling body fluids (Adler & Weller 1984).

## Alcoholic drinks and congeners

In addition to ethyl alcohol and water, alcoholic drinks contain a whole array of additives known collectively as congeners. Congeners are organic and inorganic compounds including other alcohols, tannins, colouring agents, elements and esters and it is the mix of congeners that gives each drink its particular taste and bouquet. Greizerstein (1981) has shown that wines have a particularly high content of acetaldehyde and methanol. Katlain et al (1970) showed severity of hangover and persistence of psychomotor dysfunction after heavy drinking to be increased in drinks with a high congener content.

## Classification of drug effects

A classification based on the clinical features of each substance is presented in Table 2.1. This is seen as a 'working system' and it is

**Table 2.1**   Classification of commonly misused drugs

---

*Central nervous system stimulants*
  Amphetamines
  Cocaine
  Diethylpropion, fenfluramine, methylphenidate, other appetite
  suppressants
  Bronchodilators and other sympathomimetics

*Central nervous system depressants*
  Ethyl alcohol, methyl alcohol
  Barbiturates
  Benzodiazepines
  Cannabinoids
  Glutethimide, meprobamate, other sedatives
  Dichloralphenazone, chlormethiazole, other hypnotics

*Opioids*
  Morphine, codeine, other naturally occurring opiates
  Diamorphine (heroin), other semi synthetic opiates
  Methadone, dipipanone, pethidine, other opioids

*Hallucinogens*
  LSD, mescaline, psilocybin
  Solvents
  Arylcyclohexylamines (phencyclidine)

---

This classification is based on clinically useful groupings. There is no sharp dividing line between categories: for example alcohol and LSD can both manifest stimulant properties and opioids invariably have CNS depressant effects.

acknowledged that some substances do not fit easily into their assigned category. Cannabis for example is often classified on its own but is included here under CNS Depressants on the grounds of its common usage as a tranquilliser, its cross-tolerance with alcohol and withdrawal state similar to other CNS depressant drugs. Equally solvents and phencyclidine might be placed in individual categories, but are included with Hallucinogens because of their profound effect on perception.

## Central nervous system stimulants

## Amphetamine

Amphetamines are synthetic compounds first used medically in the 1930s and during the war to sustain wakefulness and alertness; they still have medical uses in the treatment of narcolepsy, hyperkinetic disorder in children and occasionally in the management of epilepsy. *Dexamphetamine sulphate* (Dexedrine) is a commercially available preparation for oral use; the more potent *methylamphetamine* (Methedrine) is favoured for i.v. use because of its water solubility. A number of drugs with similar but attenuated action to amphetamine are available as appetite suppressants; most commonly misused of these are *methylphenidate* (Ritalin), *diethylpropion* (Tenuate) and *fenfluramine* (Ponderax). Amphetamines are known as 'speed' when used i.v.

**Mode of action**

Amphetamines have a structure similar to that of the neurotransmitters dopamine and noradrenaline. It is believed that the effects of amphetamine are mediated via displacement of these two transmitters from nerve terminals causing rapid but relatively brief sympathomimetic action.

**Effects of amphetamines**

Amphetamine is effective when taken orally or by i.v. injection. Oral use, 'uppers', tends to be a way to counter the sedative effect of other drugs. Tolerance to amphetamines develops very rapidly and from an initial dose of perhaps 20 mg three times daily a dose of 0.5 g every 2–3 hours can be reached in a matter of weeks. A common pattern of use is to inject large doses for a 'run' of several days. The effects of i.v. injection are a 'buzz' different to that described with opioids and a sense of alertness and physical strength, confidence and sustained mental activity; anorexia and prolonged wakefulness are prominent features. Tachycardia, mydriasis, raised body temperature, sweating and raised BP may also be present.

There have been claims of prolonged sexual intercourse and intensified orgasm, but these are hard to verify. Gossop et al (1974) have found little evidence of sexual dysfunction or enhanced function in oral users. There is evidence however, that amphetamines improve psychomotor performance in sleep derived subjects and they can mitigate against the effects of CNS depressant drugs.

As the dose of amphetamine increases so do toxic side effects appear. These include bruxism, stereotyped behaviour and suspiciousness which may develop into a major psychotic illness (see Chapter 3).

**Withdrawal state**

There has been considerable debate as to whether amphetamine withdrawal is a reality and many clinicians advocate no pharmacological treatment after abrupt cessation of stimulants. Other clinicians recognise a withdrawal syndrome characterised by prolonged sleep lasting 12–24 hours but often disturbed and featuring vivid, unpleasant dreams which can be monitored by measuring the rebound REM that occurs; a disturbed sleep pattern may persist for weeks after withdrawal. Depression of mood with suicidal thoughts is a serious but self-limiting problem of withdrawal and may be of such severity as to require hospitalisation. Other symptoms include extreme hunger, fatigue and lethargy. Symptoms peak at 3–4 days but may persist for months at low intensity.

Management might properly include the use of a hypnotic in mild cases but more logically as hinted at by Gossop et al (1982) a reducing dose of amphetamine would seem appropriate. The danger during withdrawal lies with the depressive symptomatology, nightmare dreams and risk of suicide; clinicians should be alert for an underlying depressive illness.

# Cocaine

Cocaine is a naturally occurring substance found in the leaves of various species of *Erythroxylon* but particularly in *Erythroxylon coca*. The trees are indigenous to Peru and Bolivia where cocaine assumes a major role in national economies. Cocaine is still used medically to induce local anaesthesia.

**Mode of action and metabolism**

Chemically cocaine is related to local anaesthetic drugs and it is thought that one of its actions is to block nerve conduction along certain, presumably central and inhibiting nerve fibres. Unlike other local anaesthetics, cocaine blocks the uptake of noradrenalin potentiating sympathetic nervous system activity and possibly central effects. Rapid absorption occurs from any mucous membrane and is enhanced by inflammation. Cocaine has a half-life of approximately 1 hour.

**Effects of cocaine**

Cocaine is a white powder usually 'snorted' in doses of 10-30 mg; the powder which may be 'cut' with procaine is set out in thin lines of a single dose which is then 'snorted' through a straw or rolled paper. The dose of cocaine can be increased by free-basing, a process that releases pure cocaine from the hydrochloride salt without loss of the active drug.

Whether or not tolerance to cocaine develops in the same way as with amphetamine remains an issue of debate. It is the case that on a 'run' 500-1000 mg may be snorted in a day and the psychological effects decay more rapidly than do plasma levels suggesting an acute tolerance. However, it has been noted that cocaine is rapidly metabolised and so high doses may be required to maintain active blood levels; also noted is that after long periods of abstinence cocaine users can, without harmful effects, revert to previous high levels of intake.

Except for the shorter duration the effects of cocaine intoxication are not readily distinguished from amphetamine intoxication, although some users have described such heightened euphoria with cocaine that any activity other than taking more cocaine is purposeless and therefore the over-activity characteristic of amphetamine use is not always seen.

**Withdrawal states**

Given the uncertainties about the development of tolerance to cocaine it is not surprising to find no clear description of cocaine withdrawal. Certainly the 'crash' an hour or so after taking cocaine is characterised by a marked dysphoria and craving for more drug. As with amphetamine withdrawal, depressive symptoms may be severe.

**Medical complications of sympathomimetics — amphetamine and cocaine**

**Cardiovascular system** Sympathetic stimulation causes vasoconstriction and tachycardia which may result in sudden elevation of blood pressure and increase the risk of cerebral haemorrhage. Hypertensive crises are sometimes a consequence of taking other pressor agents eg MAOs or inhalers, concurrently. Perforation of the nasal septum is a rare complication caused by local vasoconstriction and tissue atrophy.

**Temperature regulation** Cocaine is thought to have a central effect disrupting temperature control and the problem is compounded by additional body heat being produced by overactivity and heat loss reduced by peripheral vasoconstriction. Cooling with ice packs may be necessary.

**Malnutrition** Prolonged use of stimulant drugs will frequently be associated with severe nutritional deficits and weight loss. High protein diet and vitamin supplements are required.

**Sudden death** Sudden death may occur from cardiac arrhythmias, direct cardiotoxicity of stimulants or status epilepticus. There are several reports of sudden deaths from overdoses of cocaine in 'mules', that is, individuals smuggling cocaine in balloons or condoms that were swallowed to avoid customs detection but ruptured in passage, McCarron (1983).

**Reproduction** There have been unconfirmed reports of biliary atresia and heart defects in the offspring of amphetamine addicts. Women who use amphetamines throughout pregnancy have been noted to have an increased perinatal mortality rate and post-partum complications (Erikson et al 1981).

## Central nervous system depressants

Drugs that depress the central nervous system are very extensively prescribed as hypnotics and for the treatment of anxiety; they are also used for recreational purposes and, in social situations alcohol and marijuana enjoy popularity far ahead of their nearest rivals. All of this group of drugs have dependence forming potential (see Chapter 1) and all are prone to misuse as a universal solution for coping with difficult life situations. It is common for addicts to use CNS depressants to counteract the effects of stimulants or to potentiate the intoxication induced by another drug.

All CNS depressants have a disinhibiting effect which is often mistaken by lay people to indicate a stimulant action, although there may be transient stimulant effects. The most sophisticated cortical functions are impaired first so that thoughts become disorganised, motor functions, especially learned ones become uncoordinated and moods become labile. As the blood concentration of the drug increases so there is further depression of brain function until coma and possibly death occur. Just as the symptoms of intoxication for all this group of drugs are very similar, so too are the withdrawal states although the different pharmacokinetics of each substance cause considerable variation in the timescale of withdrawal. The modes of action and toxicity vary widely.

## Ethyl alcohol

Alcohol has been known to man for as long as man is known to have existed. Fermentation is the process whereby naturally occurring sugars are converted to carbon dioxide and ethyl alcohol in the presence of yeast fungi; the maximum alcohol concentration from this process is 10–12 per cent because at higher concentration the yeast is killed. It is said that the art of distillation and therein the ability to produce much stronger drinks was discovered about 800 AD.

### Absorption and metabolism

Alcohol is absorbed from the stomach, small intestine and colon and absorption is complete within 30 min to 3 hours, the time depending on a number of variables. Absorption is most rapid for alcohol concentrations in the 10–20 per cent range, for carbonated drinks and when there is rapid emptying of the stomach since absorption from the small intestine is very rapid and largely independent of other factors, such as the presence of food that slows gastric absorption. Post gastrectomy patients become intoxicated very quickly and women, especially premenstrually, have high absorption rates with peak BAC 35–45 per cent higher than men taking the same amount of alcohol. Alcohol is much more soluble in water than fat so that distribution throughout the fatty tissues lags behind concentrations achieved in the water soluble compartments.

Over 90 per cent of alcohol absorbed in the body is oxidised in the liver, the balance being excreted via the lungs and kidney. The rate of metabolism varies according to normal liver function, previous exposure to alcohol and liver mass, which depends on body size, but the average rate is approx 10 g per hour. The principal metabolic pathway utilises the zinc containing enzyme alcohol dehydrogenase (ADH) which converts ethanol to acetaldehyde using nicotinamide adenine dinucleotide (NAD) for the transfer of hydrogen so converting NAD to its reduced state NADH. Acetaldehyde is oxidised to acetate by aldehyde dehydrogenase. The excess of NADH caused by ethanol metabolism shifts the so called 'redox state' of the liver towards the reduced condition which in turn has important effects on the direction of a number of hepatic metabolic processes such as increased production of lactic acid with secondary hyperuricaemia, interference with amine, including neurotransmitter metabolism, impaired oxidation of fatty acids, impaired gluconeogenesis and bias towards reduced steroid compounds.

There are a number of different forms of ADH with different in vivo activity, but, unless there is serious damage to liver tissue, it is thought that the capacity to reoxidise NADH to NAD is the rate limiting factor of alcohol metabolism. In theory reoxidation of NADH can be accelerated by fructose but to achieve significant change in the rate of alcohol metabolism, huge amounts, 1–2 gm per kg body weight are required.

There are two non-ADH pathways for oxidising ethyl alcohol and between them it has been estimated, by using ADH inhibitors that they may account for up to 50 per cent of total ethanol metabolism, but the contributions depend on alcohol concentration and chronic exposure to alcohol (Matsuyuki et al 1981). The lesser of the two systems is a catalase which is peroxide dependent and accounts for no more than 2 per cent of total ethanol oxidation; the more significant system is known as the mitochondrial enzyme oxidising system (MEOS). It is the MEOS and not an increase in ADH activity that accounts for the metabolic aspect of tolerance that develops in regular drinkers.

The phenomenon of 'swift increase in alcohol metabolism' (SIAM) is well established but apparently does not occur in all individuals. The mechanism results in increased reoxidation of NADH and probably sudden release of adrenalin is in some way responsible. Lieber (1982) has made a detailed review of the metabolism of ethanol.

Alcohol is a general anaesthetic and like other drugs of that class is lipid soluble and exerts its action through entering the cell membrane; there are no specific binding sites or receptors. Alcohol interacts with phospholipid in the cell membrane and it is thought that intoxication is the result of inhibiting pre-synaptic neurotransmitter release; there are also post-synaptic effects but these seem highly complex and difficult to interpret. Littleton (1984) has proposed mechanisms at a biochemical level that can account for and differentiate between tolerance and dependence to alcohol. By dependence he refers to the manifestation of withdrawal symptoms. In essence the schema suggest that tolerance is brought about by changes in the structure of the lipid fraction of cell membranes when repeatedly exposed to alcohol; these changes make the membrane resistant to entry by alcohol and therefore resistant to disruption of neurotransmitter release. Littleton refers to this kind of tolerance as decremental because it simply resists increasing doses of the drug. Suppose however, decremental tolerance is insufficient to maintain homeostasis, then it would be possible that another kind of tolerance came into play and there is evidence that this actually happens in the form of increased sensitivity to neurotransmitter release in response to $Ca^{2+}$ influx at the presynaptic site. Littleton has called this oppositional tolerance because it involves active opposite effects to those of alcohol. If this system has any irreversibility, then on withdrawal of alcohol there will be an overshoot of neurotransmitter release which is manifest as withdrawal (or dependence).

## Effects of ethyl alcohol

The effects of ethyl alcohol intoxication are well known and they are more pronounced with a rising rather than a falling BAC. Most individuals start to show some disinhibition and mild impairment of motor function at a BAC less than 50 mg per cent, they may become talkative, feel more confident and become overactive. At blood alcohol levels between 100–200 mg per cent impaired judgement, gross motor impairment and aggressive or withdrawn behaviour can be expected and coma or death from respiratory depression are likely at levels of 400–600 mg per cent. There is considerable individual variation of response to alcohol depending substantially on the development of tolerance; a BAC of 480 mg per cent has been reported in a 35-year-old male who showed no signs of intoxication (Wakasugi et al 1976).

Modest amounts of alcohol have a number of physical effects on novice and regular drinkers alike. An initial warm feeling is followed by a fall in body temperature because of peripheral vasodilation and increased sweating. Beverages of approximately 15 per cent cause an acidic gastric secretion, whereas stronger drinks are irritant and inhibit secretions. Suppression of anti-diuretic hormone release causes a diuresis over and above excretions of any large intake of fluid and finally, sexual enjoyment may be diminished because of a reduction in penile tumescence and vaginal engorgement (Wilson 1984).

**Alcohol withdrawal states**

The exact mechanisms involved in the appearance of withdrawal symptoms await clarification. However, at a biochemical level the proposals argued for by Littleton (1984) that a regular intake of alcohol causes cellular adaptation in such a way as to increase cellular activity and therefore cause over-activity on withdrawal are convincing. If it is also the case that cell membranes can be permanently altered then this may offer an explanation for clinically observed phenomena such as persistent potential for symptoms after long periods of abstinence and reinstatement of dependence.

The manifestation of withdrawal symptoms does not require total abstinence; Mello and Mendleson (1977) have stated that a fall in BAC of 100 mg per cent from whatever level will precipitate a withdrawal syndrome. It is thought that the most severe withdrawals occur when a binge is superimposed on a high baseline level of consumption and it is for this reason that, contrary to popular belief, the vagrant population do not generally experience severe problems on detoxification (Hore 1980). The global nature of cerebral dysfunction during withdrawal has been suggested by Berglund and Risberg (1981) who found a 19 per cent decrease in cerebral blood flow during the first two days; the reduction in flow correlated with length of previous drinking bout but there were no significant regional variations to associate with symptoms.

The most common withdrawal syndrome, usually referred to as the *Tremulous State*, has its onset a matter of hours after ceasing or reducing intake. Although tremor is one of the most common features of this state there are many other symptoms and it is particularly important to recognise disturbance of mood as part of withdrawal since dysphoria frequently antedates the physical manifestation. Hershon (1977) has drawn attention to the very wide range of symptoms attributed to withdrawal. He differentiates between those symptoms that occur most commonly during withdrawal (though are not necessarily part of withdrawal) such as depression, anxiety, tiredness, craving and those symptoms that are most specific of withdrawal such as body and hand shakes, panics, can't face the day and guilt.

Disturbance of sleep is accompanied by an increase in REM sleep and vivid dreams, with hypnagogic and hypnopompic hallucinations; these hallucinations often take the form of seeing a person by the bed or seeing the pattern on wallpaper distort and turn into an object. Edwards (1982) has described a *Transient Hallucinatory State* which may be auditory, such as hearing someone call or visual such as seeing a rat move across the floor. Withdrawal seizures occur within 12–36 hours of reduced intake, usually in runs of 3–4 but sometimes in isolation. The risk of seizures is greatly increased in cases of polydrug abuse. The hallucinatory phenomena are thought to be continuous with Alcoholic Delirium (DTs) and about one-third of patients experiencing seizures develop this serious condition (see Chapter 3). Any history suggestive of the onset of DTs is an indication for hospitalisation.

The management of withdrawal is usually straightforward. The severity of symptoms peaks at 24–48 hours; if withdrawal is not complete within 5–7 days then some coexisting condition must be suspected. Major tranquillisers have no place in the routine treatment of withdrawal and *chlormethiazale* (Heminevrin) although an effective agent to cover withdrawal (McGareth 1975) has itself dependence forming potential (Reilly 1976) and should be reserved for hospitalised patients. A minor tranquilliser is the drug of choice for the tremulous state. *Chlordiazepoxide* (Librium), which has $t\frac{1}{2}$ of 12 hours has proven efficacy and sparing side effects; the dose may be as high as 50 mg qds. There is evidence that *clobazam* (Frisium) with a $t\frac{1}{2}$ of 18 hours, is superior to *chlordiazepoxide* in reducing withdrawal anxiety and improving sleep (Mukherjee 1983); doses up to 20 mg qds seem to be effective for severe withdrawal.

**Medical complications**

It is certain that not all of the toxic effects attributed to alcoholic drink are to do with ethyl alcohol but rather its metabolites acetaldehyde and acetate. Alcohol suppresses the metabolism of acetaldehyde and it has been shown that alcoholics have higher levels of acetaldehyde than non-alcoholics after receiving a standard dose of ethanol; this effect may be partially due to genetic factors. Many tissues are affected by acetaldehyde and acetate but the clinical implications are yet to be determined (Lieber 1982).

Some of the medical complications of alcohol abuse are related to the beverage consumed; for example gastritis and vitamin deficiency are more likely to occur among spirit drinkers than beer drinkers and iron accumulation is more likely in wine drinkers. For the most part, however, the medical consequences depend on the total amount of alcohol consumed. Beer contains 4–7 per cent alcohol by volume, wine 10–20 per cent and spirits 40–60 per cent. This raises the vexed question of safe levels of intake. Any figure is somewhat arbitrary but a generally accepted safe level is 80 g of alcohol daily for males and 50 g daily for females.

## Liver disease

The link between per capita alcohol consumption and liver cirrhosis is well established. It has been estimated that the risk of cirrhosis increases five times at a consumption of 80–160 g per day for men, somewhat less for women; the type of beverage and pattern of consumption are of minor importance. Wodak et al, (1983) have shown that patients who develop chronic alcoholic liver disease are usually only mildly dependent on alcohol and they suggest that the more dependent drinker will experience problems taking him into treatment earlier or will spontaneously modify drinking behaviour. Davis (1980) and Lieber (1982) have reviewed the literature on alcoholic liver disease.

**Fatty infiltration** of the liver is generally considered a reversible condition that can arise in anyone indulging in a drinking spree. Fatty liver is usually asymptomatic but in most cases there will be hepatomegaly and modest elevation of liver enzymes. Occasional deaths from fat embolism have been reported. Rarely there may be associated hyperlipidaemia, haemolysis, anaemia and jaundice; this triad is called Zieve's syndrome.

**Alcoholic hepatitis** arises in about one third of heavy drinkers, is recognised by inflammation and necrosis, and hyaline bodies are diagnostic if present. The severity of hepatitis varies from a mild anicteric malaise to a very serious illness characterised by anorexia, high fever, right hypochondrial pain, jaundice and liver failure; there is a mortality rate of 2–30 per cent. Liver enzymes are invariably raised, there may be hyperbilirubinaemia, and a low albumin; extended prothrombin time is associated with a poor prognosis.

**Alcoholic cirrhosis** is a diagnosis that must be based on histological examination. Initially there is a micronodular picture with fibrosis but later this becomes macronodular and difficult to differentiate from other causes of cirrhosis. Portal hypertension with splenomegaly, ascites and varices are secondary developments. Other stigmata of chronic liver disease are variably represented in the clinical picture. Liver enzymes are slightly raised, glucose tolerance is impaired; raised bilirubin and low albumin are poor prognostic indicators. In uncomplicated cases the 5-year survival rate for non-abstaining males is 60–70 per cent, and for women about half that. Abstention from alcohol does not invariably improve survival rates, especially not in women.

In a prospective study of 258 males who misused alcohol, Sorensen et al (1984) found 2 per cent of cases per year developed cirrhosis; the risk was unrelated to duration of misuse or intake prior to initial assessment but was increased if biopsy at assessment showed steatosis or hepatitis, or if bilirubin, AST or bromsulphthalein retention were increased.

The pathogenesis of liver cirrhosis remains somewhat unclear. It seems probable that direct toxic effects of alcohol, its metabolites or congeners in alcoholic drinks alter the hepatocyte membranes rendering them antigenically foreign; immunological mechanisms perpetuate damage. Nutritional factors play only a small part and adequate diet is not a protection against liver disease. The predominance of HLA-B5 and absence of HLA-A28 reported in some studies of patients with hepatitis and cirrhosis suggested a genetic factor but more recently association between HLA antigen states and alcohol-induced cirrhosis has been questioned (Faizallah et al 1983). Hepatoma is reported in association with liver cirrhosis.

## Cardiovascular system

There are many factors but in particular smoking and lifestyle that confuse the investigation of the relationship between alcohol consumption and heart disease. Wodak and Richardson (1982) have made a review of this area and conclude that cardiovascular damage is associated with persistent heavy drinking and rarely with acute intoxication or binge drinking.

**Ischaemic heart disease** is a very common cause of death in Western societies and the evidence for alcohol as an aetiological agent is conflicting. Some studies suggest that moderate drinking rather than abstinence or heavy drinking may protect the coronary arteries from atheroma, possibly by increasing high density lipoproteins that accelerate elimination of cholesterol.

**Cardiac Arrhythmias** may be induced by acute intoxication or alcohol withdrawal and may be fatal when there is already a diseased heart.

**Alcoholic heart muscle disease** formerly known as cardio-myopathy is a common disorder which is often unrecognised. The presentation is usually of increasing dyspnoea with signs of an enlarged heart, dysrhythmia and later cardiac failure.

## Gastrointestinal tract

Alcohol has a direct effect on the integrity of the oesophageal and gastric mucosae causing inflammation and symptoms of nausea, retching and vomiting with gastric reflux. Constant retching may tear the lower oesophagus producing the Mallory–Weiss syndrome. Although peptic ulceration is associated with heavy drinking, alcohol taken orally does not increase gastric secretions and is not thought to be a causal agent. Lieber (1982) reporting on various endoscopic studies, notes upper gastrointestinal bleeding to have varied sites in 'alcoholics': 15–25 per cent gastritis, 15–19 per cent varices, peptic ulcer 21–24 per cent and oesophagitis 7 per cent. The incidence of cancer of the pharynx, larynx and oesophagus is increased in alcoholics.

The effect of alcohol on the small intestine is complicated and an interaction between local mucosal damage and disruption of active transport systems, dysfunction in other organs and diarrhoea. The end picture is one of malabsorption of some vitamins, notably thiamin, folate, B12 and some elements such as calcium and magnesium.

**Pancreatitis** typically presents with severe upper abdominal pain radiating to the back; there may be vomiting, dehydration and shock. There is a mortality rate of up to 30 per cent depending on the severity of the attack. Alcohol induced pancreatitis usually occurs after a binge in someone with a regular baseline intake. An acute attack may progress to the chronic intermittent form of pancreatitis where complications of pancreatic dysfunction notably diabetes and malabsorption, dominate the clinical picture. Dependence on powerful analgesics often opioids, taken to relieve constant pain of chronic pancreatitis has been reported. Although an elevated serum amylase is commonly found in alcoholics without pancreatitis the reasons are not yet known.

## Musculo-skeletal system

Acute alcoholic myopathy is a rare condition characterised by sudden swelling and pain in one or several proximal muscle groups; there may be accompanying myoglobinuria of sufficient severity to cause renal failure. Much less common are subacute and chronic myopathies which typically affect the distal limb muscles and are probably neurogenic in origin (Hudgson 1984).

The evidence suggests that gout does not arise secondary to the hyperuricaemia induced by alcohol consumption but it is the case that attacks of gout will be aggravated by alcohol in those individuals already suffering from the disease. Alcoholics have been noted to have less bone density than normal and therefore to be susceptible to fractures from relatively minor injury. The exact mechanisms are not clear but are thought to be connected with hypocalcaemia and failure to respond to parathormone because of magnesium deficiency (Parsons & Cundy 1981).

**Nervous system**

**Peripheral neuropathy** is thought to be a common disorder affecting some 20 per cent of 'alcoholic' patients presenting for treatment. It is usually asymptomatic and the only clinical findings are absent ankle jerks and diminished sensation usually in the lower limbs. In more severe cases patients spontaneously complain of parasthesiae, weakness and sometimes a burning sensation under the feet. The neuropathy is caused by a direct toxic effect of alcohol on the peripheral nerves and is worsened by deficiency of the B vitamins.

**Cerebellar degeneration** is probably a more frequent consequence of alcohol misuse than is commonly recognised and is likely to coexist with other nervous system damage so that cerebellar signs may be mistaken for other disorders.

**Alcohol induced amblyopia** is a rare condition where the patient usually complains of blurred vision. Examination reveals a pale or inflamed optic disc and central scotoma.

**Endocrine system**

**Pseudo-Cushing's syndrome** can be induced by chronic alcohol intake. Patients have the classical symptoms of the disease notably obesity, menstrual irregularity and hirsutism in the female, impotence in the male, weakness, bruising, hypertension and an abnormal response to the dexamethasone suppression test.

**Sex hormone** balance is disrupted in male 'alcoholics' though the clinical significance remains unclear. Testicular production of testosterone is reduced and there is an increased elimination of the hormone. If liver disease is present there is also an increase in conversion of androgenic precursors to oestrogens which are thought to be responsible for the feminisation seen in male cirrhotics.

**Glucose regulation** is affected in a number of ways by alcohol consumption; a) 'fasting hypoglycaemia' occurs in a fasting or malnourished individual some 6–36 hours after drinking; typically the BAC is < 100 mg per cent and hypothermia is common. The cause is thought to be inhibition of gluconeogenesis by alcohol and there is a mortality rate of 10–20 per cent; b) 'reactive hypoglycaemia' may occur in both 'alcoholics' and 'normal' volunteers 3–5 hours after drinking alcohol and carbohydrate together as for example in a gin and tonic. The cause is thought to be an *excessive* output of insulin in the presence of alcohol and insulin releasing sugars; c) 'potentiated hypoglycaemia' occurs in patients taking oral hypoglycaemics and is caused by a failure to mobilise glucose from the liver. The cause is not known. The condition can be fatal (Marks 1977).

**Teratogenicity**

The fetal alcohol syndrome was independently described by workers in France and the United States as a triad of features comprising pre- and post-natal growth deficiency, especially girth, mental retardation and malformations. Common manifestations are dislocated hip joints, cleft palate heart defects, genito-urinary defects; the typical facies comprises microcephaly, flattened face, small eye sockets leaving white around the eyes, and shortened palpebral fissure.

Randall (1984) has concluded that ethanol is undoubtedly teratogenic but whether the mechanism of action is direct, mediated via effects on the mother or through the metabolite acetaldehyde is yet to be resolved. It appears that nutritional factors may aggravate but not cause the fetal alcohol syndrome.

The question arises as to what might be a safe amount to drink during pregnancy and again there are conflicting views among the experts who either see the problem of the fetal alcohol syndrome to be over-estimated or those who see serious risks in drinking anything at all during pregnancy; no doubt common sense moderation will prove an acceptable course (British Medical Journal Editorial 1983). Pratt (1981) has calculated that for every 15 g of alcohol consumed *daily* during pregnancy the risk of the baby having some anomaly increases by about 2.5 per cent.

**Acute overdose**

Acute poisoning from alcohol is most common in novice drinkers. Stupor and coma can be expected at BAC in the range of 300–400 mg per cent, that is the equivalent of approximately ¾ of a bottle of spirits. Neurological signs include hyporeflexia, respiratory depression, hypothermia and hypotension. It is important to establish the correct diagnosis and in particular consider head injury, diabetic coma, drug induced coma; treatment requires only simple supportive measures as for other CNS depressants and recovery is usually uneventful.

## Methyl alcohol

Methyl alcohol is used as an industrial solvent and is normally denatured in some way to prevent human consumption. Since there is no tax on methanol it has particular appeal to the vagrant population.

**Absorption and metabolism**

Methyl alcohol is rapidly absorbed and distributed through the body tissues. It is eliminated by oxidation to formaldehyde and formic acid in the liver and kidneys; the rate of oxidation is only 1–2 g per hour and this is reduced further in the presence of ethanol.

Methanol is fairly ineffective as an intoxicant unless taken with other substances such as ethanol.

**Medical complications**

**Acute poisoning** by methyl alcohol has serious consequences caused mainly by the metabolites; formaldehyde is toxic to retinal cells, and formic acid produces a severe acidosis. Ethyl alcohol slows the metabolism of methanol and therefore the rate of production of metabolites and so is protective against poisoning.

Symptoms may be delayed 12 hours or more after ingestion and include weakness, headache, vomiting and excitement passing on to coma. Papilloedema and blindness may be caused by small amounts of methanol and 80–150 ml is usually fatal. Treatment should include usual supportive measures, correction of acidosis and maintenance of a blood ethyl alcohol level of approximately 100 mg per cent (Lancet Editorial 1978).

## Barbiturates

The popularity of barbiturates as hypnotics and sedatives was at its peak in the 1960s. As some of the problems of dependence became more obvious and as apparently much safer preparations, notably the benzodiazepines, became available the enthusiasm for prescribing barbiturates declined and so too did the opportunity for misuse (Plant 1981). The short and ultra short acting barbiturates are still used for inducing general anaesthesia and other barbiturates are still part of the management of epileptic patients. There is no longer justification for using barbiturates as sedatives or hypnotics.

**Absorption and metabolism**

Barbiturates prescribed as hypnotics or anti-convulsants are invariably intended for oral use but are frequently taken by addicts and made into a solution for i.v. injection. Absorption is substantially from the small intestine and therefore retarded by food in the stomach.

The onset of action of barbiturates depends on their lipid solubility and the duration of action is not linked to half-life although most barbiturates have long half-lives eg; *pentobarbital*, $t\frac{1}{2} = 15-48$ hours; *amobarbital*, $t\frac{1}{2} = 8-42$ hours; *phenobarbital*, $t\frac{1}{2} = 24-140$ hours. Metabolic tolerance can increase the elimination of some barbiturates by up to 25 per cent. Filtration through the kidneys depends on the degree of binding to albumin which is greater with lipid soluble drugs.

**Mode of action**

The barbiturates have a fairly non-specific CNS depressant effect and it is thought that this occurs partly because of inhibition of neurotransmitter release presynaptically and partly by enhancing GABA pathways or mimicking GABA. This effect on GABA may account for reports of cross-tolerance with bezodiazepines. Widespread effects are indicated by the increased oxygen requirement and increased glycogen stores during regular use.

**Effects of barbiturates**

The 'therapeutic window' of barbiturate drugs is small so that the steady decline of CNS function seen with say alcohol is shortened so that sleep or coma occur at an early stage. In hypnotic doses barbiturates reduce REM sleep and increase stage 4 sleep but tolerance to this effect develops within 1 or 2 weeks. Barbiturates have no analgesic effect and indeed may increase pain perception. Hypertension is a consequence of peripheral sympathetic blockade.

**Withdrawal state**

Tolerance to barbiturates plateaus out at around six times the therapeutic dose and 25 per cent of this tolerance is mediated via enzyme induction. A withdrawal syndrome similar to that of alcohol occurs when barbiturates are abruptly stopped. The main features are depression of mood and irritability, anorexia, nausea and vomiting, malaise, weakness and sleep disturbance; tremor is not invariably a feature. Autonomic overactivity is manifest as tachycardia, sweating and fluctuating BP. The severity and onset of withdrawal depends on the barbiturate used, the shorter acting ones precipitating symptoms in 12–24 hours. The preferred treatment is a long-acting barbiturate such as *phenobarbital* and the dose is regulated to minimise withdrawal symptoms. In severe cases convulsions and delirium (see Chapter 3) may develop.

**Medical complications**

**Acute poisoning.** Tolerance to the mood altering and hypnotic effects of barbiturates is greater than the tolerance developed by the cardio-respiratory centres and since in the naive user the lethal dose is perhaps only three times the hypnotic dose, the potential risks of overdose are clear. The signs are of general CNS depression which eventually progresses to shock and circulatory collapse. The mortality rate varies from 0.5–5 per cent depending on the drug taken and treatment available. The lethal dose may be as low as 1 mg per cent for *pentobarbital* and may be reduced some 50 per cent in the presence of alcohol because of the inhibition of enzymes that metabolise barbiturates.

Barbiturates are metabolised in the liver by the microsomal enzyme oxidising system (MEOS) and competitively interfere with oxidation of other drugs such as alcohol and steroids by combining with the enzyme cytochrome P–450. The barbiturates are also potent at induction of MEOS and can therefore hasten the rate of elimination of some drugs such as phenytoin, oral contraceptives and anti-depressants as well as endogenous substances such as steroids and bile salts.

## Benzodiazepines

The benzodiazepine group of drugs dominate the market for anxiolytic and hypnotic agents. There are some twenty benzodiazepines in common usage and they are all taken to have qualitatively similar pharmacological properties though they may differ markedly with respect to pharmacokinetic properties.

### Absorption and metabolism

Since benzodiazepines are usually taken orally the rate of absorption becomes a critical factor in determining suitable applications. *Diazepam* (Valium) and *clorazepate* (Tranxene) are rapidly absorbed, *oxazepam* (Serenid-D) is slowly absorbed, while *lorazepam* (Ativan), *chlordiazepoxide* (Librium) and *flurazepam* (Dalmane) are intermediate. It is sometimes the case that the packaging rather than the physicochemical properties of the drug determine the rate of absorption as illustrated by the more rapid absorption of *temazepam* (Euhypnos) from the soft gelatin capsules marketed in the UK compared to absorption from the hard gelatin capsules marketed in North America (Luscombe, 1984).

As with barbiturates it is not simply the rate of absorption that is crucial in determining the CNS effects but also the rate at which active substance crosses the blood–brain barrier, or, to look at this another way, the extent to which plasma and grey matter form one compartment within the body; this is related to lipid solubility which in turn correlates with the extent of binding to plasma albumin. After absorption there is the distribution phase with the equilibration throughout other body tissues; if the distribution volume is large then the duration of action is short.

The benzodiazepines are metabolised through the microsomal enzyme oxidising system (MEOS). Unlike several other CNS depressants these drugs do not appear to stimulate the MEOS and metabolic tolerance is generally believed to be very small. The rate of elimination is measured in terms of plasma half-life which gives an indication of residual impairment, and drug accumulation (Table 2.2). It must be remembered that many benzodiazepines have active metabolites which in turn have very long half-lives.

**Table 2.2**  Benzodiazepine half-life values

| Benzodiazepine | t½(hours) | Active metabolite | t½(hours) |
|---|---|---|---|
| Triazolam | 2 | 7-hydroxytriazolam | 7 |
| Temazepam | 8 | none | |
| Oxazepam | 8 | none | |
| Lorazepam | 12 | none | |
| Diazepam | 32 | N-desmethyl-diazepam | 65 |
| | | oxazepam | 8 |
| Chlordiazepoxide | 12 | desmethylchlordiazepoxide | 14 |
| | | demoxepam | 37 |
| | | N-desmethyl-diazepam | 65 |
| | | oxazepam | 8 |
| Chlorazepate | 2 | N-desmethyl-diazepam | 65 |
| | | oxazepam | 8 |
| Clobazam | 18 | N-desmethyl-clobazam | 42 |
| Flurazepam | 1 | N-desalkylflurazepam | 65 |
| Nitrazepam | 28 | none | |
| Clonazepam | 53 | none | |

## Mode of action

Costa (1980) has reviewed the mechanisms of benzodiazepine action. It is thought that they enhance GABA activity but are ineffective if GABA is depleted or blocked; the suggestion is of a functional link between distinct GABA and benzodiazepine receptor sites. There is strong evidence for benzodiazepine receptors to be concentrated in the cerebral cortex and to a lesser extent the limbic system and midbrain; these findings have raised the possibility of finding an endogenous ligand for these receptors (Braestrop & Nielson 1980).

## Effects of benzodiazepines

The benzodiazepines all have properties as anxiolytics, anti-convulsants hypnotics and muscle relaxants. A hypnotic must ideally be rapidly absorbed, enter brain tissue directly and have a half-life of 8–10 hours; a shorter acting drug may cause sleep disturbance towards the end of normal sleep and a longer acting drug would cause a 'hangover' effect. The requirements for a day-time sedative are clearly different. It has been claimed that the actual structure of different compounds determines the emphasis of effect; for example *clonazepam* has marked anti-convulsant properties, *clobazam* is anxiolytic without impairing psychomotor function, *alprazolam* is an anti-depressant and *diazepam* has transient analgesic effects given i.v.

Side effects may occur at normal dosage and include drowsiness, tiredness, uncoordination, retrograde amnesia and confusion; some of these symptoms may have medico-legal implications. The benzodiazepines potentiate the effects of other CNS depressants and greatly increase the risk of prolonged psychomotor impairment, confusion, diplopia, incontinence and coma with respiratory depression. There have been case reports of paradoxical effects most notably so called 'rage-attacks' and motor stimulation with seizures after taking benzodiazepines.

People suffering from insomnia spend longer than normal in stage 0 or 1 (wakefulness or light) sleep; there appears to be a physiological requirement for stage 3 and 4 (slow wave) sleep and REM (rapid eye movement) or dreaming sleep and deprivation results in rebound of the latter sleep stages during recovery. In essence benzodiazepines increase stage 2 (deep) sleep and suppress REM and slow wave sleep. Sleep-walking and night terrors occur in stage 4 sleep and benzodiazepines have been used as a treatment for these disorders. The picture is however, much more complex. All benzodiazepines reduce the latency to stage 2 sleep and increase total sleep time (TST). This means that although the character of each sleep cycle, that is movement through stages 1–4 and REM sleep, may alter, the total number of sleep cycles and therfore net gains and losses may increase under the influence of benzodiazepines; this benefit is particularly pertinent to treatment of patients with psychiatric illness. There is also evidence that compared to longer acting drugs, short acting preparations such as *temazepam* (Euhypnos) and *triazolam* (Halcion) are associated with a 'catch up' effect of stages 3 and 4 and REM in the later part of sleep and therefore free of rebound insomnia when the drug is withdrawn and free of carryover effects into daytime (Roth et al 1980).

**Withdrawal state**

There is no doubt that tolerance can develop to the effects of benzodiazepines and patients misusing these drugs can escalate the dose to 100–200 mg *diazepam* (Valium) daily or its equivalent. The preparations most favoured by dependent users are those that are most rapidly absorbed and most readily cross the blood–brain barrier such as *flunitrazepam* (Rohypnol) (Hindmarsh & Ferreira 1984).

The problems of benzodiazepine dependence and withdrawal at

normal dosage are similar to those from high dosage and have been discussed by Lader and Petursson (1983). The withdrawal syndrome is similar to that for other CNS depressants and characterised by anxiety, dysphoria, insomnia, anorexia, headache, tremulousness, muscle pains, parasthesiae and metallic taste; some of these symptoms are of course symptoms of anxiety, the very condition for which the drugs were originally prescribed. Certainly an anxiety state may re-emerge on withdrawal of anxiolytics and Fontaine et al (1984) have demonstrated a rebound anxiety, that is an increase over and above baseline, on abrupt withdrawal of benzodiazepines after only 4 weeks of administration. The presence of perceptual disturbance or the occurence of seizures should strongly suggest withdrawal; withdrawal symptoms should have subsided within 3–4 weeks and be clear within 3 months. There are reports of delirium on benzodiazepine withdrawal (see Chapter 3). The Committee on the Review of Medicine (1980) have found little evidence for the efficacy of benzodiazepines beyond 2–3 months and a 'drug holiday' should be seen as good practice within this timescale. A long acting preparation such as *diazepam* (valium) or *chlordiazepoxide* (Librium) is most suitable for covering benzodiazepine withdrawal which may take 3–4 weeks on an initially rapid reducing dose regimen.

**Medical complications**

**Acute poisoning.** The popularity of benzodiazepines amongst prescribers must in part be to do with the immense margin of safety over therapeutic dose. Only a very small number of deaths world-wide have been attributed to benzodiazepines, although when taken in combination with other drugs effects may become unpredictable and life-threatening. Doses of 2 g of *diazepam* have been taken orally with no long term problems, used i.v. *diazepam* can cause respiratory arrest. The usual consequence of an overdose is a prolonged sleep and uneventful recovery.

## Cannabis

Cannabis is included in this section because of its sedative effects and cross-tolerance with alcohol, the cannabinoids are arguably a class of drugs on their own.

Cannabis is a mixture of some twenty cannabinoids that are

synthesised by the plant *Cannabis sativa*. It is thought that the psychoactive product is the laevo isomer of $\Delta^9$ tetrahdrocannabinol (THC) and its metabolites. All parts of the plant contain psychoactive substances but the highest concentration is in the exudate from the flowering tops which form a dark brown resin known as hashish; the amount of THC in hashish varies considerably but concentrations of 0.5-10 per cent are typical. Occasionally THC is taken orally as a cake but most often is smoked.

**Absorbtion and metabolism**

When smoked, cannabis is absorbed very rapidly and its effects are felt within minutes, lasting 2-3 hours. THC is strongly lipophilic and the absorption phase is followed by rapid redistribution into relatively inert lipid tissues, where accumulation may occur; metabolites can be detected in urine for 30 days after a single dose. It is estimated that only about half the cannabis in a cigarette is absorbed so that a typical dose from a single smoke would be 5-20 mg THC. Regular users metabolise cannabis more rapidly than non-users and this may diminish the longevity of the effects of a smoke but probably not the initial 'high'. The mechanism of action of THC is not known.

**Effects of cannabis**

Regular cannabis smokers often report using less drug than novice users to achieve consistently desirable effects; this phenomenon sometimes called reverse tolerance is probably to do with better technique of administration and more positive expectation in the regular users. A dose of approximately 5 mg THC will induce a change of mood towards a feeling of well being, euphoria, laughter and talkativeness which is quite often circumstantial; enhancement of perception in all sensory modalities has been described and associated with irritability towards others. The ability to perform simple motor tasks is retained but more complex skills such as driving and tasks requiring short-term memory function are impaired. Time is distorted and there may be dislocation of events in time. Tiredness and sleep can be prominent features.

Physical effects are rarely pronounced but include gastrointestinal upset, yawning, tachycardia, and raised systolic pressure, mydriasis and injected conjunctivi. The cardiovascular effects are reversed with $\beta$-blockers.

**Withdrawal syndrome**

Although it appears unusual for individuals to increase markedly their intake of THC there are reports of heavy regular smoking and tolerance to daily doses of 200 mg THC. Abrupt withdrawal is followed by irritability, anorexia, insomnia with rebound REM, the withdrawal syndrome is generally mild and symptoms clear within 5 days (Jones et al 1976). The mild nature of withdrawal may be due to the store of THC in lipid tissues effectively producing slow-release of THC equivalent to a reducing regimen.

## Medical complications

### Upper respiratory tract

Cannabis smokers are vulnerable to the same illnesses as cigarette smokers, notably bronchitis, respiratory infections and carcinoma of the lung; the tar from hashish may be more carcinogenic than that from nicotine.

### Reproduction

Cannabis inhibits testosterone production but sexual potency in males appears unaffected. Cannabinoids cross the placenta and in view of their long elimination time may have adverse effects on the fetus. Cannabinoids also inhibit DNA synthesis increasing the mutation potential and risk of spontaneous abortion (Hoyt 1981).

### Acute poisoning

The effects of acute poisoning are mainly psychiatric (see Chapter 3), but very high doses may cause cardiovascular collapse, hypothermia and coma.

## Other sedatives and hypnotics

There are a number of drugs that were in vogue for a time as alternatives to barbiturates, but these preparations have themselves been superseded by the benzodiazepines; all have similar effects to other CNS depressants including the potential for dependence and withdrawal problems of varying severity. Prescribing habits have changed so that these drugs are not widely available. Examples are *chloral hydrate* (Noctec), *methaqualone* with *diphenhydramine* (Mandrax), *glutethimide* (Doriden), *meprobamate* (Equanil).

Still widely prescribed, especially as hypnotics for the elderly are *dichloralphenazone* (Welldorm) a chloral derivative and *chlormethiazole* (Heminevrin) a preparation with a similar structure to the vitamin thiamin. *Chlormethiazole* has potent anticonvulsant properties and with respect to this is possibly superior to the benzodiazepines to cover severe withdrawal states; however this marginal benefit must be weighed against its dependence forming potential and incidence of delirium on its withdrawal (Gregg & Akhter 1979).

## Opioids

**Opioid** refers to all compounds, naturally occuring and synthetic whose effects are antagonised by *naloxone*. The word *opiate* is sometimes used as synonymous with *opioid* but should more correctly refer only to the alkaloids of the poppy *Papaver somniferum,* and semi-synthetic products such as heroin. The term *narcotic* originally referred to all hypnotic agents but later came to mean the class of powerful morphine-like analgesic drugs; the word no longer has a proper use and has become slang for all potent drugs of misuse.

**Opium** is the crude, unpurified exudate from the poppy which contains some twenty alkaloids and has been used for centuries as a medicine and recreational drug. Berridge (1977) describes its production and use in England prior to the mid-nineteenth century when pure alkaloids were isolated and used in preference. The opioids and their relative potencies are listed in Table 2.3. Most important of the alkaloids of *Papaver somniferum* are morphine and codeine; thebaine is also important because it is a precursor of other analgesics and naloxone.

There are many medical uses for the opioids. Analgesia such as the relief of chronic pain, particularly in the terminally ill and the relief of acute pain such as experienced with coronary thrombosis or childbirth remains the prime indication for prescribing these drugs; the risks of dependence leading to misuse are small in such circumstances. The use of oral preparations, usually including *codeine*, to control diarrhoea or suppress coughing is indeed efficacious but carries greater risks of iatrogenic opioid dependence.

**Absorption and metabolism**

Opioids are well absorbed when taken orally, smoked or snorted. *Morphine* is slow to cross the blood–brain barrier unlike heroin which is much more lipid soluble and rapidly taken up by brain tissue where it is then converted to morphine. *Codeine* is resistant to metabolism in the liver and is particularly useful as an oral preparation but its effects as with heroin are thought to be mainly the result of conversion to *morphine*; 90 per cent of *morphine* is excreted in the urine either as free drug or conjugated with glucuronic acid.

**Table 2.3** Opioid equivalents

| Drug | | Methadone equivalent |
|---|---|---|
| Street heroin | 1 g | 80 mg |
| Pharmaceutical heroin | 10 mg tablet (jack) or 10 mg freeze dried ampoule | 10 mg |
| Physeptone | 10 mg ampoule | 10 mg |
| Morphine | 10 mg ampoule | 5 mg |
| Diconal (1 tablet) | 10 mg dipipanone hydrochloride | 5 mg |
| DF11 8 | 30 mg dihydrocodeine | 2.5 mg |
| Palfium (1 tablet) | 5 mg dextromoramide | 10 mg |
| Pethidine (1 tablet) | 25 mg, 50 mg pethidine hydrochloride | 2.5 or 5 mg |
| Pethidine (1 ampoule) | 50 mg ampoule | 5 mg |
| Temgesic (1 tablet) | 0.2 mg buprenorphine hydrochloride | 2,5 mg |
| Temgesic (1 ampoule) | 0.3 mg ampoule | 4 mg |
| Fortral (1 capsule) | 50 mg pentazocine | 4 mg |
| Fortral (1 tablet) | 25 mg pentazocine | 1 mg |
| Codeine linctus (100 ml) | 300 mg codeine phosphate | 10 mg |
| Codeine Phosphate (1 tablet) | 15.30 or 60 mg codeine phosphate | 1.2 or 3 mg |
| Actified compound (100 mg) | 200 mg codeine phosphate | 6 mg |
| Gees's linctus (100 ml) | 16 mg annydrous morphine | 10 mg |
| Dr Collis Brown (100 ml) | 1.4% opium | 10 mg |

After Thorley (1983).
It is not possible to directly convert the effects, time duration and addictive potential of opioid-based drugs to a fixed equivalent of methadone. The above table is meant as a rough guideline only.

**Methadone** is well absorbed orally reaching peak levels at about 4 hours. The drug is firmly bound to protein in most tissues which act as a reservoir if the drug is abruptly stopped. The $t\frac{1}{2}$ of *methadone* is 15–20 hours compared to 3–4 hours for *morphine*.

## Mode of action

Two discoveries in the early 1970s provoked a tremendous research effort to clarify the mechanisms underlying opioid activity, but as more knowlegde has accumulated the picture has become more complicated and more questions raised rather than answers found. The first discovery was of specific opioid receptor sites in the CNS and the second was the identification of two pentapeptides, methionine (met-) enkephalin and leucine (leu-) enkephalin which has powerful opioid agonist activity (Hughes et al 1972). It was noted that these pentapeptides had sequences that could be found in the pituitary hormone $\beta$-lipotropin and there was early speculation that $\beta$-lipotropin might be the precursor for the enkephalins. This is now known to be incorrect and rather it is believed that there are at least three families of endogenous opioid peptides namely the enkephalins, the dynorphins and the endorphins. These opioid peptides may act as short acting neurotransmitters or long acting neurohormones and may show some overlap of effect.

   The earliest simplistic theories of opioid mechanisms stated that endogenous opioid had an agonist effect on opioid receptors and was produced in increasing amounts in response to stress or pain; it was postulated that chronic use of exogenous opioid would displace the endogenous opioid and by feedback systems, which are commonly seen to exist in neuro-endocrine axes, would decrease the availability of the endogenous opioid so that abrupt withdrawal of exogenous opioid drugs would leave a deficiency state that could not be met by endogenous substances. Unfortunately, this appealing explanation no longer holds up. Experiments with primates found that chronic administration of *morphine* does not in general reduce levels of $\beta$-endorphin; the significance of this with regard to opioid actions is uncertain. A second problem is that although animal studies suggest endogenous compounds are as addictive as exogenous ones, *naloxone* given to non-addicts does not precipitate a withdrawal state suggesting that there is no tonic activity from endogenous opioids (Herz 1980). Finally, five different opioid receptors, *mu, kappa, delta, epsilon* and *sigma,* have been identified and shown to have heterogenous CNS distributions. The neocortex and cerebellar cortex are especially rich in *mu* and *kappa* receptors which are thought to mediate the morphine-like action of opioids; *naloxone* is most powerfully antagonist at mu sites (Mourer et al 1983). Cross-tolerance between receptors is thought not to exist, but possibly receptors are inter-convertible. Thompson (1984) has made a helpful review of opioid peptides.

**Effects of opioids**

The opioids are powerful analgesics and are used medically almost entirely for this effect. They also have euphoriant and sedative properties and it is for these effects that they are commonly misused; heroin taken i.v. crosses the blood–brain barrier very rapidly and produces a particularly intense experience, often called a 'rush', which is sometimes likened to an orgasm. The beneficial effects are short lived for the addict and give way to depression, dysphoria, apathy and a continuous dream like state. In high doses the opioid may have excitatory effects including precipitation of seizures; pethidine is especially likely to do this.

Opioids cause a miosis by stimulating the parasympathetic pathways in the nucleus of occulomoter nerve; the effect is antagonised by *naloxone*. It was thought that miosis was resistant to opioid tolerance but there is now evidence that his is not so, but rather that it is the case that as the addict increases the drug dose, so the miosis is sustained (Murray et al 1983). Opioids act directly to reduce the mobility of the gut and usually cause constipation. Effects on the cardiovascular system are rarely severe but there may be significant hypotension with associated feelings of faintness and dizziness. There is a direct stimulatory effect on the centre for emesis so that vomiting is often an unpleasant consequence of using opioids. A degree of respiratory depression is unavoidable.

**Withdrawal state**

Tolerance to the euphoriant, analgesic and respiratory depressant effect of opioids develops within a matter of days of continuous use but constipation is a persistent problem of chronic use; while addicts might typically use 0.25 g daily, intakes as high as 5 g heroin daily have been verified. Abrupt withdrawal of heroin or morphine produces a syndrome characterised by lacrimation, rhinorrhoea, rubbing eyes, yawning, sweating within 6–8 hours progressing to irritability, dysphoria, restlessness, shivering and gooseflesh, hence the expression 'cold turkey'. The pupils dilate, there are muscle cramps, anorexia and increased mobility of the gut causing diarrhoea and vomiting. Body temperature and blood pressure may be slightly elevated and the effect on pulse is variable. Incontinence of urine and spontaneous orgasm or ejaculation may occur. The symptoms of withdrawal peak at 2–3 days and have usually gone within 7 days; tolerance to opioids substantially disappears with the end of the withdrawal syndrome. Withdrawal from other opioids is qualitatively similar to heroin but has different timescales and intensity. Abrupt withdrawal from *methadone* produces a mild syndrome that may last 1–2 months. Displacement of opioids by an antagonist such as *naloxone* produces a severe withdrawal syndrome reaching peak intensity within about 30 min. The severity of the syndrome cannot be attenuated by administering opioids. This property of opioid antagonists can be taken advantage of in a test for opioid dependence (Judson et al 1980).

A reducing dose of *methadone linctus* (Physeptone) can be used to cover withdrawal from any of the opioids. The use of linctus prevents the drug being injected and minimises the euphoriant effect of other non-prescription opioids taken simultaneously by the i.v. route. It is sometimes difficult from the history given by the addict to establish with confidence the level of opioid intake and in such cases further information can be gained from toxicological investigations, from observing the effect of a test dose of 5–10 mg *methadone* (Physeptone) or from the *naloxone* (Nalcan) test. It is rarely necessary to prescribe in excess of 50 mg of *methadone* (Physeptone) daily. Withdrawal should be complete in 5–10 days; there appears to be no benefit from longer withdrawal regimes (Sorenson et al 1982). Connell and Mitcheson (1984) have prepared useful guidelines on precautions to be taken before prescribing opioids.

**Clonidine** (Catapres) is an alpha adrenergic agonist which has been used as a non-opioid drug to cover withdrawal. In combination with an opioid antagonist withdrawal can be achieved very rapidly, apparently overcoming the problem of prolonged withdrawal symptomology sometimes associated with *methadone* withdrawal (Charney et al 1982). It is thought that *clonidine* (Catapres) acts on neurones that have projections to areas rich in opioid receptors and through these projections it diminishes the sensitivity of receptors. Electro-stimulation has also been advocated as an alternative to *methadone* (Physeptone) but it seems unlikely that this treatment is more than a placebo (Gossop et al 1984).

## Medical complications

Many of the more serious medical complications of opioid abuse are the result of improper i.v. injection. A comprehensive review of physical problems can be found in *Drug Abuse* (Sapira & Cherubin 1975).

## Acute poisoning

Although tolerance to opioids develops rapidly and for huge doses there is always a dose high enough to cause respiratory arrest; coma, respiratory depression and pin-point pupils should always suggest an overdose. An overdose of opioids can be effectively reversed with i.v. *naloxone* (Nalcan) 0.4 mg, the dose is repeated if necessary. Sudden death may occur in addicts who lose their tolerance to the respiratory depressant effect of opioid during a period of abstinence but failing to realise this they inject the same high dose of drug that they would have taken when using regularly and therefore when tolerant; so quick is the effect that the victims are often found with the needle still in their vein. There may be associated pulmonary oedema of such severity that fluid oozes from the mouth; the aetiology remains uncertain, but may be hypersensitivity to the drug or impurities injected with it.

## Reproduction

Chronic use of opioids suppress the secretion of luteinising hormone and significantly reduce plasma testosterone levels causing diminished libido in the male. There may also be impotence and prolonged time to ejaculation. In women libido is also reduced and amenorrhoea is common; menstrual disturbances have been reported in more than half the women on *methadone* maintenance. There are reports of diminished fertility in chronic users and an increase in spontaneous abortion.

## Glucose regulation

Hyperglycaemia is a common finding among chronic opioid users. Passariello et al (1983) have demonstrated that there is an impaired insulin secretion in response to i.v. glucose and glucagon secretion is stimulated.

## Urinary system

Chronic use of opioids has been implicated as a cause of the nephrotic syndrome. The mechanisms involved have not been elucidated. Acute renal failure may arise secondary to myopathy, probably caused by injection of irritant material, and myoglobinuria.

## Hallucinogenics

Hallucinogenic drugs have especially held popularity among individuals with an inclination for philosophy or creative arts. The drugs listed in this section are something of a mixed collection with regard to both mechanism of action and specific effects.

## Lysergic acid (LSD), psilocybin and mescaline

### Absorption and metabolism

The hallucinogenic drugs are all taken orally. LSD is the most powerful drug and is effective in doses of 20 μg; LSD itself is a synthetic drug but a less potent compound of a similar structure occurs naturally in the *morning glory* seed. *Psilocybin* has only 1/100 the potency of LSD and is an alkaloid of the mushroom *Psilocybe semilanceata* which grows wild in parts of the UK, and *Psilocybe americana* found in Central America; an effective dose is 20–30 mushrooms, each mushroom yielding approximately 1 mg of active drug. *Mescaline* can be synthesised or found naturally occurring in the peyote cactus; it is much less potent than the other drugs.

These drugs are thought to act at a number of different sites in the CNS and probably exert their effect by 5H.T.agonist activity at presynaptic sites; this is an inhibitory function of 5H.T.

### Effects of hallucinogens

Stimulant, (sympathomimetic) effects of hallucinogens and in particular LSD occur almost instantly. These include dilated pupils, tachycardia, elevated blood pressure, tremor and piloerection, weakness and nausea. The psychedelic effect begins after about 30 min and peaks at about 2–3 hours; although the half-life of LSD is only 3 hours the 'trip' lasts some 12 hours. Mood changes are common but not invariable. There may be euphoria, dysphoria or anxiety and panic; often the effect is labile and associated with a feeling of fragmentation of the 'ego'. The most striking effects are disturbances of perception. Time seems to be slowed down and there are usually illusions such as macroposia, microposia or distortion of colour; parts of the body may feel to be detached. Vivid visual hallucinations are notable and may take the form of single geometric shapes or more complex life-like images. The experience of synesthesia, that is a sensory disturbance such as 'hearing a colour' or 'seeing a smell', is reported. Great significance may be attached to a single note in a piece of music or a line on a picture and the user may become withdrawn and totally preoccupied with their psychedelic world. The content of the hallucinatory experience may be distressing, a 'bad trip', to the point that the user may attempt suicide. These drugs all aggravate schizophrenia and probably manic depressive psychosis also.

**Withdrawal state**

Tolerance to hallucinogens develops quickly; after perhaps 10 trips over a 2-week period the dose would have to be increased from 20 to 1000 µg. The mechanism of tolerance is not understood and no withdrawal syndrome has been reported. There is no cross-tolerance with CNS depressant drugs.

**Medical complications**

**Acute poisoning**

The physical effects of poisoning are attributable to the sympathomimetic properties of hallucinogens and may include seizures and hypothermia; treatment with *diazepam* (Valium) or beta-blocker is usually effective. There is usually an accompanying psychotic reaction.

**Reproductive system**

The possibility of an increased rate of birth defects, especially phalangeal anomalies, in children of mothers who have taken LSD has been raised but evidence remains equivocal.

## Solvents

Inhalation of solvents, or 'glue sniffing', is for the most part restricted to adolescents who are not in any way psychologically disturbed and who grow out of the habit moving on to more socially acceptable recreational drugs, usually alcohol; a few, often solitary users may be in need of psychiatric help. Possible inhalants are ubiquitous at home, in schools and in shops. Most commonly used (90 per cent) are adhesives, especially Evo-stick, which contains the active substance toluene; compared to fluorinated hydrocarbons found in aerosol propellants, toluene is thought to be relatively safe.

Inhalants have a sedative and disinhibiting effect similar to that of CNS depressant drugs causing rapid inebriation and disorientation. The level of consciousness is altered to a dream-like state associated with a feeling of well-being. Illusory rather than hallucinatory experiences are most common and users can, almost at will, conjure up whatever images they wish. The action is short-lived necessitating continuous intake of solvent to maintain an effect (Watson 1982).

Possible medical implications of solvent abuse are becoming increasingly well known. It is common practice to rebreathe solvents from a plastic bag placed over the face; in these circumstances the combined effect of hypoxia and solvent on destabilising the myocardium is exceedingly dangerous and may cause a fatal cardiac arrhythmia even in first time users. The possibility of renal failure and liver damage is also established. Coma, convulsions and encephalopathy have been reported in cases of acute poisoning (Francis et al 1982) but the question of possible longer term damage remains a matter for research.

## Arylcyclohexylamines

Phencyclidine, 'angel dust', was first used as a general anaesthetic but quickly fell from favour because of post operative problems, notably delirium; it has however been widely used as a recreational drug in the United States, partly because it is easy to synthesise. Phencyclidine causes a galaxy of subjective feelings. There is a sense of intoxication and euphoria; at lower doses there is also a weightlessness which may be to do with blocking of propriocertive impulses to the brain. There may be unwanted effects such as drooling, sweating and nausea. At higher doses, 20–30 mg, disorganisation of thought and more marked perceptual changes including visual hallucination and synesthesia occur. It is common to smoke phencyclidine with marijuana but some users inject the drug and may take 0.5–1.0 g daily.

## Conclusion

Inevitably this chapter will have omitted detail about some particular substances that are misused. The important theme here has been to consider similarities between drugs in order to have a solid framework in which to place not only those drugs that are presently misused, but also others that may come into vogue in the future. Perhaps with the exception of alcohol, drug taking habits do change quite rapidly and the practitioner is often left with a feeling of always being a few steps behind. This need not be a reason for despair since predictions can be made about the effects of most drugs simply by identifying their major class for which there are general principles of management to be applied.

REFERENCES

Adler M W, Weller I V D 1984 Aids: sense not fear. British Medical Journal
Berglund M, Risberg J 1981 Regional cerebral blood flow during alcohol withdrawal. Archives of General Psychiatry 38: 351–355
Berridge V 1977 Our own opium: cultivation of the opium poppy in Britain, 1740–1823. British Journal of Addiction 72: 90–94
Braestrup C, Nielson M 1980 Modes of action of benzodiazepines. Drug Research International Symposium, Heidelberg, Germany 30: 852–857
Charney D S et al 1982 Clonidine and naltrexone. A safe effective treatment of abrupt withdrawal from methadone therapy. Archives of General Psychiatry 39: 1327–1332
Committee on the Review of Medicines 1980 Systematic review of the benzodiazepines. British Medical Journal 2: 719–720
Connell P H, Mitcheson M 1984 Necessary safeguards when prescribing opioid drugs to addicts: experience of drug dependence clinics in London. British Medical Journal 288: 767–769
Costa E 1980 Benzodiazepines and neurotransmitters. Drug Research International Symposium Heidelberg, Germany 30: 858–868
Davis M 1980 Alcoholic liver disease: what the practising clinician needs to know. British Journal of Addiction 75: 19–26
Editorial 1978 Methanol poisoning. Lancet ii: 510–511
Editorial 1983 Alcohol and advice to the pregnant woman. British Medical Journal 286: 247–248
Edwards G 1974 Drug dependence and plasticity. Quarterly Journal of Studies on Alcohol 35: 176–195

Edwards G 1984 Alcoholism and psychiatric illness. In: McIntyre G (ed) The Treatment of Drinking Problems.

Erikson M, Larsson G, Zetterstrom R 1981 Amphetamine addiction and pregnancy. Acta Obstetrica Gynaecologica Scandinavica 60: 253–259

Faizallah R, Woodrow J C, Krasner N K, Walker R J, Morris A I 1982 Are HLA antigens important in the development of alcohol-induced liver disease? British Medical Journal 285: 533–534

Fontaine R, Chouinard G, Annable L 1984 Rebound anxiety in anxious patients after abrupt withdrawal of benzodiazepine treatment. American Journal of Psychiatry 141: 848–852

Francis J, Murray V S G, Ruprah M, Flanagan R J, Ramsay J D 1982 Suspected solvent abuse in cases referred to the poisons unit, Guy's Hospital, July 1980–June 1981. Human Toxicology 1: 271–280

Ghodse H 1981 Morbidity and mortality. In: Edwards G, Busch C (eds) Drug problems in Britain, a review of ten years, Academic Press, London ch 9, p 246

Goldstein A 1983 Some thoughts about endogenous opioids and addiction. Journal of Drug and Alcohol Dependence 11: 11–14

Gossop M R, Bradley B P, Brewis R K 1982 Amphetamine withdrawal and sleep disturbance. Journal of Drug and Alcohol Dependence 10: 177–183

Gossop M R, Stern R, Connell P H 1974 Drug dependence and sexual dysfunction: a comparison of IV users of narcotics and oral users of amphetamine. British Journal of Psychiatry 124: 431–434

Gossop M R, Bradley B, Strang J, Connell P 1984 Clinical effectiveness of electrostimulation versus oral methadone in managing opiate withdrawal. British Journal of Psychiatry 144: 203–208

Gregg E, Akhter I 1979 Chlormethiazole abuse. British Journal of Psychiatry 134: 627–629

Greizerstein H B 1981 Congener contents of alcoholic beverages. Journal of Studies on Alcohol 42: 11 1030–1037

Hershon H 1977 Alcohol withdrawal symptoms and drinking behaviour. Journal of Studies on Alcohol 38: 953–971

Herz A 1980 Opioid peptides: their role in drug dependence. In: Richter D (ed) Addiction and Brain Damage. Croom Helm, London ch 7, p 141

Hindmarch I, Ferreira L 1984 The abuse of benzodiazepines in poly drug dependents. Royal Society of Medicine Symposium Series (In Press)

Hore B D 1980 The Manchester Detoxification Centre. British Journal of Addiction 75: 197–205

Hoyt L L 1981 Effects of marijuana on fetal development. Journal of Alcohol and Drug Education 26: 30–36

Hudgson P 1984 Alcoholic myopathy. British Medical Journal 288: 584–585

Hughes J et al 1975 Identification of two related pentapeptides from the brain. Nature 258: 577–579

Jones R T, Benowitz N, Bachman J 1976 Clinical studies of cannabis tolerance and dependence. Annals of New York Academy of Science 282: 221–239

Judson B A, Himmelberger M S, Goldstein M D 1980 The naloxone test for opiate dependence. Journal of Clinical Pharmacology and Therapeutics 27: 492–501

Katlain E S, Hayes W N, Teger A J, Pruitt D G 1970 Effects of alcoholic beverages differing in congener content on psychomotor tasks and risk taking. Quarterly Journal of Studies on Alcohol

Lader M, Perturson H 1983 Long-term effects of benzodiazepines. Journal of Neuropharmacology 22: 527–533

Lieber C S (ed) 1982 Medical disorders of alcoholism. Saunders, London

Littleton J M 1984 Biochemical pharmacology of ethanol tolerance and dependence. In: Edwards G, Littleton J M (eds) Pharmacological treatments for alcoholism. Croom Helm, London & Sydney, ch 9, p 119

Luscombe D K 1984 Prescribing benzodiazepines: pharmacokinetic characteristics. Psychiatry in Practice 3(19): 22–26

Marks V 1977 Alcohol induced hypoglycaemia and endocrinopathy. In: Edwards G, Grant M (eds) Alcoholism: new knowledge and new responses. Croom Helm, London, ch 14, p 208

Marks V, Wright J W 1977 Endocrinological and metabolic effects of alcohol. Proceedings of the Royal Society of Medicine 70: 337–344

Matsuyaki S, Gordon E, Lieber C S 1981 Increased ADH Independent ethanol oxidation at high ethanol concentrations in isolated rat hepatocytes: the effect of chronic ethanol feeding. Journal of Pharmacology and Experimental Therapeutics 217: 133–137

Maurer R, Cortes R, Probst A, Palacios J M 1983 Multiple opiate receptors in human brain: an autoradiographic investigation. Journal of Life Sciences 33 Supp I: 231–234

Mayer S E, Kenneth L, Gilman M, Gilman A G 1980 Introduction: The dynamics of drug absorption, distribution and elimination. In: Gilman A G, Goodman L S, Gilman A (eds) The Pharmacological Basis of Therapeutics, 6th edn. Macmillan, London

McCarron M, Wood J D 1983 The cocaine body packer syndrome. Journal of the American Medical Association 2150: 1417–1420

McGrath S D 1975 Controlled trial of chlormethiazole and chlordiazepoxide in treatment of acute withdrawal phase of alcohol. Proceedings of the Conference on Alcoholism. Longman 81–90

Mello N K, Mendelson J H 1977 Clinical aspects of alcohol dependence. In: Springer M W R (ed) Handbook of Experimental Psychology

Mukherjee P K 1983 A comparison of the efficacy and tolerability of clobazam and chlordiazepoxide in the treatment of acute withdrawal from alcohol in patients with primary alcoholism. Journal of International Medical Research 11(4): 205–211

Murray R B, Adler M W, Korczyn A D 1983 The pupillary effects of opioids. Journal of Life Sciences 33: 495–509

Parsons V, Cundy T 1981 Alcohol and bone disease. British Journal of Addiction 76: 379–382

Passariello N et al 1983 Glucose tolerance and hormonal responses in heroin addicts. Metabolism 32: 1163–1165

Plant M 1981 What aetiologies? In: Edwards G, Busch C (eds) Drug problems in Britain, a review of ten years. Academic Press, London, ch 9, p 246

Pratt O 1981 Alcohol and the woman of child bearing age. British Journal of Addiction 76: 383–390

Randall C L 1984 The fetal alcohol syndrome. In: Edwards G, Littleton J (eds) Pharmacological treatments for alcoholism. Croom Helm, London & Sydney, ch 20, p 363

Reilly T M 1976 Physiological dependence on and symptoms of withdrawal from chlormethiazole. British Journal of Psychiatry 128: 375–378

Roth T, Hartse K M, Zorick F J, Kaffeman M E 1980 The differential effects of short and long acting benzodiazepines upon nocturnal sleep and daytime performance. Drug Research International Symposium Hiedelberg Germany 30: 891–894

Sapira J D, Cherubin C F 1975 Drug abuse — a guide for the clinician. Excerpta Medica Amsterdam. Elsevier, New York, ch 4, p 113–272

Sorenson J L, Hargreaves W A, Weinberg J A 1982 Withdrawal from heroin in three to six weeks. Comparison of methadyl acetate and methadone. Archives of General Psychiatry 39: 167–171

Sorenson T I A et al 1984 Prospective evaluation of alcohol abuse and alcoholic liver injury in men as predictors of development of cirrhosis. Lancet ii: 241–244

Tedder R S 1980 Hepatitis B in hospitals. British Journal of Hospital Medicine

Thompson J W 1984 Opioid peptides. British Medical Journal 288: 259–260

Wakasugi C, Vehima E, Matsuyawa Y, Kameda K 1976 A case of chronic alcoholism. Japanese Journal of Studies on Alcohol 11: 162–164

Watson J M 1982 Solvent abuse: presentation and clinical diagnosis. Human Toxicology 1: 249–256

Wilson G T 1984 Alcohol studies and sexual function. British Journal of Sexual Medicine 11(105): 56–60

Wodak A, Richardson P J 1982 Alcohol and the cardiovascular system. British Journal of Addiction 77(3): 251–273

Wodak A D, Saunders J B, Ewusi-Mensah I, Davis M, Williams R 1983 Severity of alcohol dependence in patients with alcoholic liver disease. British Medical Journal 287: 1420–1421

# 3

# *Psychiatric disorder*

Psychiatrists hold many different views about the importance of mental illness in relation to substance misuse and sometimes confuse other disciplines and specialists by their inconsistency of opinion which at one extreme sees everything, probably life itself, as a psychiatric disorder while at the other extreme denies the very existence of such disorder. It is no curiosity then to find the credibility of psychiatry so often questioned and yet there is ample research evidence and, for most workers in the field, clinical experience to confirm important links between addiction and psychiatric disorder. A failure to be aware of the psychiatric problems that might be found in association with substance misuse may lead to proper treatment being overlooked, case management being less successful than is possible and legal or social responsibilities being incorrectly evaluated.

Given the complexity of normal brain function, it is perhaps surprising that brain malfunction manifests itself, at least at a gross clinical level, in very few broad categories of psychiatric disorder (Table 3.1). Presumably these disorders represent final common pathways to a whole set of subsystems or mechanisms many of which have yet to be identified; it remains a mystery, for example, how withdrawal from alcohol and benzodiazepines, which have different actions at a cellular level, may result in the same delirium, or how the different biochemical effects of cannabis and cocaine can both cause the same persecutory state. For these reasons this chapter has been structured using a *differential diagnosis* approach, that is a look at the leading presenting symptoms of psychiatric disorder followed by consideration of the possible causes.

The results of epidemiological surveys depend on the criteria

**Table 3.1**   Psychiatric disorder

| | |
|---|---|
| **Affective states** | |
| Depression | Chronic alcohol and opioid use, LSD intoxication |
| | Amphetamine, cocaine withdrawal |
| Hypomania | Amphetamine, cocaine intoxication |
| | Other sympathomimetic drugs |
| Anxiety | Chronic alcohol use |
| | LSD, cannabis intoxication |
| *Delirium* | |
| Withdrawal State | Alcohol, benzodiazepines, barbiturates |
| | Other CNS depressants, PCP |
| Intoxication | Amphetamine, cocaine |
| *Paranoid psychosis* | |
| Acute Psychosis | Amphetamine, cocaine, LSD, solvents psilocybin, PCP, cannabis |
| 'Flashbacks' | LSD, cannabis |
| Chronic Psychosis | |
| morbid jealousy | Alcohol, cocaine |
| hallucinosis | Alcohol |
| **Dysmnestic states** | |
| Dementia | Alcohol, ?amphetamine, ?barbiturate, ??cannabis |
| 'Blackouts' | Alcohol, benzodiazepines, other CNS depressant intoxication |
| Wernicke-Korsakoff | Alcohol |

used to define what is to be measured and in what population it is to be measured. Definitions of dependence and psychiatric disorder remain imprecise although much has been achieved by the development of classification systems such as ICD-9 (1978) and DSM-III (1980), and the use of schedules such as the Research Diagnostic Criteria (Spitzer et al 1978). Even with these advances there remain difficulties: i) classification systems may improve inter-rater communications but as yet cannot describe descrete and homogenous disorders ii) there is no work to indicate how the evaluation of mental state might be adjusted to account for intoxication or simple withdrawal states iii) it is hard to determine whether psychiatric disorder antedated substance misuse and should therefore be declared *primary*, or, in the case of *secondary* psychiatric disorder, there is no way of knowing whether the substance misused was an aetiological agent or whether its misuse was merely coincidental.

There are a number of reasons why concomitance between substance misuse and psychiatric disorder is high. Firstly, both are common and so there are relatively frequent chance associations. The prevalence of alcoholism is estimated at 1–6 per cent depending on geographical location; the prevalence of psychiatric morbidity has been estimated at psychosis 1.7 per cent, neurosis 13–35 per cent and mental dificiency 1.2–10 per cent. Secondly, physical pain and psychological discomfort are both relieved by different psychoactive drugs and a number of individuals self-medicate with alcohol, prescribed and illicit drugs; for these *symptomatic* misusers the development of dependence may become the central problem, itself requiring treatment before the underlying disorder can be dealt with. Finally, it is clear that drugs may accelerate or uncover predisposition to psychiatric disorder as well as being causally linked to psychotic and other illness. It must be stressed that the number of patients suffering from psychiatric problems will vary considerably from one setting to another; there will obviously be many more cases referred to a psychiatric clinic than found at a housing office. It is also important to remember that not every psychological problem requires treatment and not all are amenable to treatment.

Ewusi-Mensah et al (1983) investigated psychiatric morbidity in patients with alcoholic liver disease thereby avoiding the problem of distorting the index group by selective referral and also providing a good non-alcoholic liver disease control group. They found that 60 per cent of men and 77 per cent of women in the alcoholic group had a recognisable psychiatric illness; this compared to 24 per cent and 46 per cent in the non-alcoholic group. Of the alcoholic patients 46 per cent in total had a history antedating excessive drinking, 20 per cent had a problem judged to be secondary to their drinking and 34 per cent showed no psychopathology. Comparable figures have been reported by other workers (Weissman 1978). Estimates of psychiatric morbidity in populations using illegal drugs are invariably skewed; Hall et al (1979) found that of patients admitted to a psychiatric unit 58 per cent had a history of drug misuse.

Classification systems tend to obscure grey areas and it is clear that this happens in psychiatry where it is apparent on clinical grounds that disorders have complex relationships and much overlap with each other. Connections between schizophrenia, affective disorder and substance induced psychosis are of particular importance because of the implications for prognosis and for treatment. In a detailed study Tsuang et al (1982) investigated demographic characteristics, clinical features and family history of five patient groups i) drug abusers ii) drug abusers with short duration psychosis — DAS (less than six months) iii) drug abusers with long duration psychosis — DAL iv) schizophrenics v) atypical schizophrenics. They found that all three drug misuse groups had similar rates of alcohol misuse (33–40 per cent) and amphetamine misuse (37–53 per cent) but that the drug abusers without psychosis were more likely to use opioids and non-barbiturate tranquillisers compared to both the DAS and DAL groups who were more likely to use LSD and marijuana. With regard to premorbid personality the DAL group most closely resembled the atypical schizophrenia patients with a high level of schizoid and paranoid disturbance (24 per cent). Symptoms and signs for each of the four psychotic groups differed. Depressive symptoms were reported by 80 per cent of the DAS and atypical schizophrenia groups; manic symptoms were most common in the atypical schizophrenia group (54 per cent) but also reported by one fifth to one third of all other patients. Auditory hallucinations were reported equally by all four groups (55–60 per cent); confusion, visual hallucinations and short-term memory deficits were characteristic of the DAS psychosis and Schneiderian symptoms, thought disorder, delusions and shallow affect were equally spread across the other three psychosis groups. It was noted that the DAL group had familial risks for both schizophrenia and affective disorder which were significantly greater than the DAS group. In summary, the short duration psychosis, group DAS, of patients are most like drug misusers without psychosis and the long duration psychosis group, DAL, seem to be an amalgam of at least two subtypes with characteristics of both schizophrenia and affective disorder. The authors concluded that by carefully eliciting personal and family histories and carefully assessing mental state, it is possible to sophisticate the differential diagnosis of drug induced psychosis. It was unclear from the description of methodology how many of the DAS group were diagnosed while intoxicated or in a state of withdrawal.

Most clinicians would agree that it is impossible properly to assess mental state until a patient is drug-free but it is nevertheless the case that psychiatrists and other doctors are frequently required to do so. The task is formidable and immediately throws open moral, medico-legal and resource implication questions. However, since profound changes of mood, perception and thinking may occur as a result of intoxication or withdrawal, then a positive strategy is called for. Fingarette (1981) has discussed some of the legal issues raised by problems of intoxication and dependence with reference to alcohol misuse. He concluded that becoming intoxicated is not an involuntary act and therefore is not a ground for diminished responsibility whatever the state of mind induced by the intoxication; the intent to commit a crime is embodied in the intent to become intoxicated. This pragmatic and coherent legal position does not absolve other professionals from a responsibility to their intoxicated patient. Fingarette is more expansive on the question of dependence and bases his argument on the fact that even an individual who has become markedly dependent on a substance still has a repertoire of responses and in certain circumstances at least, has control over his behaviour. He concludes that dependence cannot be put forward as a reason for diminished responsibility but might be offered in mitigation of a related infringement of the law arguing that dependence will predict future general behaviour (not specific behaviour) and it is in the best interests of society as a whole and the individual concerned to treat rather than punish the dependence if this is thought to be possible. These views are embraced by the Mental Health Act (1983) which specifically excludes alcohol or other drug states apart from psychosis, from being under the umbrella of mental illness for the purpose of the Act. ICD-9 is confusing in its categorisation of substance related mental illness and curiously still retains the dubious conditions of *pathological drunkenness* and *pathological drug intoxication.*

Legal niceties and restrictive admission policies by medical and other statutory and non-statutory agencies leave the front line clinician in the A & E Department or on a domicillary visit in a difficult predicament when faced with a patient who, for example, indicates suicidal intent or pleas for help with a drink or drugs problem but in the setting of intoxication or withdrawal. Clearly the question of service provision can only be resolved by political action at a national and local level but professionals cannot hide behind this and must set their own guidelines and standards for dealing with difficult situations. Given the universal lack of adequate detoxification facilities, most front line workers become adept at finding reasons for admission to less appropriate but more conventional facilities that do at least provide a place of safety for their patients; it is up to specialist agencies, not just in addictions, to promote more flexible responses to meet the needs of alcoholics and addicts.

In many cases where patients present in a state of intoxication or withdrawal there will be clear secondary gain prompting the attendance; it may be appropriate to collude, for example by helping a person find shelter or accommodation. Overt or threatened aggression is difficult to contain in most medical facilities and in circumstances where on-site staff cannot deal with a violent incident it may be appropriate to request that the police remove the person to a place of safety. In a number of cases, for example if it is unclear what drugs have been taken or if there is a history of delirium or seizures the patient will require hospitalisation for observation. Probably the majority of patients will require overnight observation; although a drug-free state takes weeks to achieve, a re-appraisal of an individual's condition after twenty-four hours will usually give a clear guide as to whether any psychiatric symptomatology was simply a transient disturbance or part of a more serious mental illness.

The variety of new and effective treatments for many psychological problems including frank mental illness have demanded an extension of diagnostic categories where substance misuse is concerned. A modest but useful starting point is the concept of *primary* versus *secondary* mental illness; any disorder antedating excessive use of a psychoactive substance can readily be identified as *primary* but when the age of onset of substance misuse is before the expected age of onset of a particular psychiatric disorder there is no simple way to unravel the relative contributions of drug effect, environment and genetic predisposition in order to determine primacy. Jaffe (1984) has proposed a much more complex model emphasising that post-detoxification affective disorder is both heterogenous and of multiple aetiology, and also showing how the development of dependence transcends the aetioloical significance of dysphoria in maintaining excessive substance intake.

## Affective states

Affective disturbance refers to all kinds of pathological mood states including anxiety, irritability and depression but also other less clearly defined dysphorias. The presence of affective symptomatology of which depression is ubiquitous, is common among substance misusers as a consequence of intoxication, dependence and acute or chronic withdrawal, but *symptoms* alone must by distinguished from the diagnosis of *affective illness*.

Alcohol and opioids are the principal drugs of chronic regular misuse and will be considered separately and in detail.

## Depression and alcohol misuse

Keeler et al (1979) draw attention to high rates of depression (70–98 per cent) in 'alcoholics' given self-rating questionnaires which simply record reported symptoms, against depression judged by diagnostic interview (3–10 per cent); they acknowledge that the rating scales considered were not intended to be diagnostic, but also assert that interviewers may unwittingly be biased against making a diagnosis of depression in 'alcoholics' by overcompensating for expected withdrawal dysphoria and the unfavourable social predicament of many patients.

Two large and detailed studies, one from the USA and one from Ireland, have investigated primary 'alcoholics' who were referred to psychiatric alcohol treatment units and compared patients with and without secondary depression against a range of variables. Schuckit (1983) found that almost one third of his primary 'alcoholics' had serious affective disorder meeting DSM–III criteria and O'Sullivan et al (1983) found 23 per cent of their patients met Feighner's (1972) criteria for psychiatric disorder; 10 of this latter group had bipolar illness. In the first study the depressed and non-depressed groups showed no differences in demographic variables, pattern of drinking, rates of affective disorder in first degree relatives or antisocial behaviour during childhood, but the *depressed* group did use significantly more drugs, especially marijuana and LSD, and did show a trend toward more alcohol related social problems. In the second study also, no differences were found in drinking histories, demographic profiles and rates of affective disorder in first degree relatives, however, as would be expected, the depressed group received more treatment both on an in-patient and out-patient basis and in terms of prescribed medication; the authors make the point that although treatment seemed to be effective in stabilising mood, drinking behaviour was unaltered. The relationship between mood state, dependence and pattern of drinking needs further investigation. Neither of the studies quoted report on any rating of dependence but it seems possible that dependence may be the prime determinant of maintaining drinking while depressed mood is only one albeit potent cue initiating a drinking episode. This would in part account for the equivocal results of treatment with anti-depressants and lithium.

In a study of patients with alcohol related disease referred to a liver unit Ewusi-Mensah et al (1983) found 40 per cent of men and 62 per cent of women to have an affective disorder by Research Diagnostic Criteria (Spitzer et al 1978); of these 22 per cent and 47 per cent respectively were judged primary. Schukit (1983) reported only 3 per cent of patients referred to an alcohol treatment unit had a primary affective disorder and O'Sullivan et al (1983) reported 10 per cent.

To summarise these rather confusing figures it seems reasonable to suggest that 25-30 per cent of primary 'alcoholics' referred to treatment units will have a secondary affective disorder; this figure will decrease for patients referred to non-psychiatric facilities and other non-medical agencies. The very high rate of primary affective disorder found in patients referred with alcohol related liver disease is interesting and as yet, unexplained. The rate of 'alcoholism' in patients with primary affective disorder is estimated at 8-30 per cent. Goodwin (1982) has calculated the expected concomitance for 'alcoholism' and unipolar affective disorder to be approx 0.2 per cent and for bipolar disorder 0.04 per cent.

## Depression and opioid misuse

Two studies of depression in opioid addicts use Research Diagnostic Criteria (Spitzer et al 1978) rather than symptom rating scales to estimate affective disorder and are therefore comparable to the studies of Schukit (1983) and O'Sullivan et al (1983) described above. In a six month follow-up of 157 addicts seeking help at a drug addiction unit, Rounsaville et al (1982) found that 17 per cent had a current major depressive disorder and 48 per cent had a lifetime diagnosis of depressive disorder of which some six per cent were primary cases. Using the Beck Depression Inventory to assess symptomatology they found 21 per cent reported moderate to severe symptoms (score 15 or higher) and 39 per cent mild symptoms (score 8-14); at follow-up there was a pansymptomatic improvement. Although approximately one fifth of people were judged depressed at intake and one fifth at follow-up, only 2 per cent of individuals were depressed at *both* intake and follow-up. The authors draw attention to previous work linking depressive symptomatology with treatment seeking behaviour but report that presence of depressive symptomatology and diagnosis of depressive illness were related to premature drop-out and use of illegal drugs during follow-up, suggesting that for some addicts use of opioids reduces persistent dysphoria. This theme is supported by Dackis and Marks (1983) who also found a 17 per cent prevalence of major depression using RDC criteria opioid addicts; this rose to 32 per cent at three weeks post-withdrawal. They speculate that pre-addiction depression is likely to be too debilitating to initiate the intricate manoeuvres required to obtain heroin and, again speculating, they suggest that at least some subtypes of secondary depression in opioid addicts are the result of decreased endogenous opioid output. Since *naltrexone* stimulates the release of β-endorphin this hypothesis could be tested.

## Dexamethasone suppression test

The dexamethasone suppression test (DST) has been extensively used as a clinical investigation to differentiate endogenous depression from other psychiatric disorder. It is reported to have a sensitivity of only 50 per cent but a specificity in excess of 95 per cent. *Non-suppression* (abnormal result) is not related to demographic variables, duration of symptoms or severity of anxiety or depressive symptomatology (Saleem 1984). Applying the test to 'alcoholics' Swartz and Dunner (1982) found that 33 per cent of 43 men hospitalised for alcohol misuse were *non-suppressors* at 4 pm (17 hours after 1 mg of dexamethasone); they did not differ from *suppressors* in terms of drinking history, depressive symptomatology or affective disorder in first degree relatives, but they had higher baseline cortisol levels and evidence of liver disease. The authors examine the possibility of liver damage and the possibility of withdrawal stress to account for the high frequency of *non-suppressors* but find both explanations lacking. They note that only 2 patients were *non-suppressors* at 8 am (9 hours after 1 mg dexamethasone) and suggest an early escape from suppression in 'alcoholics'; a mechanism has yet to be found. Newsom and Murray (1983) found a reversal of DST non-suppression within three weeks of continued abstinence.

In a study of opioid addicts meeting the RDC for major depression, Dackis et al (1984) found that the DST gave a sensitivity of 80 per cent and specificity of 93 per cent.

## Suicide and substance misuse

Reports of attempted suicide and completed suicide frequently avoid separating the prevalence of alcohol versus drug dependence in the study populations. Sedative drugs are the ones most frequently used and often in combinations including alcohol; more than anything else the choice of sedative reflects currently popular and available prescribed drugs. In series of attempted suicide the prevalence of drug dependence has been estimated at 10–20 per cent (Ghodse 1981) and alcohol dependence at 30–40 per cent (Soloman 1982).

Kessel and Grossman (1961) found a completed suicide rate of more than 7 per cent in male alcoholics at 1–11 year follow-up which represents a rate in excess of 80 times that expected of the general population; several other authors have replicated these findings. It is important to be aware that almost half the suicides in 'alcoholics' are committed whilst sober and at least one fifth while euthymic. Recent social loss especially separation from a spouse or loss of job are predictors of suicide (Murphy and Robins 1967) and illustrates the fragility of the 'alcoholic' in an unfavourable environment.

## Overview of depression, mania and substance misuse

That there are connections between both depressive and manic moods and substance misuse is not in dispute and there is a need for research to unravel causal links and natural histories. Several studies have shown that *excluding* those patients who are markedly dependent on alcohol, bona fide manic depressives drink less during a depressive phase and more during a manic phase. The drug of choice during a manic phase may be largely determined by cultural availability; Harding and Knight (1973) report on excessive marijuana use in manic patients in Jamaica and noted that the symptomatology was modified towards that of a schizophreniform illness. The prevalence of *primary* affective disorder is generally reported in the region of 5–10 per cent in both alcohol and opioid misusers which is in fact close to findings in the general population of 4 per cent unipolar and 2 per cent for bipolar illness (Goodwin 1982). The prevalence of *secondary* disorder is generally reported in the region of 20–30 per cent; the closeness to more normal mood states and the fluctuating and ephemeral characteristics are usually stressed. Because depressive symptoms happen to be *secondary* it does not follow that they are of diminished significance, even though the disturbance may be self-limiting. The depression associated with amphetamine or cocaine withdrawal or with use of LSD is noteworthy for its severity.

## Alcohol and anxiety

The widely accepted belief that alcohol relieves tension and anxiety has been repeatedly challenged by research findings and yet clinicians continue to affirm tension reduction as a causal factor in many cases of alcohol dependence. Unravelling these apparent contradictions from a pharmacological viewpoint Littleton (1984) has explored the connections between stress, anxiety and alcohol intake. He concludes that alcohol itself is a mild stressor but is also effective at relieving more severe kinds of tension of whatever cause; he goes on to suggest that chronic, dependent drinking is likely to generate the most stress. Anxiety can be viewed as the manifestation of a failure to cope with stress; it is one of the commonest conditions dealt with by doctors and usually treated by prescription of a minor tranquilliser. Littleton has pointed out some similarities between ethanol, barbiturates and benzodiazepines at the biochemical level of action suggesting that these drugs might all be considered as belonging to one class which has anxiolytic properties. Finally, he suggests that alcohol may itself generate an anxiety state and points out that chronic administration of alcohol increases central noradrenalin turnover (a marker of anxiety) and withdrawal increases turnover even further.

Phobic anxiety is more amenable to treatment than stress or free floating anxiety and has been the subject of several recent studies. Mullaney and Tripett (1979) found that of 102 'alcoholics' admitted to an Alcohol Treatment Unit, 33 had disabling agoraphobia or social phobia and 37 displayed minor symptoms; of 44 patients physically dependent on alcohol, only 8 had alcohol related problems antedating the phobia. In a prevalence study Smail et al (1984) found only 18 per cent of their sample of 'alcoholics' to have severe phobic symptoms and 35 per cent had mild symptoms. They found that the severity of dependence related to the severity of phobic symptoms only for male patients, but that all groups reported an anxiolytic effect from drinking. In a small second study of 18 patients referred for treatment of agoraphobia and social phobia, 12 patients described situations in which they found alcohol helpful as an anxiolytic and half of this group described deliberate use of alcohol for this purpose in certain problem situations; only 2 patients were judged to be dependent on alcohol.

Stockwell et al (1984) have concluded that anxiety may both initiate and maintain dependent drinking. It might reasonably be assumed that there are similar risks of other sedative drugs being misused and reports are available to support this contention (Reilly 1976, Peturrson & Lader 1981). It can also be speculated that any drug with dependence forming properties may itself become a stressor and generate anxiety. Patients frequently report using cannabis for its anxiolytic properties but generally speaking illegal drugs do not find favour for dealing with situational anxiety problems.

## Delirium

Delirium is a non-specific response by the brain to some intra or extra cerebral toxin, infection, metabolic or other systemic disturbance which is usually reversible. The cardinal features of delirium are i) clouded, but typically fluctuating level of consciousness ii) disorientation, impaired hierarchically for time, place and person iii) perceptual disturbance including illusions and vivid hallucinations which are predominantly visual iv) confusion. Affective disturbance and delusional beliefs may occur as secondary phenomena.

It is rarely problematic to recognise a state of delirium but it will often be impossible to determine the aetiology without extensive investigation. An assumption of substance related delirium even where there is a supporting history may result in failure to properly examine the differential diagnosis which will include a number of conditions such as trauma, heart failure and infection, common among the population of alcoholics and drug addicts.

All patients in a delirious state should be admitted to a suitable hospital unit. The patient should be nursed in a well but not too brightly lit room with plain decoration; there should be maximum constancy of staff and the patient repeatedly reassured and informed of what is happening. General supportive measures will be required until a definitive diagnosis is reached or the condition subsides.

## Delirium and withdrawal states

Abrupt withdrawal from any CNS depressant drug taken in high dosage is likely to precipitate delirium, often preceded by seizures. There is invariably a delay of 24–72 hours before the signs of delirium appear and once triggered the delirium seems to run a course of its own which may, to some extent be controlled by sedative drugs. This is in contrast to opioid withdrawal where there is no delirium and the symptoms of withdrawal can be completely reversed by giving opioids.

### Alcoholic delirium

In a classic study Isbell et al (1955) demonstrated that seizures and the condition then known as Delirium Tremens were a consequence of an abrupt cessation of alcohol intake. Six of a group of volunteers who were former morphine addicts and serving prison sentences for drug-related offences, drank 350–450 g of alcohol daily for a minimum of 48 days before abrupt withdrawal. All subjects experienced symptoms of autonomic overactivity, visual and auditory hallucinations; three subjects were disorientated and two had seizures. Kramp et al (1979) have reported on a detailed investigation of the clinical features of alcoholic delirium; they graded the severity of delirium by dividing their patient sample into two groups distinguished by the presence or absence of disorientation. On a rating scale of severity of withdrawal the disorientated group were also more agitated and more preoccupied with hallucinations; they had more likely been on a heavy binge immediately prior to admission and had a high BAC on admission. In both groups the course of the detoxification was uncomplicated and markers for autonomic overactivity, namely elevated pulse, unstable blood pressure and pyrexia had made significant movement back towards normal at 36 hours; elevated temperature was, in individual cases, correlated with the severity of withdrawal. The authors took particular care to monitor the doses of barbiturate (the sedative used to cover withdrawal) required to induce sleep and found that overall there was no difference between the two groups. If the disorientated group were simply a more severe form of a withdrawal state continuum then they should have required more barbiturate to achieve the same end point and since this was not so the authors argue that there are two factors associated with alcoholic delirium. They speculate that the tremulousness and autonomic overarousal is a component related to dependence and amenable to control by drugs cross tolerant with alcohol whereas the delirious component is related to high levels of tolerance, not susceptible to treatment with sedatives and triggered by a rapidly falling BAC. In his review of alcoholic delirium Gallant (1982) points to the observation that falling serum potassium is a good predictor of delirium, though correction of the serum level by potassium infusion has no therapeutic value. Gallant also makes a plea that the presence of auditory hallucinations should not be taken as evidence against a diagnosis of alcoholic delirium.

The phenomenology of the perceptual disturbances associated with alcoholic delirium has not been widely investigated. The classic visual hallucinations of frightening, bright coloured animals can be understood because of the patient's susceptibility to illusions. It is more difficult to understand the frequently reported well formed hallucinations such as the disembodied head described by Isbell et al (1955) or the coloured often distorted human forms which may fluctuate between lilliputian and gigantic size. Insight into the hallucinations is variable and usually more evident when the hallucinations are less threatening.

Specific pharmacological measures to treat alcoholic delirium will include adequate sedation and the drug of first choice is probably *chlormethiazole* 1–2 g qds or the equivalent by infusion. Benzodiazepines such as *chlordiazepoxide* in a divided dose of 200–300 mg daily or, if there is significant liver damage, *oxazepam* 60–180 mg daily may be useful. If additional anti-convulsant medication is required, *phenytoin* up to 1 g iv in 24 hours should be adequate. Daily vitamin supplements containing at least 200 mg of *thiamin* to protect against Wernicke's encephalopathy should be given routinely until normal diet is re-established. Alcoholic delirium is usually of short duration and intravenous infusion is rarely necessary; care must be taken not to set up a glucose infusion until thiamin has been given. Alcoholic delirium carries a mortality rate variously reported at up to 10 per cent. The most common causes of death are circulatory collapse, irreversible hyperglycaemia, malignant hyperthermia or intercurrent infection. Cutting (1978) describes a subacute confusional state which persists beyond the normal course of alcoholic delirium.

**Other sedatives and delirium**

There are reports in the literature (Barten 1965, Preskorn & Dunner 1977) of delirium and seizures occurring three to five days after withdrawal of benzodiazepines taken in doses ranging upwards from *diazepam* 100 mg daily (or its equivalent). The autonomic overarousal appears to be less prominent than for alcohol withdrawal.

The widespread use of *chlormethiazole* as an effective agent to cover alcohol withdrawal has lead to realisation that this drug itself possesses powerful dependence forming properties and doses ranging upward from 6 g daily seem well able to produce delirium, with an onset within 24 hours of abrupt withdrawal and a high propensity for seizures (Reilly 1976, Gregg & Akhter 1979). The prescription of barbiturates has been greatly reduced but misuse and therefore difficult withdrawal problems persist. Isbell et al (1950) described the occurrence of seizures and delirium 48 to 72 hours after the abrupt withdrawal of barbiturates. The severity depends on the dose of drug being taken and its half life; for *amylobarbital* withdrawal seizures or delirium are likely for doses in excess of 1 g daily. The preferred treatment is to reinstate barbiturates using a long acting preparation such as *phenobarbital* in doses adequate to alleviate symptoms which should require no more than 2 g on the first day, reducing by 100 mg per day initially.

## Delirium and intoxication

Delirium asociated with intoxication from stimulants and similar sympathomimetic drugs, occurs within hours of taking the drug and is dose related. The essential features are of delirium but tactile and olfactory hallucinations are said to be especially common. There is often a lability of mood and violent or aggressive behaviour. Snow et al (1980) report on a case of *phenylephrine* misuse which demonstrates some features typical of stimulant delirium. A twenty-six year old female presented with depression and suicidal ideation secondary to experiencing a feeling of snakes crawling over her body and bugs crawling under her skin; she believed men were watching her and that she was in great danger.

Delirium associated with stimulant intoxication subsides spontaneously within 6-12 hours. An anxiolytic and 'talking down' is the only treatment required. *Phencyclidine* delirium may last up to a week following a waxing and waning course that is thought to be due to excretion into and reabsorption from the stomach.

## Schizophrenia, delusional and hallucinatory states

Schizophreniform psychosis is taken to mean any psychotic episode that in 'cross-section' is difficult to differentiate from schizophrenia but is seen as a separate disorder when a wider view is opened and factors such as family history, premorbid personality, natural history, and response to treatment are taken into account. The cardinal features of schizophreniform psychosis are i) delusions which are often persecutory ii) disembodied auditory hallucinations iii) anxiety and agitation. Drug induced psychosis normally resolves within 4–8 weeks of the patient being in a drug-free state. If recovery is less rapid the possibility of schizophrenia arises but it is often the case that the residual symptoms of drug induced psychosis are more in the nature of a hybrid schizo-affective disorder.

### Schizophrenia

Patients suffering from schizophrenia tend to avoid drugs in the classes of stimulant and hallucinogen because they recognise that these substances exacerbate schizophrenic symptomatology. Equally a majority of schizophrenic patients say that their condition is worsened by alcohol, but for those individuals experiencing troublesome auditory hallucinations or mood disturbance there seems to be some relief gained from drinking or taking some other sedative drug, especially cannabis. Of hospitalised schizophrenic patients 20–40 per cent are said to be 'alcoholic' and of 'alcoholics', 10 per cent have schizoid personality disorder or frank psychosis. In a review of alcoholism and schizophrenia Freed (1975) was unable to find any constant themes linking the two disorders.

### Acute delusional psychoses

The delusional psychoses of acute onset all occur in the setting of recent and usually escalating drug use. There may be an associated toxic confusional state when massive doses of a drug are absorbed into the system rapidly but this is not part of the delusional disorder. The psychotic state, which usually includes hallucinations, delusions and dysphoria, can always be seen to have emerged from a state of intoxication. Some drugs such as alcohol do not feature a proclivity to acute psychotic states, possibly because the rate of intake of alcohol is usually a self-limiting factor. Opioids are not associated with paranoid psychoses.

**Amphetamine psychosis** has been described by many authors, but Connell's monograph (1958) which reports on 42 cases, remains the definitive work. He concludes that psychosis can be induced by a single dose as low as 50 mg of amphetamine, but notes that chronic users can consume much higher doses without displaying psychotic symptoms. Auditory and visual hallucinations were equally common and invariable while tactile or olfactory hallucinations were present in 20 per cent of cases. In all but two cases the symptoms persisted no more than 4 weeks from withdrawal from amphetamine. Disorientation was noted in three patients but Connell suggested that more may have experienced a toxic confusional state prior to the onset of the paranoid psychosis. Comparing amphetamine psychosis with schizophrenia Bell (1965) concluded that the two conditions were very similar in presentation but found that visual hallucinations and absence of disordered thinking were prominent features of the former. Stereotypic behaviour has been reported to be a characteristic of amphetamine psychosis (Snyder 1973) but this does not appear to be a clinically helpful marker. Kalix (1984) has drawn attention to the rare amphetamine-like psychosis caused by chewing Khat leaves.

**Cocaine psychosis** is described as having essentially the same features as amphetamine psychosis. Spotts and Schontz (1980) have commented on the potential for aggressive and violent behaviour from patients suffering from cocaine psychosis and Thornton (1984) has vividly illustrated this point from her research into use of unadulterated cocaine in the 1880s and 1890s.

**Lysergic acid diethylamide** (LSD) is a highly plastic drug and the occasion of a 'good' or 'bad trip' depends very heavily on factors such as stable premorbid personality, using the drug in a secure environment and the absence of personal crisis (McWilliam & Tuttle 1973). Given this backdrop and being mindful of the powerful and varied drug effects of LSD, most noticeably disturbances of affect and perception, it is easy to understand the emergence of an acute LSD psychosis in a vulnerable person. Comparing 52 patients diagnosed as LSD psychosis against 29 schizophrenic patients, Vardy and Kay (1983) found a high incidence of alcoholism in parents of the LSD users; the two differed on some minor points of psychological testing but no other distinguishing features were noted. In a similar exercise Young (1972) found more visual disturbance and memory impairment in the LSD patients, but similar problems of thought processes to a schizophrenic group.

**Psilocybin psychosis** has become increasingly common as more people discover and experiment with 'magic mushrooms'. 25–50 psilocybe mushrooms are sufficient to induce a psychotic state characterised by ideas of persecution or ideas of reference, delusional mood, anxiety and physical signs including dry mouth, dry skin, dilated pupils and difficulty with micturition. It has been suggested that this results not from sympathetic overactivity but rather parasympathetic blockade (atropine-like) and there is a case report of recovery from psilocybin psychosis within 30 minutes of receiving *phsysostigmine* 4.0mg iv (Benjamin 1980, van Poorton et al 1982).

**Cannabis psychosis** has been described as 'rare' (Polsson et al 1982) and 'common' (Carney & Bacelle 1984); such contrasting reports reinforce the need for research into the patterns of use of cannabis and consequences. A person who develops cannabis psychosis is typically a heavy daily smoker and often uses other drugs most usually alcohol; as with the other psychoses in this group, the disorder develops as an extension of a period of intoxication. A striking feature is lability of mood, sometimes with agitation and aggressive outbursts. Delusions are often rather vague but may sometimes be intense and frightening; auditory and visual hallucinations are usual. Confusion, disorientation and difficulty judging time or distance are not uncommon features. It may be that there are sub-types of cannabis psychosis that might most properly be classified as toxic confusional states or manic depressive states; in fact the mood changes are not as sharp or bipolar as would be expected in manic-depressive illness and there is a low hereditary base. The paranoid cannabis psychosis typically settles within 2–3 days without medication but perceptual and affective disturbance may persist for several months (Edwards 1983). Polsson et al (1982) describe symptoms of apathy, lack of initiative, shallowness of affect that are present for years after stopping the drug; this symptom cluster may be analogous to the amotivational syndrome described by Chopra and Smith (1974) in India.

# Flashback phenomena

These have been reported in individuals who have taken hallucinogenic drugs experiencing perceptual disturbances even many years after last taking the drug. Abraham (1983) in a retrospective study of patients attending a psychiatric emergency clinic found that most commonly reported were geometric pseudohallucinations, flashes or intensified colours and trailing phenomena (positive afterimages). The most common precipitants of 'flashback' were entering a dark place, intention (will), marijuana, phenothiazines, anxiety and fatigue (in rank order). He goes on to speculate a failure of inhibitory mechanism in visual pathways as the neurophysiological basis. Whatever the precise mechanism involved, 'flashbacks' seem to involve a re-emergence or release of previously established psychotic processes rather than a malfunction of memory systems.

## Non-acute delusional psychosis

**Morbid jealousy** has a rather doubtful status as a delusional disorder. It seems more likely the case that some individuals have a lifelong sensitivity and difficulty in controlling feelings of jealousy and possessiveness. The cardinal features of morbid jealousy are i) falsely believing a spouse (invariably wife) to be unfaithful ii) seeking confirmatory evidence of this iii) extreme violence directed against the spouse. Occasionally auditory hallucinations are reported in which case, treatment with a phenothiazine may be appropriate. Morbid jealousy is said to be particularly common where there is misuse of alcohol or cocaine and a dynamic explanation sees declining sexual performance from the man as fertile ground for a real risk of infidelity but in any event, loss of self esteem compensated for by hostility in the husband. It is unclear why alcohol and cocaine should be particularly associated with this problem. Even if a patient can be kept away from alcohol and drugs, the prognosis is poor and the risk for the spouse's safety, even her life, should not be underestimated; geographical separation seems to be the best approach. Shepherd (1961) has elegantly described this condition.

**Alcoholic hallucinosis** is very fully described in a classic paper by Victor and Hope (1958). In a series extending to over 1000 'alcoholic' patients they identified 76 who had auditory hallucinations, about half also had visual hallucinations which proved to be a predictor of imminent and serious withdrawal problems. The onset of hallucinations occurred within 12 hours of stopping drinking for 60 per cent of patients but for 30 per cent the onset occurred while still drinking. The hallucinations are usually of disembodied voices, often derogatory, threatening, accusatory, moralising or commanding; in almost all cases the patients responded in the appropriate way to the voices, 90 per cent of patients recovered spontaneously within one week and at this time there was a restoration of insight. The symptomatology in the 10 per cent of patients who developed the chronic illness also changed at one week to a more clearly schizophreniform character with ideas of reference and influence emerging as well as more systematised delusions albeit with disordered thinking. The authors concluded that in the benign group there was no connection between alcoholic hallucinosis and schizophrenia, indeed 3 patients in this group had a diagnosis of schizophrenia, and reverted to their previous schizophrenic state once the hallucinosis had subsided. For the chronic group the emergent symptomatology was indistinguishable from schizophrenia. The age of onset, 45–50 years, the premorbid personality usually 'cyclothymic' and the absence of any family history of schizophrenia distinguished the chronic hallucinosis group from schizophrenics.

Of the non-acute delusional psychoses it would seem reasonable to suggest re-classifying morbid jealousy perhaps with anankastic personality disorder and grouping alcoholic hallucinosis with the other drug induced delusional psychoses.

## Dementia and amnestic syndromes

### Cerebral atrophy, cognitive impairment and dementia

The availability of non-invasive CT scanning has made possible the detailed study of structural changes in the brain and allows for these to be regularly monitored. The hallmarks of dementia are: i) progressive impairment of memory function associated in the early stages with anxiety, agitation, depression and lability of mood ii) coarsening of the personality characteristics and associated behavioural problems iii) global impairment of cognitive function iv) emergence of secondary delusions and hallucinations; the onset is usually insidious but psychological testing can reveal deficits before they become clinically evident.

In testing for *alcohol* related cognitive impairment a number of psychological tests are accepted as having particular value, i) memory function: *synonym learning, Inglis paired associate learning* ii) perceptual and motor skills: *block design, digit symbol test, trail making* iii) abstracting ability: *Wisconsin card sort test, Halstead categorising*. Batteries of tests for use on micro-computers are now available and will no doubt replace pencil and paper methods in due course. However, there remains much validation work to be done before these new instruments can safely be used with patient groups. Ron (1983) has reported on a study comparing 50 alcoholics with 50 matched controls on variables of demographic data, drinking patterns, psychological tests and CT scans. The radiological findings showed that at least two thirds of the 'alcoholics' significantly differed from controls in showing widening of the Sylvian fissure and enlarged ventricles. The degree of atrophy did not, however, correlate with any of the drinking variables such as duration of excessive drinking, peak consumption, period of abstinence prior to scan or total life consumption. Other workers have reported a correlation between cognitive impairment and total life intake when this exceeded 400 gallons of absolute alcohol. Ron also noted an amelioration of the cerebral changes during periods of abstinence though the extent of the improvement varied according to age related factors. It is accepted that there is a rapid improvement in cognitive function after detoxification especially in the areas of verbal learning, visuospatial ability, and abstract thinking, and it used to be thought that the improvement could continue for some 4–6 weeks. Brandt et al (1983) in a long-term follow-up have shown that there is a selective return of cognitive function up to at least five years, indeed in all their patients who had achieved such extended abstinence, short-term retention of verbal and non-verbal material was no different to controls although long-term memory and the ability to learn novel associations remained impaired. The authors speculate that the improvement in short-term memory not matched by long-term memory may indicate a propensity for cortical but not subcortical tissue to regenerate. In a study of 20 patients dependent on benzodiazepines Ron found that 17 had abnormal CT scans which fell intermediate to normals and abstinent alcoholics; the details of the methodology are not supplied (Lader & Petursson 1983). Poser et al (1983) found cerebral atrophy on CT scan only when benzodiazepine misuse was associated with a history of heavy alcohol use. In a much criticised paper Campbell et al (1971) demonstrated cerebral atrophy using air-encephalogram techniques in a group of cannabis smokers; the index group misused other drugs so that interpretation of the findings is difficult.

Using CT scans Kuehale et al (1977) were unable to confirm the presence of structural changes in the brains of heavy marijuana smokers. Rumbraugh et al (1980) conducted a series of experiments on rhesus monkeys and also found no evidence of brain damage caused by oral marijuana; they did however, find that amphetamine, particularly when given intravenously did cause major abnormalities in angiographic studies and on CT scanning. In summary then, there is plentiful evidence to support the concept of alcoholic dementia. The diagnosis may be difficult to make since the signs can for long periods remain sub-clinical or be passed over and attributed to a 'troublesome alcoholic'; the danger of course is that incorrect management decisions may be taken and goals set that cannot be attained. Gregson and Taylor (1977) have shown impaired cognitive function to be a predictor of poor outcome. A second diagnostic confusion may arise because only rarely will pure alcoholic dementia be present and much more frequently the picture will be a mix including features of the Korsakoff's syndrome. The case for dementia being caused by other drugs most notably cannabis and minor tranquillisers has yet to be proved and needs much more intensive investigation noting interactive effects with alcohol.

## Blackouts

The *alcoholic 'blackout'* refers to memory loss associated with drinking; other sedative drugs, notably benzodiazepines (Barton 1965) and barbiturates may also cause amnesias. A rapidly rising plasma concentration of any central nervous system depressant may be associated with a dysmnestic syndrome; such conditions are encountered with intravenous drug use, either recreational or for anaesthetic purposes, or heavy spirit drinking. Goodwin et al (1969) found that two thirds of hospitalised 'alcoholics' had experienced 'blackouts' while drinking; one third had fragmentary amnesia and one third had what they described as *en bloc amnesia,* that is, a dense memory loss with a definite beginning and end. Typically the amnesias extend over a period of 2-6 hours but may occasionally run to several days. In the fragmentary type of 'blackout' a return of memory loss was often possible during subsequent episodes of intoxication and this phenomenon is referred to as state dependence. In theory, novice users could experience amnesias, but in practice 'blackouts' indicate a high level of tolerance to sedative substances otherwise the rapidly rising blood levels would induce a state of unconsciousness.

## The Wernicke-Korsakoff syndrome

The eponymous Wernicke's encephalopathy and Korsakoff's psychosis were independently described at the end of the 19th century. Wernicke's encephalopathy is a nutritional disorder caused by deficiency of vitamin B1 (thiamin); the condition is particularly likely to arise in alcoholics because i) the body has little in the way of thiamin stores, ii) nutritional status may be chronically poor (Carney et al 1982) although Wood et al (1982) note that an alcohol intake of not less than 80 g daily is required to displace dietary thiamin, iii) absorption may be impaired, iv) the metabolism of alcohol requires thiamin as a co-enzyme. It has generally been thought that an alcoholic binge can, per se, precipitate a relative B1 deficiency state, however on the strength of a single pair of MZ twins one of whom died and was diagnosed at post-mortem as Wernicke's encephalopathy and the other being healthy but with abnormal transketalase activity, Leigh et al (1981) suggest a possible contribution from an inborn error of metabolism.

Inadequately treated, Wernicke's encephalopathy may progress to permanent damage of susceptible brain tissue, the symptoms and signs of which are manifest as Korsakoff's psychosis. The intimate connection between the two disorders is fully described by Victor et al (1971) in their series of 245 patients. Neuropathological studies have identified the areas of brain most vulnerable to damage and equated these to clinical signs; lesions are found in the walls of the third ventricle, periaqueductal region, floor of the fourth ventricle, mamillary bodies and some areas of thalamus and cerebellum.

Over 90 per cent of patients with Wernicke's encephalopathy have psychiatric symptoms, typically a low grade delirium with drowsiness, fatiguableness, memory disturbance and perceptual disturbance such as misidentification but rarely hallucinations. Victor et al (1971) reported ocular abnormalities in 96 per cent of their patients and ataxia, usually truncal, in 87 per cent. This triad of confusion, opthalmoplegia, and truncal ataxia represents the core of the condition. Nearly one fifth of their series died in the acute phase and of the survivors 84 per cent developed a typical Korsakoff psychosis; the psychiatric symptoms are almost invariably resolved within 4 weeks but ataxia and ocular disturbance was sometimes persistent. The leading features of Korsakoff's psychosis are i) short term memory difficulties with grossly impaired new learning ability, ii) retrograde amnesia for the acute episode (where this occurs) antecedent to the Korsakoff's, iii) confabulation with dislocation of events in time. Cutting (1978) compared patients with acute versus gradual onset of Korsakoff's syndrome and patients with alcoholic dementia. He noted that in all three groups about three quarters of the patients showed mood change, especially euphoria. The gradual onset Korsakoff's group and alcoholic dementia group were most similar. The acute onset Korsakoff's group were younger, had shorter drinking histories and were more likely to show evidence of liver damage. Cutting found that over 25 per cent of patients in his series improved and good prognostic factors were gradual onset of the illness, in an older person with a short drinking history.

Treatment must be vigorous. Parentrovite which contains 250 mg *thiamin* is a suitable preparation for daily administration until a normal diet is restored at which time oral vitamins should be prescribed for a further six weeks. Refractory cases may respond to magnesium supplements (Traviesa 1974). The Wernicke-Korsakoff syndrome is a unique psychiatric disorder in that it can be diagnosed using a blood test, it is treatable, curable and preventable. Brewers have argued against adding thiamin supplements to beers on aesthetic grounds but Mielgaard (1982) found that a thiamin supplement of 0.25 mg per litre which would protect against Wernicke's encephalopathy could technically be introduced to drinks and was acceptable to consumers.

## Conclusion

Although this chapter has rather colluded with the classification systems that force unwilling mixtures of symptoms and signs into convenient categories, this has been done in an attempt to achieve clarity by focusing thought on the differential diagnosis for the four major groups of psychiatric disorder considered. The position taken here should be seen as a starting point from which variants or subtypes can be recognised. The presence of psychiatric disorder is often quite obvious even though its precise nature may be unclear, but practitioners must also be alert for more subtle manifestations of psychiatric illness and to achieve this a clear understanding of symptoms and signs that might be expected as a direct result of substance misuse as well as a good knowledge of psychiatry is essential.

## REFERENCES

Abraham H D 1983 Visual phenomenology of the LSD flashback. Archives of General Psychiatry 40: 884–889

Barten H H 1965 Toxic psychosis with transient dysmnestic syndrome following withdrawal from valium. American Journal of Psychiatry 121: 1210–1211

Bell D S 1965 Comparison of amphetamine psychosis and schizophrenia. British Journal of Psychiatry 111: 701–707

Benjamin C 1980 Persistent psychiatric symptoms after eating psilocybic mushrooms. British Medical Journal 19 May 1: 1319–1320

Brandt J, Butters N, Ryan C, Bayog R 1983 Cognitive loss and recovery in long-term alcohol abusers. Archives of General Psychiatry 40: 435–442

Campbell A M G, Evans M, Thomson J L G, Williams M J 1971 Cerebral atrophy in young cannabis smokers. The Lancet Dec 4: 1219–1224

Carney M W P, Bacelle L 1984 Psychosis after cannabis use. British Medical Journal 288: 1047

Carney M W P, Ravindran A, Rinsler M G, Williams D G 1982 Thiamine riboflavin and pyridoxene deficiency in psychiatric in-patients. British Journal of Psychiatry 141: 271–272

Chopra G S, Smith J W 1974 Psychotic reaction following cannabis use in east indians. Archive of General Psychiatry 30: 24–27

Connell P H 1958 Amphetamine psychosis. Maudsley Monograph No 5

Cutting J 1976 Heterogeneity in Korsakoff's syndrome. M.Phil Thesis

Cutting J 1978 The relationship between Korsakov's syndrome and 'alcoholic dementia'. British Journal of Psychiatry 132: 240–251

Dackis C A, Marks S G 1983 Opiate addiction and depression — cause or effect. Journal of Drug and Alcohol Dependence 11: 105–109

Dackis C A, Pottash A C C, Gold M S, Amitto W 1984 The dexamethasone suppression test for major depression among opiate addicts. American Journal of Psychiatry 141: 810–811

Edwards G 1983 Psychopathology of a drug experience. British Journal of Psychiatry 143: 509–512

Edwards G, Holgate S T 1979 Dependency upon salbutamol inhalers. British Journal of Psychiatry 134: 625–626

Ewusi-Mensah I, Saunders J B, Wodak A D, Murray R M, Williams R 1983 Psychiatric morbidity in patients with alcoholic liver disease. British Medical Journal 287: 1417–1422

Feighner J B et al 1972 Diagnostic criteria for use in psychiatric research. Archives of General Psychiatry 26: 57–63

Fingarette H 1981 Legal aspects of alcoholism and other addictions: some basic conceptual issues. British Journal of Addiction 76: 125–132

Freed E X 1975 Alcoholism and schizophrenia: the search for perspectives. A review. Journal of Studies on Alcohol 36: 853–881

Gallant D M 1982 Psychiatric aspects of alcohol intoxication, withdrawal and organic brain syndromes. In: Soloman J (ed) Alcoholism and clinical psychiatry. Plenum Medical, New York & London, ch 11 p 141

Ghodse H 1981 Morbidity and mortality. In: Edwards G, Busch C (eds) Drug problems in Britain, a review of ten years. Academic Press, London, ch 7 p 171

Goodwin D W 1982 Alcoholism and affective disorders, the basic questions. In: Soloman J (ed) Alcoholism and clinical psychiatry. Plenum Medical, New York & London

Goodwin D W, Crane J B, Guze S B 1969 Phenomenological aspects of the alcoholic 'blackout'. British Journal of Psychiatry 115: 1033–1038

Gregg E, Akhter I 1979 Chlormethiazole abuse. British Journal of Psychiatry 134: 627–629

Gregson R A M, Taylor G M 1977 Prediction of relapse in male alcoholics. Journal of Studies on Alcohol 38: 1749–1760

Hall R C W et al 1979 Relationship of psychiatric illness to drug use. Journal of Psychiatric Drugs 11: 337–342

Harding T, Knight F 1973 Marijuana — modified mania. Archives of General Psychiatry 29: 635–637

Isbell H et al 1950 Chronic barbiturate intoxication. Archives of Neurology and Psychiatry 64: 1–28

Isbell H, Fraser J F, Wikler A, Belleville R E, Eiseman A (ed) 1955 An experimental study of the etiology of 'rum fits' and delirium

Jaffe J H, Martin W R 1980 Opioid analgesics and antagonists. In: Gilman A G, Goodman L S, Gilman A (eds) The pharmacological basis of therapeutics. Macmillan, London, ch 22, p 494

Kalix P 1984 The pharmacology of Khat. General Pharmacology 15: 179–187

Keeler M H, Taylor O C, Miller W C 1979 Are all recently detoxified alcoholics depressed? American Journal of Psychiatry

Kessel N, Grossman J 1961 Suicide in alcoholics. British Medical Journal ii: 1671–1672

Kramp P, Nemmingsen R, Rafaelsen O J 1979 Delirium tremens — some clinical features Part 11. Acta Psychiatrica Scandinavica 60: 405–422

Kuehnle J, Mendleson J H, Davis K R, New P F J 1977 Computed tomographic examination of heavy marijuana smokers. Journal of American Medical Association 237: 1231–1232

Lader M, Petursson H 1983 Long-term effects of benzodiazepines. Neuropharmacology 22: 527–533

Leigh D, McBurney A, McIlwan H 1981 Wernicke-Korsakoff syndrome in monozygotic twins: a biochemical peculiarity. British Journal of Psychiatry 139: 156–159

Littleton J M 1984 Biochemical pharmacology of ethanol tolerance and dependence. In: Edwards G, Littleton J M (eds) Pharmacological treatments for alcoholism. Croom Helm, London & Sydney. ch 9, p 119

McWilliams S A, Tuttle R 1973 Long-term psychological effects of LSD Psychological Bulletin, American Psychological Association 79: 341–349

Meilgaard M C 1982 Technical aspects of the enrichment of beer with thiamin. Journal of Studies on Alcohol 43: 427–433

Mullaney J A, Trippett C J 1979 Alcohol dependence and phobias clinical description and relevance. British Journal of Psychiatry 135: 565–573

Murphy G E, Robins E 1967 Social factors in suicide. Journal of American Medical Association 199: 303–308

Newsom G, Murray N 1983 Reversal of DST nonsuppression in alcohol abusers. American Journal of Psychiatry 140: 353–354

O'Sullivan K et al 1983 A comparison of alcoholics with and without co-existing affective disorder. British Journal of Psychiatry 143: 133–138

Petursson H, Lader M H 1981 Benzodiazepine dependence. British Journal of Addiction 76: 133–145

Polsson A, Thulin S O, Tunving K 1982 Cannabis psychoses in South Sweden. Acta Psychiatrica Scandinavica 60: 311–321

Poser et al 1983 Do benzodiazepines cause cerebral atrophy? The Lancet March 26 715

Preskorn G H, Denner L J 1977 Benzodiazepines and withdrawal psychosis. Journal of American Medical Association 237: 36–38

Reilly T M 1976 Physiological dependence on, and symptoms of withdrawal from, chlormethiazole. British Journal of Psychiatry 128: 375–378

Ron M A 1983 The alcoholic brain: CT scan and psychological findings. Psychological Medicine. Cambridge University Press, p 1–33

Rounsaville B J, Weissman M M, Crits-Christoph K, Wilber C, Kleber H 1982 Diagnosis and symptoms of depression in opiate addicts. Archives of General Psychiatry 39: 151–156

Rumbaugh C L, Fang H C H, Wilson G H, Higgins R E, Mestek M F 1980 Cerebral CT findings in drug abuse: clinical and experimental observations. Journal of Computer Assisted Tomography 4: 330–334

Saleem P T 1984 Dexamethasone suppression test in depressive illness, its relation to anxiety symptoms. British Journal of Psychiatry 144: 181–184

Schukitt M 1983 Alcoholic patients with secondary depression. American Journal of Psychiatry 140 (6): 711–714

Shepherd M 1961 Morbid jealousy: some clinical and social aspects of a psychiatric symptom. Journal of Mental Science 107: 687–704

Smail P, Stockwell T, Canter S, Hodgson R 1984 Alcohol dependence and phobic states in a prevalence study. British Journal of Psychiatry 144: 53–57

Snow S S, Logan T P, Hollender M H 1980 Nasal spray 'addiction' and psychosis: a case report. British Journal of Psychiatry 136: 297–299

Snyder 1973 Amphetamine psychosis: a model schizophrenia mediated by catecholamines. American Journal of Psychiatry 103: 61–67

Soloman J 1982 Alcoholism and suicide. In: Soloman J (ed) Alcoholism and clinical psychiatry. Plenum Medical, New York & London, ch 8, p 97

Spitzer R L, Endicott J, Robins E 1978 Research diagnostic criteria rationale and reliability. Archives of General Psychiatry 35: 773–782

Spotts J V, Shontz F C 1980 (eds) Cocaine users, a representative case approach. Free Press, London

Stockwell T, Smail P, Hodgson R, Cater S 1984 Alcohol dependence and phobic anxiety states II a retrospective study. British Journal of Psychiatry 144: 58–63

Swartz M, Dunner F J 1982 Dexamethasone suppression testing in alcoholics. Archives of General Psychiatry 39: 1309–1312

Thornton E M 1984 Images of cocaine. Lancet Jan 7 p 46

Traviesa D C 1974 Thiamine refractoriness in Wernicke-Korsakoff. Journal of Neurology, Neurosurgery and Psychiatry 37: 959–962

Tsuang M T, Simpson J C, Kronfol Z 1982 Subtypes of drug use with psychosis, demographic characteristics, clinical features and family history. Archives of General Psychiatry 39: 141–147

Van Poorten J F, Stienstra R, Davoracek B, Moleman P Rupreht J 1982 Physostigmine reversal of psilocybin intoxication. Anaesthesiology 56: 313

Vardy M M, Kay S R 1983 LSD psychosis of LSD induced schizophrenia. Archive of General Psychiatry 40: 877–883

Victor M, Adams R D, Collins G H 1971 Wernicke-Korsakoff syndrome. Blackwell Scientific Publications, Oxford

Victor M, Hope J M 1958 Phenomenon of auditory hallucinations in chronic alcoholism. Journal of Nervous Mental Disorder 126: 451–481

Weissman M M, Myers J K 1980 Clinical depression in alcoholism. American Journal of Psychiatry 137: 372–373

Wood B, Goode A, Buttigeig R, Brian K 1982 The effect of short-term moderate alcohol consumption on health and thiamin states. Journal of Studies on Alcohol 43: 158–163

Young B G 1972 A phenomenological comparison of LSD and schizophrenic states. British Journal of Psychiatry 124: 64–74

# 4
# *Social aspects*

One of the fascinations of working in the field of addictions is to study not only the social antecedents and consequences of substance misuse but also the social policy that determines these. Building up a general model of how the environment and the individual interact with each other has taken the energy of many sociologists over the years; social consequences of substance misuse have also been rigorously investigated by researchers from various disciplines. The conclusions are sometimes conflicting and it is not the intention in this short review to discuss all the many interesting aspects of this research, but rather to pull out some key themes and look at some of the problems facing research in this area.

Social research frequently involves looking at large numbers of interacting variables and there are some pitfalls here to be aware of. First, index group selection is often quite seriously biased towards help seeking populations such as A & E attenders or psychiatric referrals; it is frequently difficult to find adequate controls for these patients. General population field studies are, of course, notoriously expensive and difficult to run, and not surprisingly they are uncommon. Secondly, many authors propose categories such as 'alcoholic' or 'addict' as though these were diagnostic groups when, in fact, the labels simply identify, at the best, one common variable, *dependence* in an otherwise heterogenous group of individuals that certainly span all of general psychiatry and probably all of the general population. The trend by researchers to record the severity of dependence on the drug of first choice is to be applauded. Thirdly, there is a problem of how properly to take account of social factors in the process of change that leads to recovery; for example the importance attached to life events might be somewhat idiosyncratic, the events may be distant in time from

101

changes in substance use and cause or effect links constantly difficult to unearth. Finally, there is the problem common to all group surveys that significant changes in individuals in terms of their substance use and personal well being are often lost in the cancelling out of positive and negative movement when group means are calculated. Edwards (1984) has discussed the need to look at not only an individual's substance use career but also at health, work, crime and other careers. Thorley (1984) and Norris (1983) have plotted the treatment careers of small numbers of cases, but to date there has been no real attempt at a statistical presentation of careers.

Sociological studies that in some way sample changes in the relationship of the individual to the environment as a way of accounting for movement in attitudes and behaviour are especially valid once substance misuse occurs and more particularly when society has invoked controls to prevent misuse, but why does misuse occur in the first place? Plant (1981) has sympathy for a universal explanation and supports the view that since substance use, especially tobacco, alcohol and cannabis, is so widespread among diverse groups of people who are neither socially deprived nor psychologically disturbed, then there may exist some fundamental need artificially to achieve altered states of mind. It is interesting that socially acceptable recreational drugs tend to have modest dependence forming properties and moderate pathoplasticity. Plant's bold statement is in itself very helpful; without looking for additional causes or vulnerability factors we can accept that human beings have an innate propensity to take psychoactive materials and that any society will start out with a substrate of users whose choice of substance will no doubt vary but who will be problem free. Given this starting point can we identify the influences that come to bear and so transform what was an innocuous, indeed rewarding habit into a major problem for the individual and for society as a whole? Robinson (1977) has reviewed some of the social factors associated with alcohol misuse.

## A balance of interests

At a national level social policies are arrived at by a compromise of conflicting demands lobbied by powerful institutions and pressure groups and inevitably this juggling trick leaves anomalies and dissatisfaction. In the case of substance misuse it is often the government itself that is ambivalent about adopting control measures. This theme is well illustrated in the excellent historical review of Williams and Brake (1980) who describe how overt drunkenness by successive monarchs, gentry, clergy and common people alike emerged by common consent as a problem that society must deal with, and in 1495 Henry VII, a sober individual, introduced legislation to control alcohol misuse. This was the first of now numerous drinking laws governing alcohol and other drugs. In 1552 drunkenness per se became an offence, and 1643 saw the critical development of a tax on liquor. The revenue raising potential of alcohol was again seized on by William III when the importation of distilled spirit was banned thereby encouraging a home industry which paid a levy to the Crown. The distilling business flourished showing an increase from 527,000 gallons of spirit in 1684 to 3,601,000 in 1727, but the toll of 'gin houses' on health and social well-being, vividly depicted in Hogarth's series 'The Rake's Progress', was so great that the government, under pressure from temperance minded people was forced to do something to reduce drinking. The Gin Act 1736, which amounted to prohibition, was passed by parliament with the effect that income was lost, an illicit trade flourished and the temperance movement strengthened.

This cameo of the fortunes of alcohol immediately throws into relief two of the issues that are at the heart of the conflict surrounding any social policy decisions, namely the dangerousness of a substance versus its revenue raising potential. It should not be supposed that an interest in making profit is necessarily at odds with safety and certainly most legitimate organisations are sufficiently concerned to protect their image, their future and their compensation contingency fund that they market their products responsibly. It can be assumed that organised crime is motivated by money and rarely philanthropic though again it would be against its own interest to sell a product that was transparently very dangerous; cynics would say this is also the view of legitimate business. There are many vested interests in both promoting and restraining the drink and drug business and lobbying produces some strange bedfellows. Different ministerial priorities often leaves the government behaving in worrying ways as for example when the 'Think Tank' report on factors influencing alcohol consumption was repressed (BJA Editorial 1983).

A point that merits amplification is the question of how, especially in social terms, harm is defined. In 1495 for example, when the first controls on alcohol were introduced, there had been no sudden change in drinking pattern but rather social historians (Trevelyan 1978) comment on a redefining of values and new sense of order in the country as the Middle Ages faded into past history. As society has become more sophisticated this intrusion of regulations has necessarily extended into many areas of life, some of which are mundane such as driving motor vehicles while others are more elite, for example flying airplanes. Another interesting example of public outrage being the prime mover of legislation is cocaine. Spotts and Schontz (1980) point out the usefulness to the poor South American Indians of chewing Coca leaves to relieve hunger and reduce exhaustion and when the cocaine alkaloid was isolated in 1860 it was seen as a drug with powers to cure many ailments and it was overenthusiastically prescribed by physicians including Freud, who believed it to be a cure for morphine addiction. Many proprietary concoctions containing cocaine appeared as medicines or tonics including, in 1888, Coca-Cola. It slowly became apparent however, that cocaine had serious dependence forming properties and frequently caused a dangerous persecutory psychosis. It was shrewdly dropped as an ingredient in Coca-Cola in 1903, three years before legislation restricting its use, in spite of strong opposition, was put on the statute book.

Government now has properly constructed committees of professional people and invariably researches the costs and benefits of a drug before taking formal action. However, there remain numerous examples where legislators seem to take the view that if a substance is of economic importance then it is acceptable to tolerate 'casualties' and to play down the harmful effects until the usage is so excessive as to be debilitating to the country as a whole. The actual use of social policy in present day preventive strategies is discussed in detail in Chapter 6.

## The personal environment

A culture is made up of a miscellaneous collection of beliefs and values handed down through the ages and usually enshrined in institutions such as the Law, the Church and the Schools; it is in this one particular social context that a child learns behaviours such as drinking alcohol and taking drugs. Clinicians need to make a detailed assessment of an individual's personal characteristics, but they must also see that individual in a dynamic social system which may well be amenable to change itself.

It is established that young children learn what alcohol and its effects are at a very early age and advocates of the so called *integration model* suggest that making alcohol a part of every day life for young people takes away the mystery, excitement and guilt associated with novice, clandestine drinking; the proposition assumes the development of healthy, moderate attitudes towards drink which will then be sufficiently robust to withstand undesirable influences in young adult life. The French and Italians tend to adopt this integrative approach and while it is true in these countries that social consequences of intoxication are few, per capita consumption is high and they experience among the highest rates of liver cirrhosis in Europe. The integration model may have merit on heuristic grounds rather than as a protection against problem drinking.

In a fascinating cross-cultural study, O'Connor (1978) collected data about drinking habits and attitudes by interviewing 774 18-21 year olds, 613 fathers and 747 mothers from Dublin and London. She found that parent's attitudes rather than actual behaviour influenced drinking habits, but that the perceived attitudes of father were the most potent influence. She supports the widely held idea that parents with particularly vehement views, for or against alcohol, are more likely to have heavy drinking children. She points to some intriguing cultural differences between the English and Irish and proposes that children are not alienated from their older generation as has been suggested but in fact, transmit to their own children their parent's beliefs with small modifications. The Irish were much more disapproving of drink and made no distinction between social drinking, drunkenness and alcoholism. Of 18-21 year olds, 70 per cent of English and 66 per cent of Irish males, and 33 per cent of English and 24 per cent of Irish females were classed as heavy or very heavy drinkers. Peer group pressure is important for determining how, when and where drinking becomes part of a lifestyle. In O'Connor's study peer group support for drinking was high: only 1 per cent of all males, 2 per cent of English females and 10 per cent of Irish females said they had no peer group support for drinking. Single sex drinking or drinking with a signficant other was most often associated with heavy consumption. The influence of peers and its interaction with personal characteristics and the political environment needs interpreting at the single case level.

Throughout most western societies there are campaigns to

legalise cannabis and there now exists a generation of parents that includes regular cannabis users. It is difficult to know in what ways this seeming approval of cannabis by some adults puts it on a par with alcohol in countries where cannabis remains illegal. The manifestations of marijuana smoking might not be as obvious to young people as drinking and where the drug is still illegal parents are likely to conceal its use. Kandel et al (1978) found that peer group use and non-conforming attitudes best predicted cannabis smoking for young people in New York. Dembo and Shern (1982), again in New York, found that there was an orderly progression from no drug use to drinking 'hard-liquor', from hard liquor to marijuana and marijuana to hard drugs; the movement up to marijuana was accounted for by street socialisation activities, while movement to opioid drugs was associated with friends using hard drugs, but only where the individual was also impaired in their personal development. In his study of drug taking in Cheltenham, Plant (1975) found that cannabis was the drug first used by 79 per cent of the population studied and all drug users had at some time taken cannabis. Plant found 14 per cent of those interviewed had exclusively used cannabis and did not intend to move to other drugs, 15 per cent had experimented with injecting drugs but only 1.5 per cent continued to do so. On this evidence Plant rejected the idea of progression from cannabis to heroin use but in fact his research is consistent with the findings of Dembo et al (1979) who suggest that cannabis is a usual stepping stone on the way to hard drugs. The point to note is the requirement of adverse personal characteristics in addition to cannabis use for the move to heroin.

Some sociologists believe there are social theories that, without calling on explanations of personal characteristics, account for how some individuals cross a rather arbitrary and ill defined line into anti-social behaviour and then find themselves placed in a new framework of interaction with society as a whole. Although *deviance* remains continuous with *normal* experiences it is as if society runs out of coping strategies and, in effect, takes *deviance* out of 'normal' society. Plant (1981) has suggested that two theories merit consideration. *Deviancy amplification* theory holds that society reacts against drug taking by attempting to control it and this leads to a vicious circle of intensification of identity with the 'drug scene' and further attempts by the state at control; this may explain the stereotyping and strong subculture images that are held about drug takers. Plant points out that the proposition that control necessarily leads to a reactive increase in drug use is debatable. The second theory which Plant considers is based on Durkheim's concept of *anomie* which holds that people who, through no personal failing, are nevertheless denied access to status and wealth as defined by a given society, establish alien subcultures that take on their own values and support systems. At the risk of over generalising it might be held that drug misusers positively reject the values of the dominant culture and identify with a drug scene, whereas the Skid Row subculture is a survival group and a serious negative consequence of alcohol misuse. Cooke (1975) and others have tended to romanticise the meaning of Skid Row as a positive alternative to the dominant culture.

There are factors in the personal environment that modify the overall influences of society to protect against or increase the risk of substance misuse. Considering first some demographic variables, males are more likely than females to drink excessively and to misuse drugs. Of clinic populations it is young people who misuse illegal drugs; over 90 per cent of patients are under 30 years. It is true that as the explosion of drug users from the mid-sixties matures so the drug clinic attender's mean age increases slightly; it is also the case that the age of presentation with an alcohol problem is falling and in recent years is increasingly found to be under 30 years. A majority of drug users have no religious inclinations and less than 10 per cent subscribe to traditional religions; Rastafarians are pro cannabis, Moslems, Jews and Hindus strongly oppose the use of alcohol.

Among other things, employment status is an indicator of how people spend their day; very little research has investigated the risks of substance misuse from being unemployed, a student or housewife. 30-40 per cent of drug users in the treatment population are in regular employment and represent the bulk of Stimson and Ogbourne's (1970) 'stable' addicts; 70-80 per cent of alcoholics are in full time employment. Empirically, certain jobs carry a high risk of substance misuse; medical, nursing and pharmaceutical practitioners are at particular risk of drug addiction, whereas publicans, seamen, servicemen, journalists and actors are at high risk of alcoholism. It is debatable whether the job leads to the substance misuse or whether it is the case that certain jobs are attractive to people dependent on drugs or alcohol; probably both are true in different cases. Plant (1979) has suggested a number of factors are important in finding high rates of alcoholism in certain occupational groups: i) availability, ii) social pressure to drink, iii) separation from normal socio-sexual relationships, iv) freedom from supervision, v) collusion and protection by colleagues, vi) stressful nature of occupation. Certain spare time activities are more likely to include heavy drinking and this notion was the basis of Wilkins' (1974) Spare Time Activities Questionnaire as an instrument of detection. Although there is conflicting evidence, it does not seem that involvement in sport is an effective protection against licit or illicit substance use with the exception of cigarette smoking (Rooney 1984).

The focus here has been on social explanations of substance use and misuse, and should be seen as part of a complex picture of interaction. Dembo and Shern (1982) have proposed a framework of understanding based on the concept of *relative deviance*, which asserts that individuals who deviate from the norms of general behaviour for their particular socio-cultural group will tend to use psycho-active substances that are also less acceptable in that group. In essence this means that the use of drugs such as tobacco, alcohol and marijuana will be predominantly accounted for by socio-cultural factors; disturbed personality variables will be increasingly important as individuals move onto drugs such as stimulants, opioids, solvents and hallucinogens (though there may be a hierarchy within these) especially when use is regular and heavy rather than experimental.

There is a substantial research literature supporting the idea that individuals move in and out of misuse of substances, be this alcohol (eg Saunders & Kershaw 1979) or opioids (eg Wille 1983) and indeed this vacillation, rather than sudden change, is the most usual way to establishing abstinence or reinstating 'normal' use of a substance (to all intents and purposes 'normal' use refers to alcohol but similarities may be seen in methadone maintenance programmes or appropriate use of tranquillisers). The social correlates of time spent in harm-free use of alcohol and other drugs are not difficult to predict but sometimes may simply reflect what has been measured rather than what is important. Favourable influences that have been identified include marriage or the establishment of an important relationship, employment per se but especially changes in employment that involve promotion or a work ethos intolerant of alcohol or drug use, financial restrictions, geographical relocation, religious or other group activity intolerant of alcohol or drug use, and adequate housing provision. Heather and Robertson (1981) comprehensively review the literature on outcome studies relating to alcohol misuse and Stimson and Oppenheimer (1982) for heroin misuse. The question to be answered is do these social correlates of overall improvement antedate and generate changes in cognitive set or does the change in cognitive set come first with social advances passively following? The answer of course does not have to be one or the other and indeed an overview of the research evidence points to both sequences happening and always an interactive progression. Edwards (1984) has pointed to the need for synthesis of psychosocial and psycho-biological approaches.

## Consequences of substance misuse

### Problems of Procurement

There are obvious differences between use of licit and illicit substances simply by virtue of their legal status. Because of the ready availability and legality of alcohol in most western cultures maintaining supplies is not in itself a problem, the limiting factor is usually finance. On average, ten pints of beer daily will cost, at 1984 prices, approx £45 per week and a daily bottle of spirits will cost approx £60 per week. Even for a wealthy person this kind of expenditure will cause hardship and deprivations relative to others of similar socio-economic status and for the less well off the only way to make ends meet is to indulge in petty crime, either by theft of alcohol directly or stealing other goods to sell or exchange for alcohol.

Maintaining an addiction to hard drugs is massively expensive. Costs fluctuate depending on simple supply and demand principles but, again at 1984 prices, a heroin user could be spending £150-250 per week and involvement in serious crime, especially resale of drugs and prostitution is the usual way of funding the habit (James et al 1979). Mott (1981) has stated that drug misuse is not associated with criminal activity except in respect of offences directly drug related, and the drug addicts who include in their repertoire offences that are not drug related are more similar to other offenders than other drug addicts. The illegality and limited availability of most drugs of misuse presents separate problems for the user. Sources of supply have to be established and the drugs have to be collected; this may be done by private arrangement or at some acknowledged 'street market'. In fascinating accounts Hughes (1977) has described the 'street-life' in a neighbourhood of Chicago and Burr (1983) has described her infiltration of the

Piccadilly drug scene in London. The essential features of both are easy accessibility, regular presence of known dealers and protection against harassment from the police or opportunist criminal elements; protection is afforded by the openness and bustle.

## Problems of intoxication

Simple public drunkenness, being drunk and disorderly or drunk and incapable are all offences although the vigour with which the police enforce these laws is quite variable. Arrests for drunkenness are taken as a marker of alcohol-related problems and in a given cultural setting the number of drink related arrests is crudely correlated with per capita consumption. Many people believe that control of public drunkenness is not likely to be achieved by penal approaches and have advocated the decriminalising of drunkenness through the setting up of detoxification centres where the police can take intoxicated individuals to sober up without pressing charges; this approach offers the possibility of screening people for health and social problems that are amenable to change and is economical on penal system resources (Home Office 1971).

Intoxication causes impairment of judgement. At a BAC of 80 mg per cent the overall risk of a road traffic accident doubles and at a BAC of 150 mg per cent the risk increases twenty five fold. Other factors, notably personality and drinking experience influence the risk of accidents; the anxious of introverted person can improve performance on motor skills with modest amounts of alcohol whereas the 'psychopath' becomes intolerant and aggressive. Several studies have found that with a BAC >150 mg per cent the risk of serious pedestrian accidents, death from drowning, house fire or other untoward event is greatly increased, and 30-50 per cent of serious accidents at work, skewed to after lunch or on the night shift are a direct result of intoxication. Although not systematically researched, there are reports of increased accident risk from intoxication with other drugs especially solvents and prescribed tranquillisers. The more stable users of illegal drugs will tend to take their drugs in a private place and therefore have some protection against the problems discussed here; the unstable drug user is likely to overdose and be taken to A&E or arrested for possession of illegal drugs.

The association between violence or aggressive acts and

intoxication is widely recognised. About half the rapes and two thirds of murders in the U.K. are committed under the influence of alcohol. The research suggests that spontaneous or opportunist offences and premeditated offences with emotional or interpersonal overlay are most likely to occur in association with intoxication. Wife battering and child abuse have traditionally been seen as resulting from the effect of alcohol as disinhibitor releasing aggressive tendencies, but the prevalence of marital violence and the true relationship with intoxication is in fact unknown. There may be advantages in terms of a defence mechanism for the drunken person to attribute drunkenness simply to a problem with alcohol rather than examining the state of their marriage or their personality characteristics (Jacob & Seilhamer 1982). Chick (1984), in a more general review of intoxication, has warned of spurious connections pointing out that it may be easier for the police to catch an intoxicated person or there may be a third unseen factor common to both crime and drinking such as a personality disorder or the nature of the situation such as a football match where there is a high expectation of violence.

Aggression from intoxication with other drugs may arise in a similar way to alcohol where misuse of other CNS depressants occurs but for other drugs is more likely to result from the emergence of ideas of persecution from taking high doses of amphetamine, cocaine or LSD, although evidence of this is conflicting. Misuse of opioids per se is not generally associated with violence against other people.

## Problems of dependence

Problems of dependence will usually, though not necessarily, include the problems of procurement and intoxication previously discussed. The timescale to achieve serious levels of dependence on different substances varies greatly. A cardinal feature of dependence is the salience of substance use over other activities and for drugs such as heroin or amphetamine, dependence develops so rapidly that a lifestyle characterised by inactivity, self-neglect and a preoccupation with procurement is often established quickly. A swift decline with burgeoning social problems or death is not inevitable and in a 10 year follow-up Stimson and Oppenheimer (1982) found that of 'stable' addicts who represented a third of their intake group one third had remained 'stable' addicts over the follow-up period; these 'successful' addicts adopted routines for taking their heroin that did not involve intoxication, they worked in jobs that allowed them to attend clinics weekly and take drugs through the day, and they moved out of friendship with other addicts so that they relied solely on clinics to supply their drugs.

Drugs where dependence develops more slowly, such as alcohol and sedatives, are also likely to be associated with a more insidious social deterioration. The more dependent alcoholics will experience problems at work; there will be morning absences occasioned by hangover, difficulty in getting on with workmates and a fall in productive work output. In earlier stages of dependence much of the heavy drinking will be restricted to weekends so that work problems are largely unnoticed. Personal relationships will suffer as the individual and family, if there is one, become alienated from friends and society in general; social contact may lessen. The 'alcoholic' is seen as a stressor of family systems; the economic problems, unpredictable behaviour and exclusion from peer group activities fuel the tensions. If children are involved then emotional problems and abnormal behaviour are commonly reported though these research findings need careful interpretation being mindful of the index group selection. Wilson (1982) draws attention to the effects of different drinking patterns on children, an observation that may equally apply to other drugs. She notes differences in male: female patterns of drinking, men being more likely to be intoxicated and women more likely to tipple at home through the day and suggests that neglect of children from constant intoxication or depression may be more damaging than aggression and conflict. About one third of children with an 'alcoholic' parent also develop a drink problem.

## Conclusion

Much of the research into the social aspects of substance misuse has centred on the study of associations and is limited by the problem of attributing cause, effect and coincidental findings. The asssessment and management of any case must include an appreciation of the social context; the complex interactions and dynamic character of any social system defy quick analysis and certainly do not fit neatly into the pigeon holes generated by research endeavours. It is often forgotten that a home visit can be one of the most instructive elements of investigation and can uncover important idiosyncrasies of a case in addition to testing the fit of more general theories to the particular situation.

## REFERENCES

Burr A 1983 The Piccadilly drug scene. British Journal of Addiction 78: 5-19
Chick J 1984 The Social and clinical importance of intoxication. In: Edwards G, Littleton J (eds) Pharmacological treatments for alcoholism. Croon Helm, London, ch 5, p 47
Cooke T (ed) 1975 Vagrant alcoholics. Routledge and Kegan Paul, London
Dembo R, Shern D 1982 Relative deviance and the process(es) of Drug involvement among inner city youths. International Journal of Addictions 17: 1373-1399
Editorial 1982 British Journal of Addiction 77: 1-2
Edwards G 1984 Drinking in longitudinal perspective: career and natural history. British Journal of Addiction 79: 175-183
Heather N, Robertson I (eds) 1981 Controlled drinking. Methuen, London
Home Office 1971 Report of working party on habitual drunken offenders. HMSO, London
Hughes M D 1977 Behind the wall of respect. Chicago, USA
Jacob T, Seilhamer R A 1982 The impact on spouses and how they cope. In: Orford J, Harwin J (eds) Alcohol and the family. Croon Helm, London
James J, Gosho C, Wohl R W 1979 The relationship between female criminality and drug use. International Journal of Addictions 14: 215-229
Kandel D B, Kessler R C, Argulies R Z 1978 Antecedents of adolescent initiation into stages of drug use: a development analysis. In: Kandel D B (ed) Longitudinal research on drug use. Washington D C
Mott J 1981 Criminal involvement and penal response. In: Edwards G, Busch C (eds) Drug problems in Britain, A review of ten years. Academic Press, London, ch 8, p 217
Norris H 1983 The frequency of relapse and the need for coping strategies. National Symposium, Northampton, UK
O'Connor J (ed) 1978 The young drinkers, A cross-national study of social and cultural influences. Tavistock, London
Plant M (ed) 1975 Drugtakers in an English town. Tavistock, London
Plant M (ed) 1979 Drinking careers. Tavistock, London
Plant M 1981 What aetiologies? In: Edwards G, Busch C (eds) Drug Problems in Britain, a review of ten years. Academic Press, London, ch 9, p 245
Robinson D 1977 Factors influencing alcohol consumption. In: Edwards G, Grant M (eds) Alcoholism, new knowledge and new responses. Croon Helm, London
Rooney J F 1984 Sports and clean living: a useful myth? Journal of Drug and Alcohol Dependence 13: 75-87
Saunders W M, Kershaw P W 1979 Spontaneous remission from alcoholism — A Community Study. British Journal of Addiction 74: 251-265
Spotts J V, Shontz F C (eds) 1980 Cocaine users, a representative case approach. Free Press, London
Stimson G V, Ogbourne A C 1970 Survey of addicts prescribed heroin at London clinics. Lancet, May 30 1163-1166
Stimson G V, Oppenheimer E (eds) 1982 Heroin addiction: treatment and control in Britain. Tavistock, London

Thorley A 1984 Drug taking careers. 3rd International Conference on Treatment of Addictive Behaviour, North Berwick

Trevelyan G M (ed) 1978 English social history. Longman, London

Wilkins R 1974 The hidden alcoholic in general practice. Elek Science, London

Wille R 1983 Processes of recovery from heroin dependence: relationship to treatment, social changes and drug use. Journal of Drug Issues 13: 333-342

Williams G P, Brake G T (eds) 1980 Drink in Great Britain 1900-1979. Edsall, London

Wilson C 1982 The impact on children. In: Orford J, Harwin J (eds) Alcohol and the family. Croon Helm, London, ch 8, p 151

# 5

# *Treatment and change*

Treatment is not an isolated curative insertion into the lives of drug misusers but rather is part of their whole matrix of experience. This interacts with past developmental events and its effect is filtered through those of the future. This in a way contradicts the more traditional view of treatment as a bridge from illness to cure and administered by external therapists to passive patients. Longitudinal studies show that drug misusers can improve without recourse to formal treatment intervention and evidence suggests that treatment processes are not qualitatively distinct from naturally occurring processes of change. Furthermore it is equally arbitrary to differentiate between aspects of the treatment process itself as the individual is a potential changer from the moment he presents: initial interview, assessment, therapy, relapse prevention and rehabilitation can all be instrumental in the initiation and maintenance of behaviour change.

The present chapter considers treatment in this broad sense. Where possible, the emphasis is on commonalities rather than differences in the management of drug and alcohol dependence and the focus is on treatment of dependence rather than acute medical crises resulting from withdrawal or overdose. The first section concentrates on a longitudinal view of change whether it be mediated by treatment or naturally occurring processes and several longitudinal studies are reviewed. It is hoped that this can help place the effects of formal therapeutic intervention in perspective. Subsequent sections deal with current issues in service provision, common therapeutic approaches and the formulation of appropriate treatment goals.

## A longitudinal view

Longitudinal studies of drinking and drug use are becoming increasingly important and provide information on change over time which allows for a more realistic interpretation of the treatment literature (Polich et al 1981, Stimson & Oppenheimer 1982, Vaillant 1983). Such studies are time consuming, expensive and beset with methodological pitfalls but nevertheless they allow for an appreciation of the process of change into and out of addiction which cross-sectional studies do not. Before reviewing a number of important longitudinal studies it is perhaps necessary to clarify some issues involved and to outline what is the first integrative model of the processes and stages of change in the area of substance misuse.

A distinction has been drawn between the constructs of *career* and *natural history* for drinkers (Edwards 1984) and other drug users (Thorley 1981). It is argued that a career is a psychosocial construct which indicates sequential role behaviour which in this case is the role of *drug user*. The various environmental influences from birth onwards which shape the drug users career must be understood in the context of the culture and society in which the individual lives. In this context treatment should be seen as an interaction between the therapeutic input and the developing unfolding career (Edwards 1980, Finney et al 1980, Yates & Norris 1981). Treatment has been described as giving the career a 'little nudge in a more hopeful direction' (Edwards 1984). Natural history on the other hand has a more biological emphasis and in medicine is applied primarily to intrapersonal pathological processes although external events may have some bearing on these. Neuroadaptive changes such as withdrawal effects or tolerance are particular examples of phenomena which can be described in terms of natural history. These develop over time and as the sequencing and mechanisms involved are still far from understood (Littleton 1984) there is clearly a need for further natural history studies of the individual's reactivity to drugs. In the future more longitudinally based studies may take into account the interaction between the career and natural history dimensions with the resultant integration of different levels of explanation. To date however virtually all longitudinal studies have focussed on drug taking careers. Edwards (1984) argues that it is essential for treatment to be matched 'to processes and phases of an unfolding career rather than to a static description of the patient'. There has recently been an attempt to integrate treatment methods with stages of change and this work is outlined below.

## The stages and processes of change

The treatment episode is normally only a short interval in a patient's life and its effect should be seen against the backdrop of the individual's past and future circumstances, as well as his preparedness for change. In line with the current search for general principles of change across various psychtherapeutic and behavioural interventions (Ryle 1984, Goldfried 1982) some workers have attempted a similar exercise for treatment in addictions (Prochaska & Di Clemente 1982, 1983). Not only have they looked at precipitants of change which are common to various therapeutic systems but those which also occur in so called *self changers*. It is argued that individuals whose addictive behaviour improves without undergoing treatment, experience similar precipitants, or what are termed, *processes of change* as those who improve with treatment. To call such change therefore, spontaneous remission is slightly misleading as it is not an instantaneous mysterious recovery but occurs over time and is similar in nature to therapeutically induced change. Prochaska & Di Clemente in their *transtheoretical model* have, as well as looking at processes of change, isolated *stages of change* which unfold over time as the successful individual alters his drug-using behaviour. The model has been generated from data on about 900 ex-smokers but the authors point out that it is appropriate for conceptualising change among substance misusers generally.

It is suggested that individuals are at various stages in their willingness or preparedness to change. First there is the *precontemplation stage* in which the person is not aware of having a particular problem perhaps as a result of denial, ambivalence or selective exposure to information. As long as the individual remains here even the most intensive intervention is unlikely to produce a favourable outcome. In this stage he actively resists self-exposure to curative influences. When the individual becomes aware that his drug use constitutes a problem and begins to think about altering his behaviour he is said to have entered the *contemplation stage*. Data on smokers suggest that this can last for up to one year although this may well vary across substances. Next the user may move to the *determination stage* when there is a serious commitment to *action*. Evidence suggests that this is a relatively short time period and is analogous to the age-old idea of reaching a turning point. The commitment and decision to change leads the individual to the *maintenance stage* in which the new habits must be actively maintained through continual vigilance. This maintenance phase can also last for some considerable time until the individual exits the change system to *termination,* i.e. favourable long term outcome. For most people, however, who are attempting to alter addictive behaviour, *relapse* is common, notably in the first six months or so. The individual either exits back to precontemplation or begins to contemplate change once again. After the vigilance of maintaining new behaviour the determinants of relapse could include strength of dependence, negative self evaluation, environment contingencies or inadequate coping styles (Marlatt & Gordon 1980, Litman 1982). The number of revolutions of change will vary across people and drugs but the data on ex-smokers suggests that they take an average of three revolutions before becoming free of the habit. As long as the individual remains in the maintenance stage the risk of relapse is ever present. The so-called *revolving door* of change is summarised in Fig. 5.1.

Prochaska & Di Clemente (1983) demonstrated that particular processes of change are more appropriate according to the stage of change. They reviewed a number of therapeutic systems ranging from verbal psychotherapy to behavioural and cognitive approaches. Although, as would be expected, these therapeutic systems differed as to which of the processes were emphasised and in terms of whether they were applied experientially or more environmentally, a number of common and central processes were isolated. Using retrospective data they then attempted to match process with stage. It was found that verbal strategies which emphasised consciousness raising, feedback and interpretation were particularly useful during contemplation. A cognitive approach which involved self re-evaluation was more widely used in the contemplation/determination stage, while behavioural strategies, for instance stimulus control and contingency management, were found to be most useful during the maintenance stage. The self report data also indicated that environmental or developmental change and experience of harm can bridge the gap between precontemplation and contemplation, while a corrective emotional experience often turned contemplation into action. As a good predictor of relapse has been shown to be degree of self efficacy (Litman 1980), the authors emphasise, as do social

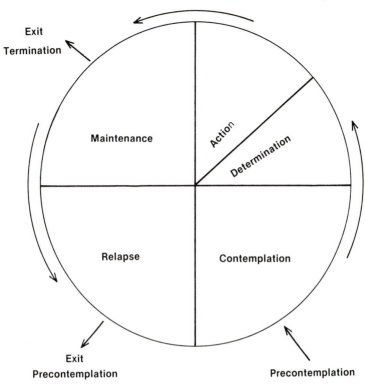

**Fig. 5.1** Stages of individual change (adapted from Prochoska & Di Clemente, 1982)

learning theorists, that successful change involves not only restructuring an individual's behaviour but also his self-evaluation. More recently Prochaska & Di Clemente (1984) have proposed that the process of change can be pursued at different *levels of change* and they propose a hierarchy starting at a *symptom and situational* level and progressing through *cognitive, interpersonal conflict, family conflict* and *intrapersonal levels.* The idea of levels of change seems to be based on a rather pragmatic approach to treatment economy rather than a Guttman style hierarchy where *symptoms* would necessarily be dealt with before *cognitive set* which would in turn have to be dealt with before *interpersonal conflict.*

This general integrative model of change has been summarised briefly and perhaps oversimplified in translation. Although developed using self report data from smokers it is currently stimulating work on users of a variety of psychotropic substances, has generated considerable interest and debate (Miller 1983) and is useful in that it emphasises integration across a range of treatment interventions as well as the essential heterogeneity of the patient group. Edwards (1984) has said that we should try to comprehend drug using behaviour in the context of what he graphically calls the 'total and unfolding play of personal evolution'. The stages of change are perhaps correlates of such evolution.

## Longitudinal studies of drug dependence

Perhaps the most intensively studied group of drug users in the United Kingdom were 128 heroin addicts who attended the London drug clinics in 1969 when they were first interviewed, and who were followed up for a period of ten years. The follow-up results have been reported in numerous studies by various authors and summarised by Stimson & Oppenheimer (1982). The sample consisted of 93 men and 35 women whose mean age was 25 years, most of whom had first used heroin in the mid-sixties. It was a representative sample of clinic users constituting about 12% of the total clinic population of England and Wales at the time and was made up of people demonstrating a diversity of backgrounds and drug using behaviour. Table 5.1 shows that record searches were

**Table 5.1**  Follow-up of 128 heroin addicts (Stimson & Oppenheimer 1982)

| Year | Attending clinic (%) | Known dead (%) | Not attending clinic (%) |
|------|------|------|------|
| 1969 (Initial interview) | 100 | | |
| 1970 (Record search) | 77 | 2 | 21 |
| 1971  " | 59 | 6 | 34 |
| 1972  " | 58 | 6 | 36 |
| 1973  " | 57 | 6 | 37 |
| 1974  " | 49 | 9 | 42 |
| 1975  " | 51 | 9 | 40 |
| 1976/77 (Second interview) | 43 | 12 | 45 |
| 1979 (Record search) | 38 | 15 | 47 |

implemented with some regularity (Stimson 1973, Ogborne & Stimson 1975, Thorley et al 1977) and the sample were actually re-interviewed some seven years later (Stimson et al 1978) when almost all of the survivors, 86% of the original group, were contacted. In total about 36% of the original sample were found not to be taking opioids. The seven year interviews also revealed that those who were not attending clinics were not hidden addicts and for this group opioid abstinence was not symptomatic of other drug use. Those who had given up were found to be less involved with the law, more likely to be in continuous employment, and have permanent accommodation (Oppenheimer et al 1979). After ten years 49 of the original sample of 128 were continuing to attend clinics, 19 had died and 60 were no longer attending (Stimson & Oppenheimer 1982). Of those who were abstinent after seven years, only one had re-attended the clinics after 10 years suggesting that those who achieve protracted abstinence continue to do so. The authors concluded that there is some cause for optimism about the outcome of addiction, as after 10 years some 38% had become abstinent from opioids, were leading reasonably normal lives and had no major problems with other drugs. Unfortunately 14% of the sample died during the decade with the cause of death being in the main drug related.

A rather different study was reported by Rathod (1977). It was a younger sample (between 16 and 20 years) most of whom lived at home with their parents in a provincial English town. Furthermore, although the predominant drug of use was heroin, virtually all of the young people were polydrug users. Of the sample of 86, about three-quarters were assessed as regular users and after six years follow-up data was collected on 85% of the original group. It was found that approximately one-third had completely stopped using illegal drugs, about one-third were rated as sporadic injectors and the remainder had either died or had a regular continuing habit. The author was particularly interested in the effect of medical and drug clinic intervention on outcome. He found that the abstinent group consisted almost entirely of users who were not originally treated by continuous opioid prescription but rather who received abstinence orientated and well integrated medical and social support, which is perhaps more likely in a small town setting. It was found that short term improvement was a good predictor of long term improvement and as Stimson & Oppenheimer demonstrated once off drugs for some time, the probability is that the individual will remain drug free.

The above investigations are two examples of a number of U.K. longitudinal studies of drug dependence (Boyd 1975, Hawks 1976, Weipert et al 1978). For the interested reader these have been comprehensively reviewed by Thorley (1981) who concludes that U.K. data broadly indicate that about one-third of addicts are likely to be abstinent after five years. Vaillant (1970) who reviewed five follow-up studies from elsewhere, three from the U.S.A., and two from Europe, reported a rather smaller rate of abstinence over a corresponding time.

Finally such a review would not be complete without mention of the Drug Abuse Reporting Program (D.A.R.P.) in the U.S.A. This was not strictly speaking a longitudinal study as there was generally only one follow-up evaluation, thus providing no information on individual variation over time. Nevertheless D.A.R.P. is the largest scale outcome study in the field and arose from a common initial assessment procedure on 44,000 patients in 52 treatment centres throughout the U.S.A. The program has been extensively reported in a number of publications (Sells & Simpson 1976, Gorsuch & Butler 1976). A particularly useful analysis was reported by Sells & Simpson (1980) in which they evaluate outcome after about five years using a sample of over 3000 from a number of different treatment groups and one control group. These included methadone maintenance (MM), therapeutic community (TC), out-patient drug free treatment programs (DF), out-patient detoxification programs (OD) and the comparison group who received no active treatment (IO). In common with other treatment evaluation studies emanating from the program, Sells & Simpson (1980) demonstrated that MM, TC and DF led to a significantly more favourable outcome than OD programs and assessment only (IO). As in most of the studies associated with D.A.R.P. the authors employed rigorous evaluative criteria and made much use of multivariate statistical measures to take account of extra-treatment variance. Nevertheless it is worth reemphasising that in any long term evaluation the treatment episode is normally only a short period in the patient's life and that outcome is a result of numerous factors past and present outside the treatment process. The findings must be viewed therefore as no more than indicators of differential treatment effects. The results of the study are summarised in Table 5.2. *Favourable* outcome is defined as total abstinence and *moderately favourable* as moderate drug use but with generally conforming behaviour and no evidence of criminal activity. The authors also concluded that DF was more beneficial for non regular opioid users and non opioid users.

**Table 5.2** Outcome evaluations of over 3,000 drug misusers

|  | Methadone maintenance (%) | Therapeutic community (%) | Drug free out-patient | Detox out-patient (%) | Assessment only (%) |
|---|---|---|---|---|---|
| Favourable | 29.5 | 36.9 | 34.4 | 19.6 | 21.0 |
| Favourable and moderately favourable | 55.1 | 52.8 | 54.3 | 35.2 | 37.1 |

Source: adapted from Sells and Simpson (1980).

These results are consistent with those reviewed above and demonstrate that a significant group of addicts improve over time even when the most rigorous evaluative criteria of all, total abstinence, is employed. The results also have implications for the efficacy of different modes of intervention and this aspect of the study is discussed more fully later.

## Longitudinal studies of alcohol dependence

In the alcohol literature there have been many reports of single point follow up studies and true longitudinal studies which trace change over time (De Morsier & Feldman 1952, Davies 1962, Kendell 1965, Goodwin et al 1971, Hyman 1976). This work has been described by Edwards (1984) as forming 'an important sector of alcohol research'. Rather than a cursory general review it is perhaps more useful to concentrate on what has arguably been the most influential and controversial study of this genre; the so called Rand Report (Armor et al 1976, Polich 1980, Armor 1980, Polich et al 1981).

In the light of increased concern about alcoholism in the U.S.A. during the early 1970s the government funded a number of treatment centres and also provided for continuous monitoring of the service by the Rand Corporation. The subject group was a sample of 758 males who were admitted to these treatment centres. A second sample of 165 males were assessed but did not receive any formal treatment. Follow up data was collected after 6 months, 18 months and 4 years. Data from the four year interview will be reviewed here but with reference to the earlier findings where appropriate. 85% of the original sample were reassessed after this time.

The subjects in the study were by any standard a substantially impaired group of drinkers. Not only were intake levels high but two-thirds were unemployed and about one-third separated or divorced. When possible, self-report outcome measures were validated against collateral evidence and outcome criteria at four years were applied over a 6 month time window. Drinkers who reported no impairment or experience of alcohol dependence symptoms over this time were classified as either *abstinent* or *non problem drinkers*. The problem drinking group were defined as those people who had experienced some alcohol related impairment or dependence symptoms over the six month period. These criteria are really quite stringent as for example short term abstainers could be included in the problem drinker group if there was any evidence of impairment or dependence during their last drinking period even if it occurred up to six months previously. This meant that outcome criteria after four years were more rigorous than after 18 months when a 30 day time window was employed although the authors made some attempt to standardise relapse criteria over the two time samples.

At four years, 14% of the initial treatment group had died with over half of these deaths being alcohol related. Among the survivors 28% had been abstinent for the six months time window although only one-quarter of this group had been completely abstinent over the entire four year period. 18% were considered to be non-problem drinkers and the remaining 54% were problem drinkers. Put another way, for 46% of the original sample their drinking did not constitute a problem after four years for at least a period of six months duration. Drinking patterns were not the only outcome criteria. On a number of psychosocial variables the two remission groups (abstainers and non problem drinkers) were found to be considerably better than the problem drinkers. Interestingly on attitudinal measures the non problem drinkers and abstainers could be distinguished, with the latter group generally describing themselves as *alcoholic* and endorsing the traditional disease view.

The so called *untreated* or *assessment only* group, some of whom the authors suggest demonstrated natural remission, were also followed up. As discussed previously it is somewhat arbitrary to categorise assessment and treatment separately as the processes involved in spontaneous remission may be similar to those involved in treatment. Nevertheless of the control group it was found that 32% showed a favourable outcome equally divided between abstention and non problem drinking. The remainder were assessed as problem drinkers or had died.

In a further analysis of the study Armor (1980) looked at relapse rates and of particular interest was the question of what behaviour at 18 months could predict successful outcome some two and a half years later. Those who were long term abstainers and non problem drinkers at 18 months were less likely to have relapsed after four years than short term abstainers. This data which plots drinking pattern over time also suggests that short term abstinence is an unstable state and many of these drinkers are constantly switching between abstinence and problem drinking.

Generally the Rand Report is one of the most methodologically sound and rigorous longitudinal studies of alcohol dependence in the literature. The four year, follow up marked a considerable improvement on the two earlier ones in terms of outcome measures, validity testing of the self report data and response rate. As would be expected of work of this magnitude and influence it has been the subject of some valuable and constructive criticism within the scientific literature (Moos et al 1980, Room 1980). What is unfortunate however is the fact that much of the Report's earlier publicity was generated by the finding, which was far from being original, that a significant minority of alcoholics returned to normal drinking. This produced hostile reaction among various groups particularly in the USA and the possible reasons for this are discussed in more detail later.

## Current issues in treatment provision

In this section, a number of questions will be raised on quantitative aspects of the treatment of substance misuse. This will include reference to the current debate on minimal versus intensive intervention as well as the most fundamental issue of all; the effectiveness of treatment as compared to the natural process of change. Other issues which can influence outcome like location of treatment and the integration of drug and alcohol users on a common therapeutic program will also be considered. Broader but related work on patient and therapist characteristics will be reviewed as this has profound implications for the assessment of treatment processes. The relative efficacy of particular types of treatment endeavour will be examined more specifically in a later section. The whole issue of treatment effectiveness is a methodological minefield and it is appropriate to consider first the difficulties of evaluative research in this area.

## Methodological considerations

Some of the problems of evaluating the efficacy of treatment have been outlined by Glaser & Ogborne (1982) and Yates & Norris (1981). First, in a study of any intervention multiple outcome measures should be taken into account and each outcome assessed by more than one method. Self and collateral reports in conjunction with record searches or blood and breath tests could for example be used to determine drug use and there should be independent assessment of other psychological, social and economic variables. These authors also suggest that outcome measures should be quantifiable, operationally defined and continuous rather than categorical in nature. The reliability and validity of such measures should be evaluated and it is important to take into account behaviour which may covary with use of a drug, notably substitute drug use. Second, patient characteristics which may add or detract from any particular intervention should be defined and assessed. The clinical importance of matching patients and treatment cannot be overemphasised. Third, there is increasing awareness of the importance of developmental and environmental influences, which prompt help seeking, maintain change, and filter any treatment effect. Indeed one can have a *treatment career* co-existing with a *drug taking career*. Influences which may maximise the effect of treatment for example the support of a significant other or continuous employment should be taken into account. Fourth, there is a need for good research design with appropriate matched or randomly assigned control groups providing comparison data. There is also increasing emphasis on the well designed single case study.

It is, however, a real world in which real people have distressing problems and often methodological considerations must take second place to practical, organisational and clinical constraints. Some authors (Sells & Simpson 1980) have even questioned whether research designs for field studies which examine treatment processes among indigenous communities should be bound by the rules of traditional laboratory-based quality control procedures.

Finally in the alcohol and drug literature there have been several major influential meta-analytic studies (Vaillant 1970, Emrick

1975, Costello 1980). These have been attempts to synthesise a whole series of primary investigations in search of general treatment or patient characteristics associated with positive outcome. Some of these studies are often quoted in support of the view that treatment is at best only minimally effective. Meta-analysis should be regarded however with some caution and the use of such a technique has been critically appraised by Strube & Hartmann (1982). It can for example mask changes in outcome when different performance indices are compared. If different outcome measures are translated into a single category information may be altered in the conversion. Other limitations can include biased selection of studies, poor quality data and a high degree of error variance normally present in interstudy comparisons. Nevertheless, meta-analysis is a popular and relatively objective method of summarising a body of empirical data, and despite the potential problems Strube and Hartmann argue that it deserves routine use as an aid to summarizing treatment literatures.

## Intensity of treatment

Longitudinal studies have led some people to question whether the rate of spontaneous remission and treatment remission is much the same. The question 'does treatment work?' has been raised on numerous occasions in the alcohol literature (Clare 1977, Smith 1982) and rather less often in the drug literature (Sells & Simpson 1980). Two related issues will be discussed in this section. First, is treatment better than no treatment at all? Second, is minimal intervention as effective as intensive intervention? These questions are really only quantitatively distinct as 'assessment only' groups are often described as having had no treatment in spite of the fact that assessment is part of the treatment process. Furthermore as outlined above, even for genuine no treatment groups the naturally occurring precipitants of change are unlikely to be different in kind from those which are applied to treatment. As the question of treatment intensity has been particularly common in alcohol studies this literature will be separately reviewed.

### Alcohol studies

Emrick (1975) in a major meta-analytic study summarised some 384 treatment investigations. He could find little evidence that any one treatment method was better than another, but did conclude that 'more treated than untreated alcoholics improved suggesting that formal treatment at least increases the alcoholic's chance of reducing his drinking problem'. However, given that his outcome evaluation was a simple drinking pattern measure and his review involved few studies in which cognitive therapy or individual counselling were the major components of the treatment program, the results must be seen as broad indicators of a trend. Costello (1975, 1980) also summarised the literature and this work is reviewed more fully later. However he did find that formal treatment made a significant and direct contribution to outcome variance. Polich et al (1981) also demonstrated a modest but nevertheless statistically significant relationship between amount of treatment received and four year outcome status. 32% of the assessment only group and 42% of those who received less intense intervention were rated as improved as were 53% of the group who received more intensive therapy. It is possible however that the more effective programs initially filtered out patients with poor prognostic indicators.

In the influential and often quoted *treatment and advice* study Edwards et al (1977) compared intensive treatment with a single session of assessment and directive advice. One hundred married men were randomly allocated to one of two groups. The conventional *treatment* included group work, social support, introduction to A.A., drug assisted withdrawal and psychiatric support in an in-patient or out-patient setting. In short the treatment group were afforded what could be regarded as the highest level of care available in the U.K. The *advice* group had a three hour assessment, were given advice to remain abstinent and they were not seen until a one year follow up interview. After one year there were no significant differences between the groups in terms of drinking pattern or social adjustment. Orford (1980) carried out a critical analysis of the study and concluded that it was a heterogeneous sample, therapist variables were not taken into account, it was carried out in a particular and prestigious hospital setting and outcome assessment procedures were perhaps less methodologically sound than the authors would have wished. Nevertheless the results have been seriously received (Glaser 1977) and have focused the minds of clinicians on simple cheaper forms of therapeutic intervention. Room (1980) does council caution, however, when considering the currently popular trend towards low cost treatment and points out that as alcohol treatment is at best only moderately effective, even the cheapest treatment is unlikely to be cost effective in purely economic terms. The basic justification of providing treatment is primarily for reasons of humanity rather than cost benefit analysis although obviously the latter must be taken into account.

Results in the alcohol literature suggest that treatment can be effective although whether intense treatment is better than minimal treatment for most of the alcoholic population is open to doubt. Given the present state of knowledge it is important for workers to steer a line somewhere between therapeutic nihilism on the one hand and uncritical acceptance of the efficacy of all therapeutic intervention on the other. Most commentators would agree with Longabaugh et al (1983) that one of the few generalisations about alcohol treatment which can be made with some confidence is that 'some treatment is better than no treatment'.

**Drug studies**

A number of years ago Winick (1962) suggested that some drug users mature out of their habit and as time goes by grow into voluntary abstinence. However current evidence suggests that this is something of an oversimplification. Abstinence seems more likely to occur in the three years following first use after which time the rate of remission slows down considerably. Thorley (1981) demonstrates that younger samples whose drug use history is relatively short (d'Orban 1974) will have a higher rate of abstinence after three or four years than older samples with a longer pre-assessment history (Smart et al 1977). Thorley calls this the 'rush and trickle' with abstinence coming in a rush in the first three or so years and then reducing to a trickle. The implication is that if a user is going to stop he will do so sooner rather than later.

The Advisory Council Report (1982) draws attention to a survey of studies of users who received minimal treatment (Vaillant 1970), which the report calls the closest data we have to a 'spontaneous remission rate depending on naturally occurring processes of change.' Approximately one-quarter of this group were drug free after five years while the rate of abstinence of more intensively treated addicts seems, with some exceptions (Chapple et al 1972), to be higher (Stimson & Oppenheimer 1982, Rathod 1977). The report argues that in general, interstudy comparisons suggest that those who undergo more intensive treatment and rehabilitation programs show superior remission rates and this gives us some indication of treatment efficacy. However comparisons of studies on different populations from diverse geographical locations must be treated with some caution.

The Sells & Simpson (1980) study which was methodologically rigorous showed that the intake only group had an abstinence rate of 21% at up to six years while some treatment groups had rates of well over 30%. The authors, while admitting the limitations of field research suggest that if a particular therapeutic program produces significant and consistent change which does not occur in the non treatment situation then treatment can be said to work. Their results which are reviewed more fully above provide perhaps the best evidence we have on drug misuse treatment effectiveness.

## Treatment setting

The issue of whether substance misuse is best treated in an inpatient or outpatient setting has profound implications for resources and service provision. It has been demonstrated (Herz et al 1971, Washburn et al 1976) that for some general psychiatric disorders, day patient care as opposed to inpatient treatment is associated with lower relapse and fewer days spent in hospital after discharge. It must be emphasised that discussion of treatment location is complicated by the fact that different patients are admitted to different treatment settings. Skinner (1981) for example compared almost 300 patients assigned to inpatient (IP) and outpatient (OP) treatment for alcohol and drug dependence. Those who had inpatient care tended towards higher consumption and greater impairment. They had also fewer community supports and demonstrated a greater degree of psychopathology.

Treatment settings for drug misusers vary considerably from long term community residential groups to short outpatient clinic withdrawal and there have been no well controlled comparative studies. It has been shown (Sells & Simpson 1976) that regular opioid misusers do benefit from care delivered in a residential or IP setting while non regular opioid users or non opioid users may do just as well as outpatients. Such conclusions are tentative and the question warrants further investigation. The work on alcohol treatment setting is rather more substantial. Costello (1975) demonstrated that IP care for alcohol dependent patients was an indicator of positive outcome. This may be somewhat artifactual as inpatient treatment was by far the dominant type of intervention for well motivated patients among the studies in his review.

Edwards & Guthrie (1967) could find no significant outcome differences in an IP group and a well matched OP group and the treatment and advice study would tend to confirm this finding. Baekeland et al (1975) found no significant differences and commented on the role of the patient 'as opposed to the kind of treatment on attrition rate and outcome irrespective of the setting'. McLachlan & Stein (1982) carried out a one year follow-up assessment of patients randomly assigned to a four week program of IP or OP care and found no significant differences in either drinking pattern or employment status. They went on to compare the cost of treatment in the two settings and as would be expected found OP care to be less expensive. Longabaugh et al (1983) also randomly allocated two groups of patients to IP or OP treatment programs, both groups having undergone inpatient detoxification for up to eight days. Not only did the two groups experience the same behaviourally based program but it was administered by the same staff to control for therapist differences. After six months it was found that the two groups were comparable in terms of alcohol consumption and other social and vocational variables. Furthermore it was found that subjective well being and interpersonal functioning were better for the OP group. There were some problems with this study notably the short follow up and furthermore, little attempt was made to assess which patient characteristics made IP care a more viable option. Nevertheless the authors do suggest that an OP program has a number of advantages. Patients are exposed to difficult situations and are attempting to develop appropriate coping strategies while still in treatment. It also enables a more accurate assessment of environmental, cognitive and emotional antecedents as well as giving patients increased opportunity to rehearse new skills in a natural environment.

It would seem that for the majority of alcohol misusers OP care is as beneficial as IP care, perhaps even more so. The next level of sophistication of this type of study is investigation of the interaction between patient characteristics and the most appropriate treatment setting.

## Combined alcohol and drug treatment

There are an increasing number of addiction units where alcohol and drug dependent patients are admitted to the same treatment program. Aumark (1980) compared a combined with a separate therapeutic program in a residential unit. The multimodel 60 day program consisted of a variety of physical, psychological and social treatment activities.

He used multiple outcome measures of substance usage, social activity, employment and quality of family relationships although no collateral evidence was sought. A total of 689 patients were assigned to separate and combined treatment programs. About two-thirds of the original sample were followed up some six months later and after partialling out the pre-treatment variance there was no significant difference between patients from the segregated and integrated programs. This study would have been rather better if more demographic details and information on the history, nature and type of drug use had been included.

La Porte et al (1980) also evaluated combined treatment for alcohol and drug misusers. They argued that combined treatment is resource efficient and also that the theoretical commonalities of all forms of substance abuse would favour integration.

Mitigating against the combination of the two populations in treatment is the fact that alcohol is legally accepted and indeed a social facilitator. The natural history of dependence will vary across drugs and acute physiological effects can be very different. So while there exists evidence that integration may make economic and practical sense, La Porte and his colleagues admit that it could be counter productive under some circumstances and specifically set out to examine the compatability of drug and alcohol users in a combined treatment setting. They assessed patient opinions on the nature of addiction generally and in particular the attitudes of alcoholics to drug addicts and vice versa. Despite the fact that the two populations differed notably in terms of age and intelligence, the main finding was that the vast majority in both groups felt comfortable with the other and were of the opinion that combined treatment actually helped. Only 10% felt that integration had a negative effect on their response to treatment. Some anecdotal evidence from the study suggests that it was not uncommon for the more verbally aggressive young drug user to bring out the more passive withdrawn alcoholic and this was reciprocated in the sense that the alcoholic group acted on occasions as a calming influence on the younger, more agitated drug user. It was also noted that younger addicts often expressed insight into the relationship with their father through association with the older alcohol dependent patients. Treatment outcome was also assessed and the authors conclude that the reported level of post treatment adjustment was on a par with that of programs which separate the two populations. The evidence from these studies and other similar work would suggest that integration of drug and alcohol users, although not without its practical and clinical difficulties, can be at least as beneficial under some circumstances as separate treatment programs.

## Therapist characteristics

It has been demonstrated that in the treatment of general psychological disorder (Murphy et al 1984) most patients tend to attribute effectiveness of therapy to empathy and understanding on the part of the therapist while most therapists attribute success to their technique. The failure to demonstrate consistent differences between psychotherapeutic treatment methods generally (Shapiro & Shapiro 1982) would support the idea that further investigation of what used to be called *error variance,* much of which was a result of patient and therapist characteristics, would be a fruitful line of research endeavour. There is no reason to suppose that these general observations should not apply to the treatment of addiction in which it is becoming increasingly clear that so called *non specific factors* like therapist characteristics can influence therapeutic outcome. An interesting study quoted by Hodgson (1980) underlines this.

Rapid smoking is a behavioural technique involving, as the name suggests, rapid smoking of a number of cigarettes to the point of nausea. It is argued that continued association of smoking with the aversive experience reduces craving. One group of 18 smokers were given rapid smoking therapy by a mechanical, coldly efficient therapist and received no praise for successfully abstaining between treatment sessions. For a second group rapid smoking was administered by a friendly therapist who recounted his own experience of using the technique and who was enthusiastic about abstinence between sessions. Thus the same treatment technique was administered in two different ways. At three months follow up the abstinence rate was 6% for the cold therapist and 72% for the warm encouraging therapist. Although these differences may be vastly reduced given a longer follow up, the study does make the point rather dramatically that therapist variables, independent of treatment method, can influence the future pattern of substance use. Some professionals could for example learn a lot from Alcoholics and Narcotics Anonymous where first time attenders are made to feel welcome and the warmth and empathy extended to them is very obvious.

As the treatment literature has been technique rather than therapist oriented, little attention has been paid to the outcome effect of particular characteristics which the therapist brings to the treatment situation. Cartwright (1981) could find only two studies which examined the therapist's perspective. There are a number of therapist characteristics which he regarded as important. These are empathy, experience, commitment and a positive attitude towards self, patient and the therapeutic process. He suggests that treatment research in the field of addiction should be guided by the question 'what type of patient improves with what type of treatment given by what type of therapist?' Orford (1980) felt that one of the important limitations of the treatment and advice study (Edwards et al 1977) was that therapist and setting variables could not be taken into account. All of the patients in the study were seen by virtually the same staff in the same setting. He goes on to say that authors of such research should describe therapist characteristics for example in terms of training, orientation and experience as routinely as they describe the characteristics of patients.

## Patient characteristics

The third element of the outcome triad after nature of treatment and type of therapist is type of patient. Luborsky et al (1971) looked at the role of patient characteristics in determining outcome in general psychological disorders. As would be expected they were able to make a fairly broad statement on the prognostic significance of age, intelligence, motivation, educational and social achievement. Patient variables which influence outcome of alcohol treatments have been the subject of considerable study.

Individuals who use drugs which incur social disapproval are not necessarily, as is often suggested a more homogeneous group than alcohol users (Blumberg 1981). Nevertheless the predictive significance of pre-treatment patient characteristics has been less thoroughly investigated for this group.

The long term outlook for alcohol dependent patients whether or not they undergo treatment can to some extent be determined by the inter-relationship of personality and environment variables.

There has been broad agreement over the years that social stability as defined for example by a supportive marriage, regular employment and the absence of legal problems are positive prognostic factors (Straus & Bacon 1951, McCance & McCance 1969, Bromet & Moos 1979). Perhaps the best evidence for this in the alcohol literature is a series of reports by Costello (1975, 1977, 1980).

In a summary of the treatment literature he attempted to identify factors associated with positive outcome. In the 1980 study he analysed data from 35 studies and computed a social stability index (SSI). This was a broad measure of degree of participation in the social system outside treatment with the studies under consideration ranging from reports on homeless skid row men to homogeneous professional groups. A treatment index (TI) was calculated on the basis of nature and intensity of treatment. A follow through (FT) measure gave some indication of intensity of post treatment follow up and outcome (OUT) was assessed in terms of drinking pattern. The problems of such meta-analytic studies have been outlined above but despite the methodological difficulties the results of this study are particularly enlightening. Costello (1980) used a path analysis which essentially allows for causal rather than correlational statements to be inputed to inter-related variables. He found SSI had a powerful and direct link with outcome i.e. SSI could effect outcome independent of TI and FT. There was a modest TI-OUT effect which was considerably enhanced when FT was included. This suggests that the intensity of treatment follow up makes an important and often underestimated contribution to favourable outcome. The amount of direct outcome variance attributable to treatment was 26% and that attributable to social stability 49%. In other words while treatment effects were significant they were considerably less powerful determinants of outcome than pre-treatment social stability. There was also some interaction between SSI and TI.

Although other patient characteristics associated with favourable outcome may vary from clinic to clinic and among different populations (Gillies et al 1974) there are some which occur so regularly in the literature that they cannot be discounted. These have been listed by Rix & Rix (1983) and include high motivation, short drinking history, high socioeconomic status, youth, and less marked alcohol dependence. Personal characteristics can also interact with the nature of future drinking. Armor (1980) found in his four year follow up that older highly dependent men were less likely to relapse if they were abstainers rather than non-problem drinkers 18 months after treatment. For younger, less dependent men the reverse was true and for both of these groups, marital status seemed not to be particularly important. For old men of medium dependence and young men of high dependence on the other hand, marital status had a much greater predictive significance. This work suggests that what is considered a positive pre-treatment characteristic is partly dependent on how favourable outcome is defined.

With regard to drug misusers the prognostic influence of individual characteristics is less clear. Oppenheimer et al (1979), in the seven year follow up of 128 heroin addicts, attempted to compare abstainers with continuing users on a range of pre-treatment variables including employment, social class, income and degree of criminal activity. The two groups could not be discriminated. What did seem to predict future outcome was age and length of drug taking history before first clinic attendance in that those who were younger with a shorter history of addiction were more likely to be abstinent after seven years. Stimson & Oppenheimer (1982) do however concede that at the onset it would have been 'difficult to choose individual characteristics of prognostic value'. Later differences were more related to withdrawal from opioids than pre-treatment characteristics. Chapple et al (1972) in a follow up study of 108 opioid users confirmed that younger short term addicts were significantly more likely to be drug free after five years than older chronic addicts.

There also appear to be subgroups whose pattern of use on presentation can be differentiated and categorised, and this can have implications for treatment and outcome. Stimson (1973) developed a typology of four distinctive patterns of behaviour among users. *Stables* suffered the fewest psychosocial and physical complications of drug use, were not part of the drug subculture and were in employment. They had homes and were conventional in their attitudes. The *junkies* tended to support their habit by stealing and criminal activity, did not work and were highly involved with the drug subculture. The *loners* had a low rate of criminal activity and little involvement with other addicts. Finally the *two worlders* seemed to straddle the junkie and stable categories in that they mixed with other addicts, had a high rate of criminal activity but yet were employed, residentially stable and had few physical complications. After three years the stables had changed least of all for better or for worse while 50% of the loners and 40% of the two worlders were in the abstinent category (Ogborne & Stimson 1975). Interestingly after 10 years it was the stables who were still most likely to be receiving continued prescriptions while the junkies were not represented at all in the continuing user group. It does seem that there are different outcomes for different types of users, which are not immediately obvious. This work may help in the development of treatment strategies which take account of individual differences in behaviour on initial presentation.

## Modes of intervention

It is artificial in some ways to catalogue a list of treatment methods as if each existed in isolation. It is unlikely that disulfiram is prescribed in silence or that the complex social learning processes of the therapeutic community involve only one particular type of group therapy. Some workers would regard the offering of a short term maintenance prescription as merely a prelude to engaging the patient in a therapeutic relationship while others may see it as an important aspect of the treatment process.

In the field of drug dependence, treatment invariably includes many therapeutic procedures which overlap, thus making efficacy statements about particular methods less than definitive. Furthermore, as there is no such thing as a typical addict or typical alcoholic, no particular treatment strategy can be appropriate for all and on the other hand one individual can gain from a range of methods. The treatment effort is a multidisciplinary exercise so that intervention can occur at various levels of reality. The addict on methadone prescribed by the doctor could at the same time benefit from family casework by the social worker and individual cognitive therapy from the psychologist. Unfortunately however, in a specialism not renowned for attracting an unlimited supply of funds, treatment may be employed as a result of economic pragmatism or organisational constraints rather than sound empirical research or thorough assessment of individual needs.

The following section is by no means an exhaustive list of commonly used therapeutic interventions but rather an attempt to illustrate the range of procedures available which can influence the process of change out of addiction. More comprehensive reviews of alcohol and drug treatment methods can be found elsewhere (Callahan 1980, Miller & Herster 1980).

## Pharmacological treatment

### Alcohol dependence

Apart from pharmacological intervention to attenuate withdrawal effects, current drug treatments for alcohol dependence itself and the treatment of alcohol related impairment are very limited. Therapy, particularly over the past decade or so, is seen mainly in terms of cognitive or behavioural approaches with an emphasis on group work. Drugs tend to be viewed perhaps as a temporary palliative or as a prelude to *real* treatment activity. The reader will already be aware that the emphasis of the present text is on treating the whole individual in the context of his social and cultural environment. Nevertheless this need not, and indeed should not, preclude research into drugs which can operate at different stages in the development of dependence. There has been in recent years renewed discussion on pharmacological approaches to alcohol dependence and several commentators (Murray 1980, Telling-Smith 1984) have suggested that the drugs industry should show more interest in the field.

Perhaps the only currently employed pharmacological intervention in the development of dependence per se is the use of deterrent drugs. Disulfiram (Antabuse) and calcium carbimide (Abstem) are preparations which produce an unpleasant reaction when taken with alcohol as a result of high blood levels of acetaldehyde. The symptoms of the ethanol-disulfiram reaction arise about half an hour after drinking and include palpitations, sweating, nausea, headache and dyspnoea while a severe reaction can produce arrythmias, myocardial infarction and convulsions with on occasions fatal results. Contraindications are notably evidence of coronary, liver or brain disease and diabetes. Unpleasant side effects which have been reported in the absence of alcohol can include drowsiness, skin rashes, impotence, headaches and mild depression. The clinician's view of an optimum dose has come down over recent years with a maximum of 200 mg daily now accepted as sufficient for most people. Abstem has a shorter half life than Antabuse and the patient can safely drink one day after its discontinuation. It also seems to have fewer side effects and contraindications for prescription although it has received little systematic investigation primarily as it is not currently approved for use by prescription in the U.S.A.

Such deterrent oral preparations are not without their value especially when taken in the context of a supportive relationship when intake is sympathetically supervised and regulated. They can also be used to help people over a crisis or at the beginning of a relapse. The major problem with these drugs is perhaps the tendency for individuals to attribute successful abstinence to external agents rather than themselves and this does not really help their evaluation of self efficacy. An added difficulty is patient compliance. Many years ago Pullar-Strecker (1950) made the comment, still relevant today, that you can 'lead an alcoholic to Antabuse but you can't make him swallow it'. Although deterrent drugs are becoming more fashionable and the pharmaceutical industry marketing policy has recently been more aggressive it is estimated that only about 5% of alcoholics in treatment in Britain are using Abstem or Antabuse (Telling-Smith 1984).

Sterile tablets of disulfiram have also been implanted in the subcutaneous tissue or into muscle and implants are said to be effective for up to one year. Their use has recently been reviewed by Morland et al (1984). Initial evidence suggested the implants could be modestly effective (Whyte & O'Brien 1974) although some patients could clearly drink on them without producing a disulfiram–ethanol reaction (Obholzer 1974). Doubts about the effectiveness of implants arose when blood tests of serum levels indicated that absorption rate was inconsistent and so on occasions insufficient to deter drinking indicating that implants do not seem to have a sustained pharmacological effect (Kitson 1978, Madden 1979). There is also the possibility of interference with the metabolism of other endogenous compounds which utilise the same pathways. At a psychological level it is quite possible that patients who volunteer for implants are highly motivated anyway thus leading to a considerable placebo effect. It has been suggested (Madden 1984) that there is a place for a longer acting injectable deterrent drug although this has not been pursued by industry in view of the fact that the large quantities required for injections would make it rather impractical. A further refinement might be a deterrent drug which allowed for moderate drinking as opposed to abstinence.

Other possible areas of investigation on pharmacological approaches to the treatment of alcohol misuse and alcohol related harm have been summarised by Littleton (1984). Although the suggestions are speculative and impressionistic they provide an interesting indication of possible future research directions. There is the development of drugs which reduce the positive reinforcing effect of alcohol although this would require a clearer understanding of the neurochemical factors involved than is presently the case. Perhaps a more hopeful area is in the reduction of the negative aspects of withdrawal and abstinence. This would be similar in some respects to the use of clonidine among heroin users and any such drug which modifies catecholamine release may also have some potential in alleviating alcohol withdrawal. Another suggested area is the use of drugs to reduce the rate of absorption, and in turn the rate of increase of blood alcohol content, thereby altering reinforcement contingencies. A related issue is rate of metabolism. If this were increased then it may limit maximum blood alcohol concentration or alternatively reduce it more rapidly. Such a *sobering-up pill* may unfortunately be of more interest to a driver about to leave a party than an alcoholic wishing to minimise his subjective feeling of intoxication. In theory however such intervention may be useful if it could prevent blood alcohol concentration reaching the level which normally primes a craving for further drinking. Another area of interest is interference with the natural history of tolerance and withdrawal symptomatology. Although the C.N.S. mechanisms which mediate tolerance are unclear there is evidence that one such process is at the level of the synaptic membrane. If this were the case then a preparation which for example modified neurotransmitter release or membrane lipid composition would be a strong candidate for use at various stages in the development of dependence.

Littleton (1984) and others emphasise that the ideas reviewed above are still more the subject of speculation than empirically based assertion and many issues relating to pharmaceutical intervention in this area remain unresolved.

**Drug dependence**

The debate on pharmacological approaches to drug dependence has focused on two broad but nevertheless important issues notably opioid prescribing versus no prescribing and injectable versus oral maintenance medication. With regard to the latter question virtually all of the U.K. treatment centres have stopped prescribing maintenance injectable heroin to new addicts. This is perhaps as much in spite of, as because of, evidence comparing heroin with methadone maintenance (Hartnoll et al 1980). There is also differing expert opinion on whether total abstinence or long term maintenance prescribing is the most appropriate therapeutic response for a significant group of addicts (Rathod 1977, Blumberg 1976). Those who argue for an increased emphasis in U.K. clinics on withdrawal and abstinence seemed to be holding sway although a significant number of addicts continue to receive long term maintenance. Discussion of pharmacological treatments for acute drug related medical crises is beyond the scope of this chapter and treatment of withdrawal is discussed in Chapter 2. This section will deal specifically with the use of methadone and opioid antagonists in the treatment of heroin dependence.

Methadone, a synthetic opioid, has several advantages over heroin for longer term treatment of dependence. Its action is longer than that of heroin. Withdrawal effects do not manifest themselves for about 24 hours as opposed to four hours after taking heroin. This leads to a potentially more ordered life style with one daily dose being sufficient and avoids the exaggerated ups and downs associated with intravenous heroin use. It produces less euphoria and larger blockade doses can eliminate the euphoric effect of heroin altogether as a result of cross tolerance, although little use is made of blockade doses as doctors in the main prefer to prescribe the minimum necessary dose. Perhaps the most important advantage is that methadone is effective when taken orally. This reduces the obvious hazards of injection as well as the risk of overdose and methadone is normally dispensed in linctus form which rules out the possibility of injecting in most cases.

The initial dose has gone down over the years. Ashton (1981) calculated that the average dose for U.K. addicts in N.H.S. hospitals was 62 mg daily and Stimson & Oppenheimer (1982) note that some clinics now adopt a unilateral policy of prescribing no more than 40 mg daily to new patients irrespective of the degree of pretreatment opioid use. Methadone is normally dispensed in the clinic on a daily basis although for longer term stabilised addicts more flexibility can be introduced. The problems associated with giving two or three days supply at once highlight the need for a clinically useful longer acting opioid like acetylmethadol which acts for up to three days. For the patient who is stabilised the possibility of graded withdrawal should always be considered.

Antagonists which block the effect of opioids by occupying their receptor sites have been used extensively in the U.S.A. but rarely in the U.K. Such preparations, for example naloxone, cyclazocine and naltrexone, have been employed as a long term relapse prevention strategy. In learning theory terms the repeated use of opioids without the accompanying pleasurable effect should lead to the eventual extinction of the behaviour (Wikler 1973) and serve to reduce craving (Resnick et al 1974, Meyer et al 1976).

Cyclazocine is long acting as it blocks opioids for up to 24 hours.

Initial unpleasant side effects can include irritability, uncoordination and occasional hallucinations. Naloxone is relatively free from side effects but is short acting and therefore of limited clinical use. Naltrexone is longer acting than naloxone with fewer side effects than cyclazocine and Resnick and his colleagues found that in the dose range 125 to 500 mg it could block the effect of 25 mg of heroin for up to three days. Longer acting depot preparations are currently being developed but still await extensive clinical trials. Schecter (1980) reviewed the use of naltrexone in the U.S.A. and concluded that it was a relatively safe and effective blocking medication which produced no withdrawal effects or euphoria and so would not be likely to be misused. Some of the problems with antagonists in general are expense, high attrition rates and their unpopularity among addicts themselves.

## Community groups

The therapeutic community plays a major role in the management of drug misuse particularly in the U.S.A. although there are a number of such groups or concept houses in the U.K. In the main, communities of this type are run by ex-addicts with an emphasis on residents remaining drug free. Alcoholics Anonymous (A.A.) too is a community group run by ex-alcoholics with total abstinence being a central requirement so it is not surprising that A.A. and drug therapeutic communities have similar historical roots (Glaser 1977, 1981).

Both were significantly influenced by the Oxford group which was a religious organisation in the evangelical protestant tradition and which flourished during the early part of this century in Britain and the U.S.A. The central features of the Oxford group were sharing, open confession of sins, guidance from other group members and change or rebirth. Bill W, the founder of A.A. acknowledged the importance of Oxford group practices in the development of A.A.'s ideas on self examination, acknowledgement of character deficits and restitution (Bill W 1957). Charles Dederick who founded Synanon, the archetypal drug therapeutic community, was an A.A. graduate and incorporated much A.A. practice into its development. Indeed there was close initial rapport between A.A. and Synanon with joint meetings and cross fertilisation of ideas. Glaser (1981) points out that while A.A. have retained their religious emphasis, the drug communities have shifted over the years from theology to ideology although this is a change of content rather than form. He comments that both ideology and theology represent a basic belief system and structure which can give the individual a sense of order and purpose in what may otherwise be perceived as a chaotic and rather random lifestyle. Although the drug communities and A.A. have grown apart over the past two decades the similarities remain more striking than the differences.

**Therapeutic communities**

The drug communities are non-statutory services which as mentioned above are usually run by ex-addicts although some involve trained staff. Synanon which began in 1958 was set up for heroin users and is characterised by an aggressive and directive style of group therapy. New residents are required to cease all drug intake immediately on admission and are *talked through* withdrawal. There is a hierarchical structure within the communities. Progress through the hierarchy and privileges incurred are contingent on the individual's compliance with group norms and values in terms of appropriate behaviour and attitudes. Most of the emergent communities in the U.S.A. like Daytop Village, New York can trace their roots back to the Synanon program. In the U.K. too such communities, for instance the Ley community, Oxford, and concept houses like Alpha House, have an influential part to play in the national response to drug misuse.

For the use of relevant referral agents the therapeutic community facilities in the U.K. have been listed and described by Banks & Waller (1983). The Advisory Council Report (1982) recommends that residential therapeutic communities should have a role within the provision of a comprehensive system of managing drug misuse although the report comments that they need not necessarily be provided by the non statutory sector.

The results of the effectiveness of drug free communities are mixed and the attrition rate is high although individuals who do complete the program tend to feel positive about their contribution and do better than drop outs (Romond et al 1975). In a review of outcome studies on community graduates Smart (1976) showed that recovery rate when defined in terms of pattern of drug use was generally quite good although highly variable across studies. He felt that when other outcome indices were used, for instance future employment, the positive contribution of therapeutic communities was less notable. Most of the studies paid little attention to differences in outcome among those who misused drugs other than heroin. Thorley (1981) reviewed some U.K. follow up studies on ex-community residents (Melotte & Ogborne 1975, Wilson & Kennard 1978) and concluded that the therapeutic community is a powerful experience which can greatly benefit some individuals but actively harm others. He stressed the need to develop more discriminating assessment procedures and a greater understanding of the social learning processes involved in order that potential harm may be minimised. Most commentators would agree that therapeutic communities can be an effective rehabilitation procedure, but as they are relatively few in number and have strict entrance requirements this renders them only genuinely available for, and acceptable to, a small percentage of the addict population.

**Alcoholics anonymous**

From small beginnings in 1930s America, A.A. has now reached 90 countries and has been described as the 'dominant treatment initiative in the field' (Glaser & Ogborne 1982). Wherever they are held, A.A. meetings take much the same form. The new member, called a *recovering alcoholic,* will be introduced by the chairman and will give an account of his drinking history. Other members of the group may discuss their own experiences or those of the speaking member. After a reading from the A.A. big book, which includes prescriptions and recommendations as well as outlines of various problems, the members will talk informally over a cup of tea. A.A. members follow a program as outlined in the famous *12 steps* which stress a personal inability to control one's drinking and a reliance on God to restore sanity and maintain sobriety. It is the experience of many workers in the field (Robinson 1979) that the quasi religious influence can deter some people from seeking A.A. help although it must be said that the organisation does not in practice insist on conventional Christian belief among members. Some of the A.A. adages like 'one drink — one drunk' or 'once an alcoholic always an alcoholic' have become what could be termed a folk science of alcoholism. As outlined in Chapter 1 such beliefs have little scientific basis (Heather & Robertson 1983) but nevertheless this need not negate the usefulness of A.A. for individuals who subscribe to such beliefs. Many therapists who for example do not agree with the underlying assumptions of A.A. will, despite this, recommend attendance as part of a multimodal treatment package.

It is said that A.A. does seem in very broad terms to attract a particular type of drinker namely the more severe, chronically dependent, rigid individual (Saunders 1982). As for the effectiveness of continued attendance at A.A. once again reports are mixed. Bebbington (1976) outlined some particular difficulties in assessing A.A., namely: anonymous membership, self selection, and varying degrees of commitment among members. Nevertheless some studies have attempted to assess its efficacy (Ditman et al 1967, Brandsma et al 1980). The results would tend to refute A.A. claims that it is particularly effective and Brandsma and his colleagues found that some commonly used behavioural psychotherapeutic methods had a more positive outcome. What is needed as with most other treatment interventions are well controlled evaluative studies.

A.A. does continue to be used by a significant minority of the alcohol dependent population as well as being recommended by professional clinicians. Many people have undoubtedly been helped in the past and there are currently over half a million members worldwide. It is probably fair to say that it would take more than well controlled outcome studies in scientific journals to substantially affect its continued development and philosophy of care.

## Psychological approaches

### Behaviour therapy

*Classical, operant* and *self control* approaches to treatment are based on the principle that behaviour is learned as a result of the person/environment interaction.

Craving is regarded as a classically conditioned response (Wikler 1973) as it can be linked with previously neutral stimuli and a number of behavioural treatments have been developed accordingly. *Aversion therapy* is a procedure which involves repeated pairing of an unpleasant unconditioned stimulus (usually nausea, electric shock or covert aversion imagery) with the conditioned stimulus. The idea is that after treatment the availability of drugs or drink will produce an unpleasant subjective state rather than craving. Aversion therapy has been applied to alcoholics (Voegtlin 1940, Caddy & Covibond 1976) and drug users (Thompson & Rathod 1968, Boudin 1972) over the years. More recently it has become unfashionable primarily because it is unpleasant for therapist as well as patient, there is a high drop out rate and it is not particularly effective (Davidson 1974), although there is some evidence that chemical aversion seems to have a slight edge over electrical aversion for some highly selected populations. Craving can perhaps be more effectively reduced by extinction. This is said to occur if the conditioned stimulus is presented but the usual behaviour prevented; a strategy normally termed *cue exposure.* For example a patient who experiences craving on entering a public house and so invariably drinks, could be accompanied by a therapist who urges him to resist. After a few sessions, craving in this situation would be reduced and this technique has been used successfully in a number of studies (Gotestam & Melin 1972, Rankin & Hodgson 1977). It has been argued that opioid antagonists are a special form of cue exposure. By repeatedly injecting without the accompanying euphoria, craving can be attenuated and heroin loses its stimulus control (Callahan 1980).

Operant strategies deal with environmental contingencies which maintain behaviour through negative or positive reinforcement. For example, drug use is usually reinforced by the contingent effect and relief drug use quickly reduces unpleasant withdrawal symptoms and so is also powerfully reinforced. The idea that behaviour is to some extent influenced by consequences does appear, at first sight contraindicated by clinical observation in the case of drug use. Health, family and job may be lost, yet the behaviour maintained. It is however contingency and immediacy of reinforcement which are most important in shaping behaviour and these can outweigh the effect of a more aversive longer term outcome. Many treatment programs particularly in the U.S.A. have been based on the principles of operant conditioning (Cohen et al 1972, Nathan & O'Brien 1971).

More recently these simple, technique based, behavioural methods have become less popular as psychologists have moved towards the view that man shapes his environment as much as he is influenced by it. In other words the individual can actively organise his environment to influence the probability of certain behaviours occurring. This has given rise to the *self control* or *self management* approach. Although behaviourally based it is not tied to any therapeutic system but rather is a strategy for generating treatment possibilities. A behavioural analysis may reveal that an individual's drinking or drug use occurs in specific places at particular times or in the presence of certain mood states. Such events are regarded as *antecedent cues* which, with the actual or expected *consequences,* serve to influence the occurrence of behaviour. **Antecedent cues** can fall into a number of categories (Miller 1980). These include situational (time of day, type of company), emotional (tension, boredom, anger), cognitive (low self esteem, expectation of loss of control) and physiological (the effect of a priming dose of the drug, withdrawal symptoms).

**Consequences** which are contingent on behaviour and serve to regulate its probability of occurrence can also operate at different levels ranging from social facilitation to relief of withdrawal effects. A self control approach is essentially an attempt to train the patient to identify cues and expected consequences and so generate appropriate coping responses. A self analysis of drug using behaviour would suggest *stimulus control* strategies for modifying the cues or introducing responses incompatible with drug use. *Contingency management* strategies would alter the perceived relationship between behaviour and consequences. The individual could be taught to avoid situational or social pressure or learn appropriate coping strategies when faced with unavoidable cues (Litman 1980). Relaxation or assertion training could circumvent a build up of tension or pharmacological intervention could reduce the immediate positive impact of the drug (Stockwell 1984). Such behavioural interventions which alter the individual's internal and external environment thus weakening the bond between behaviour, cues and consequences, have been extensively reviewed elsewhere (Hodgson 1980, Stockwell et al 1982, Robertson et al 1984).

Self control training has been central to a number of major drug and alcohol treatment programmes. (Boudin et al 1977, Sobell & Sobell 1978). This latter work is of particular interest in that it is one of the few treatment programs to demonstrate a consistent and substantially better outcome than more traditional therapeutic interventions.

## A cognitive view

A treatment approach based on animal models of behaviour obviously fails to take account of individual cognitions in the mediation of learning (Meichebaum 1977). A broadly based cognitive approach allows for such mediating influences to be considered (Bandura 1977).

**Cognitive therapy** is essentially an attempt to help the patient recognise and alter maladaptive thought patterns. Miller (1980) has listed the common cognitive factors involved in drug and alcohol misuse namely *expectations,* thoughts on *self efficacy* and what has been called the *abstinence violation effect.*

A number of alcohol studies have demonstrated that an individual's *beliefs* and *expectations* can profoundly influence behaviour. Many investigations over the years have used a balanced placebo design in which one group of alcoholics receives alcohol without being aware of it while a second group drinks a non-alcoholic beverage but believe it to be alcohol. Two further groups knowingly drink either alcohol or non alcoholic beverages (Hodgson 1984). In general what this work demonstrates is that moderately dependent alcoholics who think they have consumed alcohol are more likely to continue drinking. This idea that a pharmacological effect can be overridden by expectations or beliefs also applies to other behaviours for instance sexual arousal or anxiety (Wilson 1978). In other words what people think alcohol or other drugs do may be an important mediator of future behaviour.

Associated with this is the *abstinence violation effect.* Although first developed on drinkers this relapse model has now been applied across the range of addictive behaviours (Cummings et al 1980). These authors suggest that during a period of abstinence the individual experiences personal control which arises from an increasing ability to cope with difficult situations without recourse to drug use. As time goes on he will come to expect to be able to deal with high-risk situations and consequently what has been called *self efficacy* will increase. If the individual however does succumb to drug use he will experience the abstinence violation effect. This produces cognitive dissonance in that the individual views himself as an abstainer yet has slipped into drug use. The dissonance is usually resolved by a change of self image (I suppose I am still an incurable addict) or cognitive defence strategies like denial or rationalisation. The individual also feels that he has given in and will normally attribute the cause of relapse to personal weakness or lack of will power rather than external events. This in turn reduces self efficacy with regard to future situations and so the probability is that the relapse will continue and former pattern of use will be reinstated. The adage 'once an addict always an addict' becomes a self fulfilling prophesy. Thus expectancy, abstinence violation and efficacy effects and indeed other cognitive mediating factors can influence the initiation and development of addiction behaviour although the nature and extent of such influences is the subject of much current research. A full account of cognitive models of drug use is inappropriate here but for the interested reader there are several good reviews of the area (Wilson 1978, Donovan & Marlatt 1980).

This work has clear implications for treatment. Relapse prevention strategies for example can be developed by analysing the circumstances in which the individual is most at risk and so allowing for the development of more adaptive coping styles (Litman 1982, Marlatt & George 1984). As the individual copes with such situations the greater his self efficacy which in turn reduces the probability of future relapse. A wide variety of cognitive strategies aimed at re-aligning the individual's self evaluation have been described. These are extensively reviewed elsewhere (Cummings et al 1980, Goldfried & Goldfried 1980) and a clear comprehensive alcoholism counselling procedure, *motivational interviewing,* based on the ideas of cognitive restructuring has recently been outlined by Miller (1983). There is little doubt that an increasing number of workers in the field are using cognitive methods, whether in the context of individual or group work, as an integral part of their treatment program. This is in contrast to insight based psychotherapeutic approaches which seem to have waned in popularity over recent years.

**Psychotherapy**

While behavioural and cognitive therapy primarily focuses on current behaviour and psychosocial functioning, psychoanalytic models emphasise the conflicts underlying drug misuse. These are commonly based on the view of drug misuse as a chronic and hopeless attempt to satisfy unfulfilled oral dependency needs due to fixation at the oral stage of development. Some more specific analytic hypotheses have been listed by Miller & Herster (1980) examples of which are self-destructive behaviour resulting from hostility towards a depriving mother or a defence against latent homosexuality. The main aim of psychotherapy is towards achievement of some insight into unconsciously repressed painful material through the interpretative process.

Most commentators who have reviewed treatment methods in drug misuse conclude that deeper psychotherapy is as a rule neither feasible nor particularly effective (Platt & Labat 1976, Madden 1979, Saunders 1982). Evidence suggests that addicts and alcoholics rarely remain in treatment for the requisite time period and psychotherapists tend to view them as rather unrewarding patients

(Chappell 1977). In what few outcome studies there have been, results have generally, with some exceptions, been disappointing (Harding 1973). There is also some disagreement among clinicians as to when insight based psychotherapy can be optimally effective. Some would argue that interpretative methods are most useful before any overt commitment to change drug using behaviour (Prochaska & Di Clemente 1983) while others suggest that it is more appropriate in the consolidation and maintenance of behaviour change (Blane 1977, Lynn 1976).

Although by general consensus insight based psychotherapy is not the treatment of choice for addicts and alcoholics it is not unreasonable to suppose however that it can have some value for rather specific patient groups notably those who are verbally fluent, highly motivated and socially stable. The problem with evaluative research on psychotherapeutic methods is that these characteristics are often associated with a favourable outcome irrespective of what therapeutic intervention the individual experiences.

## Treatment goal

For a significant number of drug users who present for help, total abstinence associated with a return to a drug free life style is the stated objective. For some therapists too withdrawal followed by continued abstinence is the only acceptable treatment goal. However the question of whether abstinence is feasible, or indeed necessary, for everyone has been the subject of some debate over a number of years. A related question concerns the desirability of promoting substitute substance use as a treatment method in itself. Perhaps the two most common treatment goals which do not involve abstinence are maintenance and controlled drinking and these will be considered below.

## Maintenance

Although the ultimate aim of treating addicts is withdrawal then abstinence accompanied by a return to normal social functioning many still request maintenance therapy. They argue that this would stabilise them enough to function normally in the community by avoiding the problems inherent in the obtaining of illegal drugs.

The pharmacological aspects of methadone maintenance were discussed above and it was suggested that maintenance is now a much less favoured option among clinicians. There has been what Stimson & Oppenheimer (1982) termed a move from 'maintenance to confrontation' and they have traced the development of this change in emphasis since the London drug clinics opened in 1968. It was originally argued that a maintenance rather than an abstinence policy did more to ensure that addicts attended clinics, kept off the streets and were less troublesome to the authorities. It was also in some ways the easiest and cheapest response to addiction. It can, however, neutralise the urgency of employing treatment which could help the individual deal more constructively with his psychosocial problems. Furthermore it conflicts with traditional notions of cure as people are not actively changing but rather maintaing the status quo. Thus many workers now feel that a general policy of maintenance has more to do with social control than treatment and it is argued that social control of addiction is more the role of legislators than clinicians. It also became clear by the mid 1970s that legally available opioids did not prevent illegal drugs from reaching the streets and over the past few years drugs which are legally prescribed represent only a tiny percentage of the weight and number of seizures.

Since the clinics opened therefore there has been a move from maintenance on injectable heroin to oral methadone then to increased emphasis on withdrawal and abstinence. This is perhaps more likely to stimulate a more active and less rigid view of therapy. It may however be unwise to throw 'the baby out with the linctus' and maintenance should still be considered for some of the addict population who are unable or unwilling to participate in alternative forms of therapeutic intervention.

## Controlled drinking

While there is a trend towards abstinence in the treatment of opioid misuse there has been in recent years a move away from the view that abstinence is the only viable treatment goal for the alcohol dependent population. The traditional idea that alcoholism was inevitably a chronically relapsing condition was questioned by Davies (1962) in perhaps the single most influential piece of research in the field. He demonstrated that a small number of alcoholics were drinking normally up to 11 years after discharge from treatment. Although this discovery was not original even then, it was the Davies study which generated controversy and stimulated debate in the scientific literature and popular press as the idea that some alcoholics could return to harm free drinking undermined the traditional view. Perhaps the most consistent criticism levelled at this study was that if people could drink again they were not genuine alcoholics in the first place (Williams 1963). This assertion was squarely refuted by Davies et al (1969) who showed that some of the normal drinking group had symptoms of severe dependence on initial assessment. The general finding that some, albeit a minority of alcoholics, can resume normal drinking has since been replicated in a number of longitudinal studies (Pattison et al 1969, Smart 1978, Hyman 1976, Polich et al 1981).

In the light of these findings the 1970s saw a boom in the development of treatment strategies specifically tailored to a controlled drinking outcome, undoubtedly the most influential of which was that of Sobell and Sobell (1978) who in a series of studies developed a comprehensive controlled drinking treatment program.

One of their major findings was that a group of gamma alcoholics who had been trained in controlled drinking did much better at two year follow up than matched groups who had been treated by abstinence orientated traditional methods, for example A.A., group therapy and chemotherapy.

The debate on harm-free drinking among alcoholics simmered in the literature during the 1970s but over recent years has once again become more vigorous. This may be a result of a number of factors. First, the four year results of the large scale Rand Report (Polich et al 1981), showed quite clearly that a substantial minority of those followed up were carrying out *non problem drinking*. Second was the publication of the only book to deal specifically and systematically with controlled drinking (Heather & Robertson 1981, 1983). This was a studious and thorough review although the authors adopted a radical stance on their interpretation of the literature. Third was criticism of the work of Mark and Lynda Sobell (Pendery et al 1982) which by general concensus had been regarded as methodologically sophisticated and a most impressive demonstration of the efficacy of controlled drinking treatment strategies. The issue of controlled drinking perhaps more than anything else symbolises the differences between the traditional and more recent conceptualisation of alcoholism and its management. For this reason the debate has been conducted in a much more personal and emotionally charged manner than is normally the case in scientific discourse. The motives of the authors of the Rand Report have been questioned and their work described in emotive terms like 'dangerous'. The integrity of the Sobells has been publicly discussed with allegations being made of fraudulent research (Pendery et al 1982, Walker & Roach 1984) in spite of much evidence that their work has been of an exemplary scientific standard (Dickens et al 1982, Marlatt 1983, Doob 1984, Sobell & Sobell 1984). It is unfortunate that the time, effort and commitment which has gone into the controlled drinking debate has not been devoted to other more pressing issues in the treatment and prevention of alcoholism. So called ideological witch hunts do little to advance the sum of knowledge in the field.

The question should not be 'can some alcoholics drink normally?' as the literature is replete with examples to show that they can. Rather we should be asking which individual would benefit from a controlled drinking treatment goal and who should aim for abstinence. Some clinicians continue to believe in abstinence for all while others advocate controlled drinking for everyone except those with alcohol related brain damage (Heather & Robertson 1981). Perhaps most workers confronted with the day to day problems of the treatment and management of alcoholic patients would adopt a position somewhere between these extremes. Hodgson (1980) for instance suggests that degree of dependence may be an indicator of the optimum treatment goal. He suggests that controlled drinking is an attainable goal for the moderately dependent alcoholic while abstinence is perhaps more realistic for those who are severely dependent. There is an urgent need for the development of further indicators which have some predictive validity in terms of treatment goal. These could for example be based on the stages of change, pattern of past behaviour, attribution style or expectancy effects. Systematic assessment of such variables could help the clinician and patient in their formulation of an appropriate treatment plan.

## Conclusions

A review of treatment issues in the management of drug and alcohol misuse almost invariably raises as many questions as it answers. Based on current evidence however some general statements can be made with a degree of assurance.

(1) Treatment, however defined, is not qualitatively different from the naturally occurring processes of change.

(2) Treatment does seem generally to produce better outcome than no treatment for users of all psychotropic substances although no particular treatment approach has emerged as being consistently superior to others.

(3) Some alcoholics and addicts do however improve irrespective of whether they undergo formal treatment or not.

(4) For most alcohol users, minimal treatment intervention seems to be as effective as long term, intensive multimodal programs. For users of other drugs the effect of treatment intensity would appear to interact with type of drug and pattern of use.

(5) A significant minority of alcoholics can return to a normal drinking pattern.

(6) Improvement in terms of psychosocial functioning and pattern of use if it is to occur is more likely in those with a shorter history of alcohol and other drug use.

(7) For most individuals out-patient care can be as effective as in-patient care.

(8) Thorough assessment is a necessary prelude to the formulation of any treatment program.

(9) Finally and perhaps most important, therapy should be tailored to the individual. What is useful for one person may be singularly inappropriate for another.

REFERENCES

Armor D J 1980 The Rand Reports and the analysis of relapse. In: Edwards G, Grant M (eds) Alcoholism treatment in transition. Croom Helm, London, Ch 5

Armor D J, Polich J M, Stambul H B 1976 Alcoholism and treatment. Rand Corporation, Santa Monica

Ashton M 1981 Theory and practice in the British system. Druglink 16: 1–5

Aumark L 1980 The effectiveness of combined vs separate treatment of alcoholics and drug addicts. In: Madden J S, Walker R, Kenyon W H (eds) Aspects of alcohol and drug dependence. Pitman Medical, Bath

Baekeland F, Lundwall L, Kissin B 1975 Methods for the treatment of chronic alcoholism: a critical appraisal. In: Gibbons R J, Israel Y, Kalant H, Popham R E, Schmidt W, Smart R G (eds) Research advances in alcohol and drug problems. Wiley, London

Bandura A 1977 Social learning theory. Prentice Hall, New Jersey

Banks A, Waller T A N 1983 Drug addiction and polydrug abuse: The Role of the general practitioner. I.S.D.D., London

Bebbington P E 1976 The efficacy of alcoholics anonymous: the elusiveness of hard data. British Journal of Psychiatry 128: 572–580

Bill W 1957 Alcoholics Anonymous comes of age: A Brief History of A.A. Alcoholics Anonymous, World Services, New York

Blane H T 1977 Psychotherapeutic approach. In: Kissin B, Begleiter H (eds). The biology of addiction. Vol 5. Treatment and rehabilitation of the chronic alcoholic. Plenum, New York

Blumberg H H 1976 British users of opiate-type drugs: a follow-up study. British Journal of Addiction 71: 65-77

Blumberg H H 1981 Characteristics of people coming to treatment. In: Edwards G, Busch C (eds). Drug problems in Britain: a review of ten years. Academic Press, London

Boudin A M 1972 Contingency contracting as a therapeutic tool in the deceleration of amphetamine use. Behaviour Therapy 3: 604-605

Boudin H M, Valentine V E et al 1977 Contingency contracting with drug abusers in the natural environment. The International Journal of Addictions 12: 1-16

Boyd P 1975 Problems and treatment of drug abuse in adolescence. Proceedings of the Royal Society of Medicine 68: 566-570

Brandsma J M, Maultsby M C, Welsh R J 1980 The out-patient treatment of alcoholism: a review and comparative study. University Park Press, Baltimore

Bromet C J, Moos R 1979 Prognosis of alcoholic patients: comparisons of abstainers and moderate drinkers. British Journal of Addiction 74: 183-188

Caddy G R, Lovibond S H 1976 Self-regulation and discriminated aversive conditioning in the modification of alcoholic's drinking behaviour. Behaviour Therapy 7: 223-230

Callahan E J 1980 Alternative strategies in the treatment of narcotic addiction: a review. In: Miller W R (ed) The addictive behaviours. Treatment of alcoholism, drug abuse, smoking and obesity. Pergamon Press, Oxford, Ch 3

Cartwright A K J 1981 Are different therapeutic perspectives important in the treatment of alcoholism? British Journal of Addiction 76: 347-361

Chapple P A L, Somekh D E, Taylor M E 1972 Follow-up of cases of opiate addiction from time of notification to the Home Office. British Medical Journal 2: 680-683

Clare A W 1977 How good is treatment? In: Edwards G, Grant M (eds) Alcoholism: new knowledge and new responses. Croom Helm, London, Ch 23

Cohen M, Liebson I A, Faillace C A 1972 A technique for establishing controlled drinking in chronic alcoholics. Diseases of the Nervous System 33: 46-49

Costello R M 1975 Alcoholism treatment and evaluation. In search of methods. International Journal of the Addictions 10: 251-263

Costello R M 1977 Programming alcoholism treatment: historical trends. In: Madden J S, Walker R, Kenyon W H (eds) Alcoholism and drug dependence: a multidisciplinary approach. Plenum, New York

Costello R M 1980 Alcoholism treatment effectiveness: slicing the outcome variance pie. In: Edwards G, Grant M (eds) Alcoholism treatment in transition. Croom Helm, London, Ch 7

Cummings C, Gordon J R, Marlatt A 1980 Relapse prevention and prediction. In: Miller W R (ed) The addictive behaviours. Treatment of alcoholism, drug abuse, smoking and obesity. Pergamon Press, Oxford

Davidson W S 1974 Studies of aversive conditioning for alcoholics. A critical review of theory and research methodology. Psychological Bulletin 81: 571-581

Davies D L 1962 Normal drinking in recovered alcohol addicts. Quarterly Journal of Studies on Alcohol 23: 64-104

Davies D L, Scott D F, Malherbe M E L, 1969 Resumed normal drinking in recovered alcohol addicts.

De Morsier G, Feldman H 1952 Le traitement de l'alcoolisme par l'apomorphine: etude de 500 cas. Schiveizer Archier fur Neurologic Psychiatrie 70: 434–440

Dickens B M, Doob A N, Warwick O H, Winegard W C 1982 Report of the Committee of Enquiry into Allegations Concerning Drs Linda and Mark Sobell. Addiction Research Foundation, Toronto

Ditman K S, Crawford G G, Forgy E W, Moskowitz H, MacAndrew C 1967 A controlled experiment on the use of court probation for drink arrests. American Journal of Psychiatry 124: 160–163

Donovan D M, Marlatt G A 1980 Assessment of expectancies and behaviours associated with alcohol consumption: a cognitive-behavioural approach. Journal of Studies on Alcohol 41: 1153–1187

Doob A N 1984 Understanding the nature of investigations into alleged fraud in alcohol research: a reply to Walker and Roach. British Journal of Addiction 79: 160–174

d'Orban P T 1974 A follow-up study of female narcotic addicts: variables related to outcome. British Journal of Psychiatry 124: 28–33

Edwards G 1980 Alcoholism treatment: between guesswork and certainty. In: Edwards G, Grant M (eds). Alcoholism treatment in transition. Croom Helm, London, Ch 21

Edwards G 1984 Drinking in longitudinal prospective: career and natural history. British Journal of Addiction 79: 175–184

Edwards G, Guthrie S 1967 A controlled trial of in-patient and out-patient treatment of alcohol dependency. Lancet i, 555–559

Edwards G, Orford J et al 1977 Alcoholism: a controlled trial of 'treatment' and 'advice'. Journal of Studies on Alcohol 38: 1004–1031

Emrick C D 1975 A review of psychologically orientated treatment of alcoholism II. The relative effectiveness of different treatment approaches and the effectiveness of treatment vs no treatment. Quarterly Journal of Studies on Alcohol 36: 88–109

Finney J W, Moss R H, Mewborn C R 1980 Post treatment experiences and treatment outcome of alcoholic patients six months and two years after hospitalization. Journal of Consulting and Clinical Psychology 48: 17–29

Gillies M, Laverty S G et al 1974 Outcomes in treated alcoholics. Journal of Alcoholism 9: 125–134

Glaser F B 1977 Comments on "alcoholism: a controlled trial of 'treatment' and 'advice' ". Journal of Studies on Alcohol 38: 1810–1827

Glaser F B 1977 The first therapeutic community. The addiction therapist 2: 8–15

Glaser F B 1981 The origins of the drug-free therapeutic community. British Journal of Addiction 76: 13–25

Glaser F B, Ogbourne A C 1982 Does AA really work? British Journal of Addiction 77: 123–130

Goldfried M R 1982 Converging themes in psychotherapy. Springer, New York

Goldfried M R, Goldfried A P 1980 Cognitive change methods. In: Kanfer F H, Goldstein A P (eds) Helping people change, 2nd Edition, Pergamon Press, New York

Goodwin D W, Crane J B, Guze S B 1971 Felons who drink: an eight-year follow-up. Quarterly Journal of Studies on alcohol 32: 136–147

Gorsuch R L Butler M C 1976 Initial drug abuse: a review of predisposing social psychological factors. Psychological Bulletin 83: 120–137

Gotestam K G, Melin L 1972 Covert extinction of amphetamine addiction. Behaviour Therapy 5: 90–92

Harding G T 1973 Psychotherapy in the treatment of drug abuse. In: Bostrom H, Carson T, Ljungstedt N (eds) Drug dependence — treatment and treatment evaluation. Almquist and Wiksell, Stockholm

Hartnoll R L, Mitsheson M C et al 1980 Evaluation of heroin maintenance in controlled trial. Archives of General Psychiatry 37: 877

Hawks D 1976 Heroin users in a provincial town and their follow-up over a three-year period. In: Edwards G, Russell M A H, Hawks D, MacCafferty M (eds) Drugs and grud dependence. Saxon House, London

Heather N, Robertson I 1981 Controlled drinking. Methuen, London

Heather N, Robertson I 1983 Controlled Drinking 2nd edn. Methuen, London

Herz M I, Endicott J, Spitzer R L, Mesnikoff A 1971 Day versus in-patient hospitalization: a controlled study. American Journal of Psychology 127: 107–118

Hodgson R J 1980 Treatment strategies for the early problem drinker. In: Edwards G, Grant M (eds) Alcoholism treatment in transition. Croom Helm, London

Hodgson R J 1984 Craving and priming. In: Edwards A, Littleton J (eds) Pharmacological treatments for alcoholism. Croom Helm, London, Methuen, New York

Hodgson R J, Stockwell T R 1983 The theoretical and empirical basis of the alcohol dependence model: a social learning perspective. In: Heather N, Robertson I, Davies P (eds) Alcohol misuse: three crucial questions. Junction Books, London

Hunt G M, Azrin N H 1973 A community-reinforcement approach to alcoholism. Behaviour Research and Therapy 11: 91–104

Hyman H H 1976 Alcoholics fifteen years later. Annals of the New York Academy of Sciences 273: 613–622

Jaffe J H 1980 Drug addiction and drug abuse. In: Gilman A G, Goodman L S, Gilman A (eds) The pharmacological basis of therapeutics. MacMillan, Toronto

Kendell R E 1965 Normal drinking by former alcohol addicts. Quarterly Journal of Studies on Alcohol 26: 247–257

Kitson T M 1978 On the probability of implanted disulfirams causing a reaction to ethanol. Journal of Studies on alcohol 39: 183–191

La Porte D J, McLellan A T, MacGahan J A 1980 Evaluation of combined treatment for alcohol and drug abusers: importance of patient compatibility. In: Madden J S, Walker R, Kenyon E H (eds) Aspects of alcohol and drug dependence. Pitman Medical, Bath

Litman G K 1980 Relapse in alcoholism: traditional and current approaches. In: Edwards G, Grant M (eds) Alcoholism treatment in transition. Croom Helm, London

Litman G 1982 Factors in the breakdown of abstinence. Paper presented at the Annual Conference of the New Directions in the Study of Alcohol Group. Bollington

Littleton J M 1984 The future could be bright. In: Edwards G, Littleton J (eds) Pharmacological treatments for alcoholism. Croom Helm, London, Methuen, New York, Ch 31

Longabaugh R, McCrady B et al 1983 Cost effectiveness of alcoholism treatment in partial vs in-patient settings. Six month outcomes. Journal of Studies on Alcohol 44: 1049–1071

Luborsky L, Chandler M, Auerbach A H, Cohen L, Bachrach T 1971 Factors influencing the outcome of psychotherapy. A review of quantitative research. Psychological Bulletin 75: 145–185

Lynn E J 1976 Treatment for alcoholism. Psychotherapy is still alive and well. Hospital and Community Psychiatry 27: 282–283

McCance C, McCance P F 1969 Alcoholism in North-East Scotland: its treatment and outcome. British Journal of Psychiatry 115: 189–198

McLachlan J F C, Stein R L 1982 Evaluation of a day clinic for alcoholics. Journal of Studies on Alcohol 43: 261–272

Madden J S 1979a Annotation: disulfiram implants. British Journal on Alcohol and Alcoholism 14: 7–10

Madden J S 1979b A guide to alcohol and drug dependence. Wright, Bristol
Madden J S 1984 What would a pharmacological treatment for alcohol dependence look like? In: Edwards G, Littleton J (eds) Pharmacological treatments for alcoholism. Croom Helm, London, Methuen, New York
Marlatt G A 1983 The controlled-drinking controversy: a commentary. American Psychologist 38, 1097–1110
Marlatt G A, George W H 1984 Relapse prevention: introduction and overview of the model. British Journal of Addiction 79: 261–274
Meichebaum D 1977 Cognitive behaviour modification. Plenum, New York
Melotte C J, Ogborne A C 1975 Strategies for the successful follow-up of treated drug users. Journal of Drug Issues 5: 79–82
Meyer R E, Mirin S M, Altman J, McNamee H B 1976 A behavioural paradigm for the evaluation of narcotic antagonists. Archives of General Psychiatry 33: 376
Miller W R 1980 The addictive behaviours. In: Miller W R (ed) The addictive behaviours. Treatment of alcoholism, drug abuse, smoking and obesity. Pergamon Press, Oxford, Ch 1
Miller W R 1983 Motivational interviewing with problem drinkers. Behavioural Psychotherapy 11: 147–172
Miller W R, Herster R K 1980 Treating the problem drinker: modern approaches. In: Miller W R (ed) The addictive behaviours. Treatment of alcoholism, drug abuse, smoking and obesity. Pergamon Press, Oxford
Moos R H, Finney J W, Cronkite R C 1980 The need for a paradigm shift in evaluations of treatment outcome: extrapolations from the Rand research. British Journal of Addictions 75: 347–350
Morland J (et al) 1984 Lack of pharmacological effects of implanted disulfiran. In: Edwards G, Littleton J (eds) Pharmacological treatments for alcoholism, Croom Helm, London, Methuen, New York, Ch 29
Murphy P M, Cramer D, Lillie F J 1984 The relationship between curative factors perceived by patients in their psychotherapy and treatment outcome: an exploratory study. British Journal of Medical Psychology 57: 187–192
Murray R M 1980 Why are the drug companies so disinterested in alcoholism? British Journal of Addiction 75: 113–115
Nathan P E, O'Brien J S 1971 An experimental analysis of the behaviour of alcoholics and non-alcoholics during prolonged experimental drinking: a necessary precursor to behaviour therapy. Behaviour Therapy 2: 455–476
Obholzer A M 1974 A follow-up study of nineteen alcoholic patients treated by means of tetraethylthiuram disulphide (Antabuse) implants. British Journal of Addiction 69: 19–23
Ogborne A C, Stimson G V 1975 Follow-up of a representative sample of heroin addicts. International Journal of the Addictions 10: 1061
Oppenheimer E, Stimson G V, Thorley A 1979 Seven-year follow-up of heroin addicts: abstinence and continued use compared. British Medical Journal 2: 627
Orford J 1980 Understanding treatment: controlled trials and other strategies. In: Edwards G, Grant M (eds) Alcoholism treatment in transition. Croom Helm, London, Ch 9
Pattison E M, Coe R, Rhodes R J 1969 Evaluation of alcoholism treatment: a comparison of three facilities. Archives of General Psychiatry 20: 478–488
Pendery M L, Maltzman I M, West L J 1982 Controlled drinking by alcoholics? new findings and a re-evaluation of a major affirmative study. Science 217: 169–175
Platt J J, Labate C 1976 Heroin addiction: theory research and treatment. Wiley, New York
Polich J M 1980 Patterns of remission in alcoholism. In: Edwards G, Grant M (eds) Alcoholism treatment in transition. Croom Helm, London, Ch 6

Polich J M, Armor D J, Braiker H B 1981 The course of alcoholism: four years after treatment. Wiley-Interscience, New York

Prochaska J O, Di Clemente C C 1982 Transtheoretical therapy toward a more integrated model of change. Psychotherapy: Theory, Research and Practice: 19: 276–288

Prochaska J O, Di Clemente C C 1983 Stages and processes of self-change of smoking: toward and integrated model of change. Journal of Consulting Clinical Psychology 51: 390–395

Prochaska J O, Di Clemente C C 1984 Proceedings 3rd International Conference on the Treatment of Addictive Behaviour, Scotland, In Press

Pullar-Strecker H 1950 Discussion on modern techniques for the treatment of acute and prolonged alcoholism. British Journal of Addiction 47: 16–20

Rankin H, Hodgson R 1977 Cue exposure: one approach to the extinction of addictive behaviours. In: Gross M (ed) Alcohol intoxication and withdrawal Vol 3b, Plenum Press, New York

Rathod N H 1977 Follow-up study of injectors in a provincial town. Drug and Alcohol Dependence 2: 1–21

Report of the Advisory Council on the Misuse of Drugs 1982 Treatment and rehabilitation. HMSO, London

Resnick R, Volauka J, Freedman A M, Thomas M 1974 Studies of EN-1639A (naltrexone): a new narcotic antagonist. American Journal of Psychiatry 131: 646

Rix J B, Rix E L 1983 Alcohol problems. A guide for nurses and other health professionals. Wright, Bristol

Robertson I, Hodgson R, Orford J, McKechnie R 1984 Psychology and problem drinking. British Psychological Society Working Party Report

Robinson D 1979 Talking out of alcoholism: the self-help process of A.A. Croom Helm, London

Romond A M, Forrest C K, Kleber H D 1975 Follow-up of participants in a drug dependence therapeutic community. Archives of General Psychiatry 32: 369–374

Room R 1980 New curves in the course: a comment on Polich, Armor and Braiker, 'The Course of Alcoholism'. British Journal of Addiction 75: 351–360

Ryle A 1984 How can we compare different psychotherapies? Why are they all effective? British Journal of Medical Psychology 57: 261–264

Saunders W M 1982 Prevention. In: Plant M A (ed) Drinking and problem drinking. Junction Books, London Ch 7

Schecter A 1980 The role of narcotic antagonists in the rehabilitation of opiate addicts: a review of naltrexone. American Journal of Alcohol Abuse 7: 1–18

Sells S B, Simpson D D (eds) 1976 Effectiveness of drug abuse treatment (Vol 3): further studies of drug users, treatment, typologies and assessment of outcome during treatment in the DARP. Ballinger Publishing Co, Cambridge

Sells S B, Simpson D D 1980 The case for drug abuse treatment effectiveness, Based on the DARP Research Programme. British Journal of Addiction 75: 117–131

Shapiro D A, Shapiro D 1982 Meta-analysis of comparative theory outcome studies: a replication and refinement. Psychological Bulletin 92: 581–604

Skinner H 1981 Comparison of clients assigned to in-patient and out-patient treatment for alcoholism and drug addiction. British Journal of Psychiatry 138: 312–320

Smart R G 1976 Outcome studies of therapeutic community and halfway house treatment for addicts. International Journal of Addictions 11: 143–159

Smart R G 1978 Characteristics of alcoholics who drink socially after treatment. Alcoholism: Clinical and Experimental Research 2: 49–52

Smart R G, Everson A, Segal R, Finley J, Ballah B 1977 A four-year follow-up study of narcotic-dependent persons receiving methadone maintenance substitute therapy. Canadian Journal of Public Health 68: 55–58

Smith R 1982 Alcohol and alcoholism. Leagrave Press, London

Sobell M B, Sobell L C 1978 Behavioural treatment of alcohol problems: individualized therapy and controlled drinking. Plenum, New York

Sobel M B, Sobell L C 1984 The aftermath of heresy: a response to Pendery et al's (1982) Critique of "Individualized Behaviour Therapy for Alcoholics". Behaviour Research and Therapy 22: 413–440

Stimson G V 1973 Heroin and behaviour. Irish University Press, Shannon

Stimson G V, Oppenheimer A 1982 Heroin addiction treatment and control in Britain. Tavistock, London

Stimson G V, Oppenheimer E, Thorley A 1978 Seven year follow-up of heroin addicts: drug use and outcome. British Medical Journal 1: 11–90

Stockwell T 1984 Sensitising drugs in behavioural perspective. In: Edwards G, Littleton J (eds) Pharmacological treatments for alcoholism. Croom Helm, London, Methuen, New York

Stockwell T, Hodgson R J, Rankin H 1982 Alcohol dependence, beliefs and the priming effect. Behaviour Research and Therapy 20: 513–522

Straus R, Bacon S D 1951 Alcoholism and Overall Stability. A study of occupational integration in 2023 male clinic patients. Quarterly Journal of Studies on Alcohol 12: 231–260

Strube M J, Hartmann D P 1982 A critical appraisal of meta-analysis. British Journal of Clinical Psychology 21: 129–140

Telling-Smith G 1984 Pharmacological treatments for alcohol problems as a challenge to pharmaceutical intervention. In: Edwards G, Littleton J (eds). Pharmacological treatments for alcoholism. Croom Helm, London, Methuen, New York

Thompson I G, Rathod N H 1968 Aversion therapy for heroin dependence. The Lancet ii: 282–384

Thorley A 1981 Longitudinal studies of drug dependence. In: Edwards G, Busch C (eds) Drug problems in Britain: a review of ten years. Academic Press, London, Ch 6

Thorley A, Oppenheimer E, Stimson G V 1977 Clinic attendance and opiate prescription status of heroin addicts over a six year period. British Journal of Psychiatry 130: 565

Vaillant G 1970 The natural history of narcotic drug addiction. Seminars in Psychiatry 2: 486–498

Vaillant G E 1983 The natural history of alcoholism: causes, patterns and paths to recovery. Harvard University Press, Cambridge

Voegtlin W L 1940 The treatment of alcoholism by establishing a conditioned reflex. American Journal of the Medical Sciences 199: 802–810

Vogler R E, Weissbach T A, Compton J V 1977 Learning techniques for alcohol abuse. Behaviour Research and Therapy 15: 31–38

Walker K D, Roach C A 1984 A critique of the report of the Dickens Enquiry into the controlled drinking research of the Sobells. British Journal of Addiction 79: 147–156

Washburn S, Vannicelli M, Longabaugh R, Scheff B J 1976 A controlled comparison of psychiatric day treatment and in-patient hospitalization. Journal of Consulting and Clinical Psychology 44: 665–675

Weipert G D, Bewley T H, d'Orban P T 1978 Outcome for 575 British opiate addicts treatment between 1968 and 1975. Bulletin on Narcotics 30: 21–32

Whyte R C, O'Brien P M J 1974 Disulfiram implant: a controlled trial. British Journal of Psychiatry 124: 42–44

Wikler A 1973 Dynamics of drug dependence: Implications of a conditioning theory for research and treatment. In: Fischer S, Greedman A M (eds) Opiate addiction: origin and treatment. Wiley, New York

Williams L 1963 Comment on Davies D L 'Normal drinking in recovered alcohol addicts'. Quarterly Journal of Studies on Alcohol 24: 109–121

Wilson G T 1978 Booze, beliefs and behaviour: cognitive processes in alcohol use and abuse. In: Nathan P E, Marlatt G A , Loberg T (eds) Alcoholism: new directions in behavioural research and treatment. Plenum Press, New York

Wilson S, Kennard D 1978 The extraverting effect of treatment in a therapeutic community for drug abusers. British Journal of Psychiatry 132: 296–299

Winick C 1962 Maturing out of narcotic addiction. Bulletin on Narcotics 14: 1–7

Yates F E, Norris H 1981 The use made of treatment: an alternative approach to the evaluation of alcoholism services. New Directions in the Study of Alcohol 2: 32–48

# 6
# *Prevention*

Within the context of an increasing awareness of the importance of prevention in a wide range of social and medical problems, attention is more than ever focusing on preventive strategies for drug and alcohol misuse. As the aetiology of drug and alcohol misuse is multiple and interactive a comprehensive prevention policy must operate at the level of the individual, the agent and the environment. Such a policy may have a variety of aims. These include a reduction or elimination of consumption, a reduction of the psychological, social and physiological correlates of excessive consumption or an altering of people's perception of what constitutes a problem. As these aims are not necessarily compatible, it is clear that a broadly based prevention policy subsumes a number of different approaches. While there is some overlap between strategies employed for recreational and controlled drugs there are differences in approach which must be taken into account. Limits on advertising for example may reduce nicotine use but would have no effect on cannabis demand. Possession of solvents is not an offence while possession of cocaine can result in a severe custodial penalty. Government fiscal policy may reduce per capita alcohol consumption but has no part to play in the control of blackmarket heroin. On the other hand health educators now take the view that it is inappropriate to separate recreational, prescribed and illegal drugs and they argue that teaching about all drugs should be seen in the context of wider health, social and political education.

McKechnie (1982) emphasises that the word prevention is used in two different ways. It can mean *to hinder* or curtail the progress of, and when used in its absolute sense it means *to stop*. The main thrust of the preventive effort with regard to illegal drug use is towards eradication and so prevention is used in the latter sense. On the other hand when applied to recreational drugs which are not the subject of legal control it normally means to hinder or at the very least maintain the frequency of use at present levels.

For the purpose of the present discussion, preventive approaches are broadly divided into *control* and *demand* strategies with the former consisting of legal and fiscal measures imposed to hinder or stop consumption. Demand strategies take into account measures aimed at manipulation of public attitudes or promotion of a greater understanding of the problems associated with drug and alcohol misuse. Except where appropriate, for example in the area of drug and alcohol education, alcohol prevention policy will be considered separately.

## Alcohol consumption

Alcohol consumption in the U.K. is relatively modest in relation to other economically comparable countries. The people of Luxembourg generally seem to be the most prolific imbibers in the world with the U.K. remaining consistently in a mid-league position. U.K. data, however, over the past two decades reflects the general increase in consumption in most western countries and indeed many third world countries. Appendix 6.1 demonstrates an almost exact doubling of alcohol consumption in England between 1962 and 1982.

In the U.K. highest consumption tends to be among young unmarried males (Taylor 1981) although there has been a significant increase in female-drinking over the past 10 years (McConville 1983). Ten years ago, alcoholic cirrhosis was about 5 times more common in men than women; the male:female ratio is now in the order of 2:1. It has been estimated (OPSC 1980) that in mainland Britain some 94% of men and 89% of women drink alcohol. Some occupational groups have an increased risk of problems. These include workers in the catering industry, fishermen, members of the armed forces, journalists and medical practitioners (Paton et al 1982). Whitehead et al (1978) demonstrated that 11% of healthy men attending a health screening programme were found to have biochemical evidence of heavy alcohol consumption in the form of raised gammaglutamyltranspeptidase levels.

Prevalence data and the problems associated with the application of epidemiological methods to the field of alcohol drinking, dependence and harm have been extensively reviewed elsewhere (Hore 1980, Shaw 1982, Paton et al 1982, Rix & Rix 1983). Suffice to say that most issues in the area are related to what Kreitman (1977) called the inter-connected triad: the prevalence and definition of a clinical problem, the distribution of alcohol drinking practices in the normal population and the analysis and assessment of alcohol related disability or harm.

Taylor (1981) has collated data from various sources on the numbers of heavy, problem and dependent drinkers in England and Wales (Table 6.1). Such estimates must of course be interpreted with caution and restraint. He uses alcohol dependence in the sense

**Table 6.1**   Numbers of heavy, problem and dependent drinkers in England and Wales

|  | Heavy drinkers | Problem drinkers | Dependent drinkers |
| --- | --- | --- | --- |
| High estimate | 3 000 000 (8%) | 1 300 000 (3%) | 240 000 (0.6%) |
| Low estimate | 1 300 000 (3%) | 500 000 (1.5%) | 70 000 (0.2%) |

Percentages of the total population are shown in parentheses.

of the full syndrome as described in Chapter 1. Problem drinkers are defined as those who sometimes behave in a manner harmful to themselves or others but whose overall consumption is not necessarily excessive. Heavy drinkers are those who consume more than the generally accepted limits over which the probability of incurring physical damage increases. The oft quoted 1979 report of the Royal College of Psychiatrists cites 8 units daily as the upper acceptable limit for men and 6 units for women where 1 unit is equivalent to one half pint of ordinary strength beer or one sixth gill of spirits. His upper estimate of heavy drinkers is based on the Whitehead study referred to above, but weighted to include women.

With regard to the distribution question the work of the French alcoholist Ledermann (1956) has had a profound effect on the field of alcohol studies. He suggested that the distribution of alcohol consumption in any random sample of population is depicted by an approximation to a log normal curve. The aetiological significance of this is that in any sample the proportion of at risk drinkers can be predicted from per capita consumption and that a rise in consumption is a result of proportionately heavier drinking throughout the entire population. Ledermann has been arguably the most influential worker in determining the current and widely held view of alcohol dependence as dimensional rather than categorical in nature.

The evidence that increased per capita consumption produces proportionately more heavier drinkers and consequently a higher prevalence of alcohol related damage, is more empirically than theoretically based. A positive correlation between national consumption levels and indices of harm, for example alcohol deaths, alcohol related accidents, incidents of drunken drinking and hospital admissions for alcohol dependence has consistently been demonstrated (Osterberg 1979, Colon et al 1982). National and regional statistics do not however give us any information on the intermediate step; namely that increases in demand produce generally heavier drinking throughout the *entire* drinking population and not only those in the potentially at risk category. The most appropriate validation procedure for the Ledermann proposition is the use of longitudinal surveys with at least two data points. The Camberwell study is perhaps the most comprehensive example of such a survey (Edwards et al 1972, Cartwright et al 1975, 1977). In this study two matched samples from the same London suburb were interviewed in 1965 and 1974 during which time per capita consumption had increased by some 5.6%. A general increase was demonstrated across all categories of consumption with proportionately more people experiencing alcohol related problems; thus supporting the validity of per capita consumption as an indicator of problem prevalence. The proportion of abstainers remained constant. Although a longitudinal study analysing drinking pattern practices in a district of the Shetland Islands (Caetano et al 1983) supported the Camberwell conclusion on the rate of abstinence this has been challenged in a review of a number of North American studies which demonstrated an inverse relationship between proportion of abstainers and per capita consumption (McIntosh & Chir 1981). Ledermann's work has been criticised with regard to mathematical inconsistencies (Duffy 1977, Skog 1980). Furthermore, dispersion around the mean which does vary from region to region (Plant et al 1979, Singh 1979) can influence the extent to which per capita consumption predicts heavy drinking. Nevertheless, survey results are invariably similar in that they are always skewed and unimodal. Taylor (1981) observes that detailed demonstrations of the failing of Ledermann's work should not be allowed to draw attention away from the fact that limitation of global consumption is at present the best proven alcohol harm control policy.

The third element namely the analysis and assessment of alcohol related problems remains a difficult alcohol related problem in itself. As well as the direct effects of acute intoxication, long term alcohol misuse is associated with a range of psychological and physical damage. Many of the problems must be defined within the socio-cultural and interpersonal context in which they occur. Drinking on the way to work in the morning for example may be perceived as down and out in London but not in Paris. In an interesting comparative survey of drinking practices Yates (1983) points out that alcohol problems in France could be described as a result of over use as opposed to misuse in the U.K. Delint (1977) suggests that the route from consumption pattern to problem may be short and direct, for example acute pancreatitis, or long and insidious, for example a gradually deteriorating marriage finally ending in divorce. A related issue is the directness of alcohol's influence. In some problems regarded as alcohol related, few factors other than alcohol may be implicated, while alternatively alcohol may be only one of many factors involved.

McKechnie (1982) suggests that alcohol related problems can be sub-divided into those which arise as a direct result of alcohol consumption, those which occur as a result of the context or situation in which the drinking takes place and those which are a result of the interaction between the effect of drinking and the context in which the effect is experienced.

In summary there is no doubt that alcohol consumption and the individual and social problems associated with its misuse have increased significantly over the past two to three decades. Most people now agree that the more alcohol a group consumes the more damage will result and this has prompted Kendell (1979) to comment that the answer to alcohol problems lies less with the health workers and more with politicians.

## Drug consumption

While alcohol demand can be monitored fairly precisely there is no single reliable indicator of the nature and extent of illegal drug misuse. Parameters of drug misuse for example the U.K. Home Office Addicts Index, weight and number of seizures, the incidence of drug offences, and local reports and surveys do however provide useful information on trends in the prevalence of addiction.

The Addicts Index is the number of notifications of people who doctors reasonably suspect are addicted to certain controlled drugs namely cocaine, dextromoramide, diamorphine, dipipanone, hydrocodone, hydromorphone, levorphanol, methadone, morphine, opium, oxycodone, pethidine, phenazocine and pipitramide. Even if a doctor refused to accept a person onto his list he is legally obliged to notify the Chief Medical Officer of the Home Office within seven days of attending the patient. If the patient continues to attend the doctor there is a responsibility to notify annually. Perhaps the most important figure is the number of new notifications per annum (see Appendix 6.2). The Addicts Index is recognised to be a significant underestimate for a number of reasons. Many drug misusers do not seek treatment and if they do, not all doctors are necessarily aware of the notification regulations. The Report of the Advisory Council (1982) suggests that the number of addicts in the U.K. is at least five times greater than the figures, derived from the Index, would suggest. It is possible that the number of unregistered addicts has increased even more disproportionately to the number of notifications since the publication of this report as a result of the significant escalation of blackmarket heroin in the U.K. A treatment system which cannot cope with the increasing demand means that notification will account for a diminishing proportion of the addict population. Nevertheless it is clear that the number of addicts known to be receiving treatment in the U.K. is increasing and the rate of increase has accelerated during the early 1980s. Approximately one third of the known addicts are now female as opposed to one quarter in the first half of the 1970s. There has also been an increase in the 1970s in the number of notifications from G.P.s which may in part be accounted for by the lengthening clinic waiting lists particularly in the London area.

A further trend during the 1970s has been toward polydrug misuse. The interim report of the Advisory Council (1977) noted a significant move in this direction. The 1982 report confirms this and comments 'for some years it has been accepted by experts in the field that most drug misusers are not solely dependent on one drug. The same person may be using a number of drugs and may be dependent on more than one of them'. The report cites data from a London crisis intervention clinic which demonstrated that of 308 admissions 95% had taken barbiturates, 85% had taken opioids and all had taken stimulants. Almost half the sample were using three types of drugs. Although the number of barbiturate prescriptions decreased as a result of the Campaign on the Use and

Restriction of Barbiturates (CURB), these drugs clearly continue to be widely available on the blackmarket. This trend towards multiple drug misuse has also been noted in the U.S.A. In an examination of drug use trends in the U.S.A. Senay (1983) comments that 'drug users now tend to use multiple drugs in a rotating fashion. This contrasts with the drug taking behaviour of the past in which users tended to use one drug preferentially'.

H.M. Customs and Excise figures indicate that the weight and number of seizures have also increased significantly over the past decade (See appendix 6.3) although there has been a differential rate of increase for different classes of drugs. The increase in quantity of heroin and cocaine in the early 1980s is illustrated in Fig. 6.1. The relationship between the weight and number of seizures and the volume of illicit drugs on the street is unclear. Ashton (1981) estimates that seizures account for approximately 10% of illicit heroin entering the U.K. although approximately only one in every hundred people entering the U.K. is searched at customs.

While the proportion of seizure intercepts is more guess work than anything else, the estimates indicate that Customs and Excise intercept a relatively small percentage of the U.K. drug traffic. Nevertheless in recent years the number of seizures in non-public premises, and on the street, as well as at ports and airports have been increasing.

The most disturbing trend is the significant increase in the availability of heroin throughout the British Isles. It is interesting to note that the first major seizure of heroin (over 1 kilogram) in the U.K. occurred as late as 1971 while a decade later in 1981 there were 30 seizures of over 1 kilogram. It seems that traditional importers of cannabis and organised crime began turning to heroin import in the early 1980s. Experts agree that blackmarket heroin as opposed to over zealous prescribing or pharmacy thefts is the major source of opioid supply in the U.K. In 1982 almost 200 kilograms of heroin and morphine were seized in Britain the majority of which was destined for home consumption rather than re-export. Of opioids commonly prescribed by clinics and G.P.s, only .09 kilograms were seized indicating that this is clearly a minor problem in comparison to blackmarket heroin addiction. A further indication of heroin availability is its street price. Despite inflation and massive price fluctuation the price of heroin in 1984 at approximately £40 to £80 per gram at 20% to 80% purity mirrors almost exactly its price a decade before. Thus in real terms the price

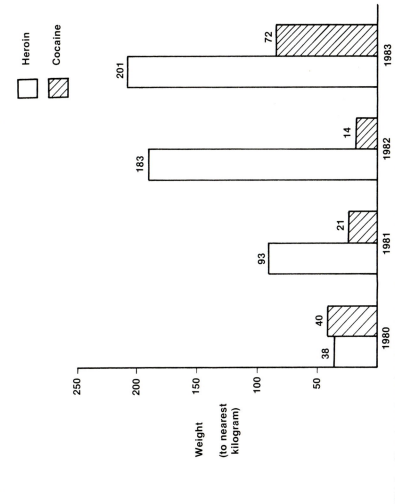

**Fig. 6.1** Weight of heroin and cocaine seizures in the UK between 1980 and 1983

of heroin in the U.K. has fallen considerably over the past few years reflecting increased availability on world markets. Accounts from statutory and voluntary treatment agencies in major urban centres in the British Isles have also indicated a steep rise in the availability of blackmarket heroin during the early 1980s. One such account was a survey carried out by local workers and volunteers in north central Dublin (Bradshaw et al 1983). The authors estimated that the 1982/1983 prevalence of heroin among young people in the area aged 15 to 19 years was in the order of 12% with approximately a one to one male:female ratio. The report noted that this 'epidemic' was all the more alarming as there had been very little heroin in Dublin before the Spring of 1981. Since this time increases have been noted in various U.K. cities where, unlike Dublin, young people generally prefer to inhale rather than inject.

While the 1980s have seen a slowing down in the rate of increase of alcohol use the Advisory Council 1982 report concludes that all the indicators point to a substantial increase in the number of people misusing other psychoactive substances. This increase applies not only to opioids but also amphetamines, barbiturates and minor tranquillizers.

## Preventive action: control strategies

### International drug control

The attraction of a relatively low detection rate and large profits has drawn organised crime to international drug trafficking. The dramatic increase in heroin availability in the U.K. as outlined in the previous section bears witness to this. In the 1960s the heroin trade consisted of individuals smuggling comparatively small amounts to Europe from the so called Golden Triangle of Burma, Laos and Thailand. In the 1970s Iran was the major European source until the revolution of 1979 pushed out the middle class producers. The Russian invasion of Afghanistan and the Iranian revolution brought together an unlimited pool of refugee labour, the production expertise and favourable climatic conditions in Afghanistan and Northern Pakistan for growing the lucrative poppy with onsite conversion from opium to heroin. The increase of both heroin and South American cocaine on the world market highlights the increasing need for international cooperation.

The aim of international drug control is primarily to ensure that effective control of dangerous drugs in one country is not impeded by lack of control in another. The international control system requires governments to exert control over the production, trade and distribution of dangerous drugs, to combat illegal trafficking across the borders, to maintain the necessary administrative machinery and to report their actions to special international bodies. The most important international agreement to date is the Single Convention on Narcotic Drugs 1961 which was signed in New York and amalgamated several international treaties. It covered opioids, cocaine and cannabis. The 1971 Convention on Psychotropic Substances signed in Vienna extended control to barbiturates, amphetamines and hallucinogens. The International Narcotics Control Board was set up to supervise international agreements and the drugs branch of the U.K. Home Office maintains continual liaison with the I.N.C.B. regarding Britain's needs for narcotic raw materials.

The Commission on Narcotic Drugs of the U.N. Economic and Social Council while having no legislative powers is an advisory body which makes policy recommendations to the Council and represented governments. The Commission itself is advised by the W.H.O. Expert Committee on Drug Dependence. In 1971 the U.N. Fund for Drug Abuse Control was established with the aim of promoting and funding projects in such diverse areas as crop replacement, law enforcement, education and the treatment and rehabilitation of addicts. The fund is made up of voluntary contributions. At European level the Council of Europe accepted recommendations in 1975 for increased exchange of information and broad based studies to be implemented under the auspices of the Council. One such study for example concerned the problem of young drug misusers and travellers trafficking in Europe.

As an indication that international cooperation is vital in bringing the problem under control the British Government in 1984 doubled its contribution to the U.N. Fund for Drug Abuse Control, ratified the 1971 Convention on Pschotropic Substances by including barbiturates in the Misuse of Drugs Act, introduced legislation to confiscate the proceeds of drugs dealing from international traffickers and contributed directly to the policing of the heroin district in North Pakistan.

## Drug control in Britain

The first major Government report in the U.K. was that of the Rolleston Committee (1926) whose remit was to advise on the treatment of morphine and heroin users and on the administrative arrangements for control of supply. An interesting historical note is that the committee adopted the general view that addiction should be regarded as an 'illness' and not as 'a mere form of vicious indulgence'. One of the recommendations of the committee was that in certain circumstances addicts could be prescribed a 'non progressive quantity, usually small, of the drug of addiction'. This gave rise to the so called 'British System' which was essentially the management of addiction by prescription of a maintenance dose over a long period. The Committee also preserved the right of all doctors to prescribe heroin and morphine to addicts. These policies remained until the publication of the second Brain Committee Report (1965) which also considered new opioids, cannabis, sedatives and barbiturates. The main recommendations which were embodied in the Dangerous Drugs Act (1967) were that heroin and cocaine should be prescribed to addicts by doctors licensed from the Home Secretary and that such a licence could only be issued to those working in treatment units or hospitals. The right to prescribe other dangerous drugs was retained. The Brain Committee sought to achieve a balance of control: 'if there is insufficient control it may lead to a spread of addictions... if on the other hand the restrictions are so severe as to seriously discourage the addict from obtaining any supplies from legitimate sources it may lead to the development of an organised illicit traffic'. The Dangerous Drugs Act also introduced *notification* whereby doctors were required to report details of addicts to the Home Office Medical Officer.

All drugs legislation, particularly the Dangerous Drugs Act of 1920 and 1967 were consolidated into the Misuse of Drugs Act (1971). This came fully into force on 1 July 1973, and forms the basis of present control policy over those drugs listed in Schedule II of the Act. It specifies three categories of controlled drugs according to their accepted degree of harmfulness in the light of current knowledge, and changes can be made in the classification on new scientific evidence or to meet new forms of misuse. Class A includes the major opioid drugs (individually named), cocaine and the coca leaf, L.S.D., injectable amphetamines, cannabinol and its derivatives. Class B includes amphetamines, codeine and cannabis leaf and resin. Class C includes methaqualone and some amphetamine like drugs. Other sections of the Act deal with the limitations on the right to prescribe, regulations for import and export of drugs and the setting up of offences for cultivation, manufacture, supply and possession. The main feature of the penal side of the Misuse of Drugs Act is the sharp distinction between offences of supply which carry severe penalties and offences of possession which carry relatively less severe, but nevertheless substantial penalties (Table 6.2).

**Table 6.2** Penalties for unlawful possession and supply of controlled drugs in the United Kingdom

| Class of drugs | A | B | C |
|---|---|---|---|
| Supply (1) | 6 months £1000 fine or both | 6 months £1000 fine or both | 3 months £500 fine or both |
| Supply (2) | 14 years unlimited fine or both | 14 years unlimited fine or both | 5 years unlimited fine or both |
| Possession (1) | 6 months £1000 fine or both | 3 months £500 fine or both | 3 months £200 fine or both |
| Possession (2) | 7 years unlimited fine or both | 5 years unlimited fine or both | 2 years unlimited fine or both |

(1) Maximum penalty: Summary prosecution (Magistrate Court).
(2) Maximum penalty: Indictment (Crown Court).

The Act also endows the Home Secretary with powers to introduce regulations, in conjunction with the Advisory Council on Misuse of Drugs, without Parliamentary consent to allow for rapidly changing circumstances. In 1984 the U.K. Government used this provision to control barbiturates under Class B in Section II of the Act. Barbiturates were previously included in the Medicines Act (1968) which exerts control over minor tranquillizers and other sedatives and hypnotics. A 1984 amendment to the Act also prohibited doctors from prescribing dipipanone except under licence.

The efficacy of the provisions in the 1971 Act with regard to prevention of consumption and its related problems is as yet uncertain. Edwards and Busch (1981) suggest that the preventive significance of prescribing controls has never been the subject of a comprehensive analysis. They also point out that the enforcement system for implementing controls has never been investigated and a full understanding of the prevention of drug misuse with a large slice of the preventive activity unassessed is clearly a continuing problem. They question the assumption that Police and Customs action is 'unresearchable and that drug squads are less investigatable than drug clinics'. The political view however as stated by the U.K. Secretary of State in 1980 is that Customs surveillance and Police campaigns are the most vital lines of defence in the prevention of drug misuse in this country. Traditionally in the U.K. there has been a balance between treatment and control although there seems to be an increasing emphasis in recent years on the latter. In their review of heroin addiction in Britain, Stimson and Oppenheimer (1982) suggest that this may be a result of the growing emphasis in the Britain of the 1980s on law and order and the corollary of this is that strong policing is seen as the central element in the response to drug addiction.

## Alcohol availability

Legal measures aimed at controlling excessive alcohol use have been developed to attenuate rather than eliminate consumption. As possession and manufacture of alcohol is not an offence, legislation takes the form of tax measures or limitations on the sale and distribution. The results on the effectiveness of restricting availability by manipulating the number of retail outlets, stringency of licensing control and minimum legal drinking age have been somewhat equivocal and should be considered within the context of styles, customs and social norms governing drinking behaviour. It is also likely that the marketing policy of the drinks industry will influence the effectiveness of legal controls. Roberts (1983) has noted that the U.K. alcohol industry has begun to market its products as adjuncts to other recreational activities and so there has been an increase in consumption outside the public house. The alcohol industry has made drinking first acceptable, and then expected on a wide range of social occasions. As a result of this the impact of restricting the number of licensed premises for example maybe less marked than in the past. National differences in drinking styles and customs as well as the prevailing marketing policy of the drinks industry may account in part for the conflicting findings regarding the efficacy of alcohol control policy.

In the U.S.A. Smart (1977) found that when the variance attributable to differential income was controlled the density of licensed retail outlets, licensing hours and minimum legal age did not effect alcohol problem rates. Popham et al (1975) suggest that increasing retail outlets would have no more effect on alcohol consumption than increasing the number of television shops would have on the prevalence of television sets. However there is evidence that the number of retail outlets can effect consumption and the prevalence of alcohol related harm. Spellman and Jorgenson (1983) demonstrated that in the U.S.A. the monopoly control system, which operates in some states and effectively cuts the number of retail outlets, does appear to reduce consumption. Whitehead (1975) noted a significant increase in consumption in Finland after a relaxation of restrictions on sale and a consequent dramatic increase in retail outlets. This more liberal Finnish system seemed to lead to an increase in the number of drinking occasions and is an impressive demonstration of the effects on consumption of increased availability. Caetano et al (1983) in their analysis of drinking patterns in the Shetland Islands over a period of rapid social change concluded that the main effect of affluence and an increase in number of outlets was an increased level of intake. Their findings were similar to those in Finland in that drinking episodes became more frequent without a concomitant substantial change in the quantity drunk per occasion. Between 1960 and 1980 the number of on-licensed premises in the U.K. increased by one third and this was accompanied by an even greater increase in off-licensed outlets, particularly supermarkets. This latter development has been linked to market investigation reports which demonstrate increases in drink purchasing among women. McGuinness (1980) in an important and widely quoted economic analysis of alcohol demand in the U.K. was impressed by the importance of the number of outlets. He calculated that a 1% decrease in the number of licensed premises in the U.K. might reduce consumption by something in the order of 2%. It would seem that on balance, the evidence available to date demonstrates a significant relationship between the number of licensed retail outlets and the amount of alcohol consumed.

The effect of licensing hours as a control of availability is perhaps more contentious. Smith (1982) comments that over the years what is probably 'a disproportionate amount of energy has been devoted to arguments about licensing hours'. He goes on to say that the evidence on the specific effect of licensing hours in sparse. The report of the Departmental Committee on Scottish Licensing Laws (Clayson 1973) recommended that in Scotland they should be relaxed in line with the rest of Britain. It was argued that the pressure to drink in Scottish public houses was higher because less time was available and as a consequence there was a greater misuse of alcohol. Although the argument was conducted more at an anecdotal than empirical level it does seem that the subsequent increase in Scottish licensing hours has not produced any increase in consumption or related problems and appears to have produced a style of drinking which is less concentrated and pressured (Wilson 1980). The equivalent English report was the report of the Departmental Committee on Liquor Licensing (Errol 1972), which recommended extending licensing hours still further. The proposal met with considerable opposition not least from the licensed trade itself. The DHSS Advisory Committee on Alcoholism (1979) concluded that the outcome of such changes would be uncertain and advised against them. It would seem that as so little is known about the effect of increasing licensing hours it is probably more prudent to err on the side of caution in the face of an ever increasing alcohol problem.

In view of the controversy generated by the licensing hours issue it is surprising that the nature of the drinking environment has received relatively little attention. Taylor (1981) does point out however that the idea of allowing accompanied children to pubs and 'cafe pubs' as advocated by Clayson (1977) has been criticised by both the temperance movement in politics and the drinks industry who regard any shift in the traditional arrangements as threatening. The Errol Report also recommended a reduction in the minimum legal drinking age from 18 to 17 years in the U.K. It was argued that such a change would not lead to further alcohol related problems as there are many under age drinkers although strictly speaking it is illegal. However, available evidence suggests that a reduction in the minimum age leads to a substantial increase in the level of consumption in the new legal age group and also increases the number of road traffic accidents among young people (Smart & Goodstadt 1977). Trethowan (1977) comments that where the legal age falls there seems to be a parallel fall in the age at which young people actually start to drink.

What evidence there is suggests that a reduction in the number of retail outlets and an increase in the minimum age may reduce alcohol consumption although the magnitude of such a reduction is unclear. It seems unlikely however that there will be more restrictive licensing laws as it would entail most western governments risking support in what are largely alcohol drinking electorates.

## Fiscal measures

There is little doubt that fiscal control is a politically sensitive issue in view of the fact that production, distribution and tax return from alcohol are of considerable economic importance. It is the widely held view nevertheless that price manipulation is the most effective alcohol control policy (Kendell 1979, Smith 1982, Rix & Rix 1983); increases in the real price of alcohol are said to reduce per capita consumption and as a consequence alcohol related harm. Popham et al (1975) commented that almost universally 'relative price was found to be very closely associated with indices of consumption and alcoholism'. National statistics can be misleading however in that they may not validate the assertion that per capita reduction due to relative price increases indicates generally reduced drinking throughout the entire population. To derive more appropriate data, surveys of a drinking population before and after a real price increase are required. As there have been very few recent examples of Governments imposing substantial taxes on alcohol there is arguably only one such study (Kendell et al 1983). This was carried out in the Lothian area of Scotland between 1979 and 1982 during which time the rate of increase of the Retail Price Index (RPI). Before reviewing the Lothian study it would be appropriate to comment on more general economic aspects of alcohol use, as it is often argued that alcoholic beverages behave on the markets like any other commodity (Delint 1977).

*Elasticity of demand* for a product can be computed for any number of variables particularly price, income, substitution, advertising and perhaps in the case of alcohol, dependence. A further complicating factor is that alcohol has a number of different usages. For example ritual, social and medical and each of these may have a very different demand elasticity. *Price elasticity* of demand is calculated by dividing percentage change in demand by percentage change in price. Estimates of price elasticity (Duffy 1980, Wilson 1980) suggest that the beverage with the greatest share of the market, for example beer in the U.K. and wine in France is the least elastic, indicating that the level of demand is relatively less sensitive to price increases. A recent estimate of price elasticity for beer in the U.K. of $-0.2$ suggests that a 1% increase in real price would reduce beer demand by only 0.2%. On the other hand the calculation for spirits was $-1.16$ indicating that a 1% increase in the price of spirits would reduce demand by 1.16% Ornstein (1980) however counsels caution in drawing conclusions for policy purposes from estimates of price elasticity as it varies considerably across studies. Levy and Sheflin (1983) also comment that as existing estimates of price effects are based on very small changes in price it is quite possible that their reliability will decrease with larger price changes. A sudden and substantial increase in price may lead to illegal manufacture and acquisition of alcohol thus upsetting the econometric estimates. Economists do tend to view consumers as inherently logical in that they maximise the *total net utility* or benefit obtained from consumption of a product. The concept of *diminishing marginal utility* suggests that successive purchases of a product add to the stock of utility in diminishing quantities and the *opportunity cost* i.e. cost of the next best alternative forgone, increases with total consumption. It seems not unreasonable that an individual's perception of what constitutes the next best purchase or the benefit obtained from successive purchases of alcohol may vary according to the degree of dependence. Some people, in the face of a significant price increase of alcohol, may reduce expenditure on other items deemed less important.

The Lothian study does however support the prevailing view that a small increase in price substantially alters drinking patterns throughout the whole drinking population. A sample of 676 regular drinkers were interviewed in 1978/1979 with 69% of this group being re-interviewed in 1981/1982. During this period the increase in the retail price of alcohol was some nine points greater than the RPI. The authors comment that this was the first U.K. example of alcohol outstripping other prices in the past three decades. Some commentators would disagree with this however, for instance (Newton 1984) who argues that between the years 1961 and 1965 the price of alcohol increased relative to the RPI yet national consumption also maintained a steady increase. In the period between the two Lothian surveys personal disposable income among wage earners increased in line with inflation although this is complicated by the fact that unemployment in the region virtually doubled over the same time. The results of the study indicate that over the three year period alcohol consumption fell by some 18% with the heaviest drinkers reducing their absolute intake most of all. The majority of respondents who curtailed consumption reported that the increase in price was a major contributing factor. A simple 'harm index' was computed and this too decreased in line with consumption. The authors suggest that although interpretation of the results is complicated by a regression to the mean effect, heavy drinkers did seem to cut down proportionately by at least as much as light to moderate drinkers. They conclude that the findings indicate 'an increase in the Excise Duty on alcoholic beverages can be an effective means of reducing the ill effects of excessive alcohol consumption'. The fall in demand in Lothian was in fact consistent with a national decrease in consumption over the same period. Although the study demonstrates a striking and significant relationship between price and consumption the results should be interpreted with some caution. The drop out rate was high particularly among young, unmarried, male respondents; a particularly heavy drinking group. As with survey methods in general there is the problem of selective under reporting. Care must also be taken when extrapolating from region to region as alcohol is used in a variety of ways with different beverages being consumed in different contexts all of which affect demand elasticity.

The view of the U.K. Government that an increase in the real price of alcohol 'will not influence many problem drinkers' does nevertheless seem to be unwarranted in the light of what little available evidence there is. The Government view may be in part a result of economic expedience and need to retain electoral support. Despite the revenue consequences of alcohol misuse the value of alcohol in terms of export earnings, tax income and jobs is considerable and a national survey (Sunday Times 1980) showed that some three-quarters of the British electorate were opposed to large increases in the price of alcohol. On the other hand the idea that a broad brush fiscal policy is the only real effective control strategy is an over simplification. The indications are that if the price of alcohol rises in line with the RPI and differential taxation is linked to market share of the beverage, per capita consumption may be stabilized. The effect of more substantial and sudden real price increases is as yet far from clear. While fiscal control is an important part of the prevention armoury, price remains a crude weapon which affects rich and poor in different ways. As Maynard and Kennan (1981) suggest it is to be hoped that the alcohologist and the economist can continue to cooperate in years to come in order to clarify the nature of the relationship between price and consumption.

## Preventive action: demand strategies

### Education

As well as control strategies like price regulation and drug legislation, action which seeks to alter demand by changing public attitudes and promoting greater understanding of the problems associated with substance misuse is an integral part of an eclectic approach to prevention. The role of educating young people, teachers and non specialist health personnel on drug and alcohol misuse has been the subject of much debate and there have been several reviews summarising the outcome of drug and alcohol education programs (Kinder et al 1980, Schaps et al 1981, Staulcup et al 1979). What has emerged is the apparent failure of such programs to substantially influence patterns of use. The evaluators suggest that despite short term penetration the behaviour of the consumer remains relatively intransigent. Budd et al (1983) point out that attitudinal change does not necessarily result in behavioural change and the traditionally assumed linear progression from information gain through attitudinal change to modification of behaviour is over simplified and has little empirical basis. Dorn (1981) comments that 'attitudes to abstractions such as "drugs"... can have precious little relevance to behaviour when faced with normal recreational drug offer situations'. Several other authors have questioned the relationship between attitudes and alcohol or drug use (Schlegel & Norris 1980, Yates & Hebblethwaite 1983) and at least one has suggested that increased knowledge may actually lead to increased use (Stuart 1974). Weisheit (1983) suggests that health education when directed at problems of social concern is often seen as a symbolic act or a visible public response which makes political and philosophical sense but fails to take into account the need for scientific outcome evaluation.

Despite these, often justified, criticisms many commentators feel that drug and alcohol education when considered in a wider context has a role in the prevention effort. Education can for example influence the implementation and the effect of other social and legal controls. Smith (1982) suggests that unpopular political action may only be possible if the electorate is fully informed and aware of the issues involved. Plant (1980) comments that public attitudes on alcohol and drugs resulting at least partly from the education process can influence social policy in the direction of humanity and restraint. Alcohol and drug education particularly in schools, has only recently become less substance specific and more 'person orientated'. It has come to be regarded as part of a more broadly based health and social education program, although it may be as yet too early to assess the longer term impact of this type of approach. The goal of improved general health, rather than specific attitudinal and behaviour change, is now seen as the primary focus. It is increasingly clear that alcohol and drug education can do little to reduce experimentation but it may reduce the proportion of experimenters who would ultimately suffer physical or psychological damage. Should such damage begin to manifest itself some health educators would argue that dissemination of knowledge may equip the target group with an increased awareness of a wider range of options for coping with problems when they arise (Tomes 1977).

Behavioural change is sometimes regarded as an isolated event rather than a process and this could be a contributory factor to the rather pessimistic view of the efficacy of drug and alcohol education. An educative approach may be optimally effective at a particular point in the process of individual change. Prochaska & Di Clemente's (1982) integrative model of change suggests five stages in the process namely precontemplation contemplation, action, maintenance and relapse. The model was developed by investigating change in smoking behaviour (Prochaska & Di Clemente 1983) and is outlined in more detail in Chapter 5.

They suggest that in the precontemplation stage the individual pays little attention to information even if it is available. People who do not see their behaviour as problematic will not respond to even the most intensive educational input. The authors demonstrate however that those in the contemplation stage are most likely to respond to feedback and education and have an increased openness to appropriate information. This leads to a gradual re-evaluation process which can ultimately carry the individual from contemplation to action. During the action and maintenance stages, behavioural strategies are seen as most important while relapse itself can be viewed as an integral part of the whole change process. This model is relevant to the present discussion on education in that it provides a framework for evaluation of outcome. It emphasises the importance of individual differences and the developmental nature of behavioural change, although further comparative studies are needed to clarify differences in this process according to the substance of misuse. It is clear however, that individuals at a particular stage may benefit from consciousness raising and information input but they may not translate it into action for some considerable time. Immediate behavioural assessment may mask this potential for longer term change.

Dorn (1981) in a review of the literature on drug education also emphasises that immediate behavioural measures can be positively misleading about longer term effects. He has outlined practical guidelines for the setting up and monitoring of drug educational programs which are equally relevant to alcohol education. He suggests that teaching should be carried out by professional educators rather than imported experts and inservice training for the educators should concentrate on problem assessment rather than stigmatising alcohol and drug experimentation. The positive goal of such education should be to reduce the expectation of inevitable addiction thus increasing people's belief that they need not necessarily lose control of the experimentation. Dorn also suggests that, as well as factual information, situational education is important and this may lead to small group discussions on the kinds of situation for example in which drugs may be offered. With regard to evaluation Dorn emphasises the point made by several authors that outcome measures should reflect a program's stated goals and that small well defined controlled experiments can often be more useful than large badly designed studies. Educators should also be prepared to challenge the prevailing stereotypes and climate of thought as presented by the media so that their message will be interpreted in adaptive ways at the individual level. A Guardian Editorial (1984) on drug prevention in the U.K. highlights the prevailing media view by suggesting that public education, particularly directed at school children should be in the most graphic form possible to 'bring home to them the horrors that lie in store if they succumb to a fad which most do not perceive as inevitably destructive'. The point has been made by several authors (Madden 1979, Plant 1980) that concentration on the risks produces few tangible results. The educator, whether he be talking about alcohol or drugs does not necessarily gain credibility by the use of shock tactics, distortions and half truths.

There does seem to be a continuing need for the provision of well evaluated drug and alcohol education input for the consumer, the primary worker and the general population. What is needed however is more information from well controlled longitudinal studies to assess its immediate and longer term impact. Alcohol and drug education should be a sustained process rather than a once and for all effort.

## Media campaigns

The use of the media is a particular aspect of alcohol education which has become increasingly important in Western countries over the past decade. In the financial year 1980/1981 for example over

60% of the British Health Education Council budget was earmarked for mass media campaigns in the light of the recommendation of the Royal Commission on the NHS Report (1979). The efficacy and cost effectiveness of a number of U.K. alcohol campaigns have been comprehensively assessed in recent years (Plant et al 1979, Cust 1980, Budd et al 1983).

In 1976 the Scottish Health Education Unit carried out a national T.V. and press campaign with the aim of encouraging people to seek treatment. The evaluation showed that while penetration was high the level of public knowledge on alcohol did not significantly increase and the pattern of drinking remained unchanged. Immediately after the campaign however more people did come forward for treatment.

The most extensive media campaign aimed at educating the public about *sensible alcohol drinking* was the Tyne Tees programme which developed through three distinct stages between 1974 and 1981. The target area had a population of some three and a half million and the campaign was originally conceived as a pilot scheme which would form the basis of a national media prevention strategy. The campaign emphasised media advertising accompanied by an individual counselling programme with the stated aim of curtailing the increasing level of alcohol consumption and alcohol related problems in the North East of England. The first phase concentrated on secondary prevention by encouraging people to seek help and alerting them to early indicators of harm. The second phase made more use of local newspapers as well as radio and television. During this period primary prevention was stressed through education of the public, particularly young people, on the sensible use of alcohol and promotion of social controls against alcohol misuse. The third phase included specific guidelines on what constitutes mild, moderate and heavy drinking with extensive information on beverage equivalents. This last phase adopted a factual rather than a moralising approach. The DHSS Report 'Drinking Sensibly' (1981) has expressed some ambivalence on the idea of *safe limits* in that they 'may confer official approval on drinking levels which were in fact quite high'. Thorley (1982) counters this by citing data from the final stage of the campaign which indicated that the limit setting was more successful than any previous media alcohol education approach.

In his analysis of the earlier stages of the Tyne Tees campaign Cust (1980) established that there was an increase in enquiries and interest from social service departments, G.P.s and companies exploring the possibility of introducing a company policy on alcohol. In the evaluation of public response to the latter phases of the campaign Budd et al (1983) administered self completion questionnaires and interviewed some 250 people from the Newcastle area with a Leicestershire sample as a control. The Newcastle group demonstrated significantly greater awareness of the nature of alcohol and its potential harm. The level of penetration was high in that 80% of the sample were exposed to some aspect of the campaign although again very few of the respondents actually attempted to alter their own drinking behaviour. The data did not demonstrate any causal link between degree of information acquired and increased probability of behavioural change. The authors do suggest however that after exposure to a campaign of this nature people will be better informed should problems arise in their own drinking or that of family and friends.

The limit setting approach pioneered in North East England gave rise to the national 'That's the Limit' campaign (1984). Essentially this was a series of short peak time T.V. programmes aimed at providing the public with a simple safe limit message and concise information on beverage equivalents. This was repeated in various ways and viewer participation was encouraged. Initial impressions are that this approach has had a favourable public response.

This seems to indicate that for national campaigns the message should be simple and amenable to repeated presentation in different forms. More abstract ideas such as the nature of dependence or the relationship between consumption and harm do not lend themselves to sharp media presentation. Smith (1982) suggests that transmission of a complex message may over-estimate both the interest of the public and the power of the educator. He adds that health educators should not emphasise the medical consequences of alcohol abuse at the expense of social consequences. A necessary prerequisite for local media campaigns is an understanding of the particular regional context of alcohol use so that information and the nature of its presentation may be tailored accordingly. The individual who does not understand the message or interprets it as having little relevance for his own life and drinking routine will be less likely to respond. The results of the Tyne Tees and Scottish surveys also suggest that as more people tend to come forward for treatment after a campaign sufficient local support facilities should be available to follow up and maintain any change which may be initiated.

## Advertising

The budget of the alcohol educator is small in comparison to that of the alcohol advertiser and the health message can be eclipsed by alcohol advertising. As in much of the prevention debate the effectiveness or otherwise of alcohol advertising is the subject of much rhetoric but little empirical evidence.

The advertising industry would argue that in a mature market such as alcohol sales the role of advertising is primarily to generate brand loyalty or to encourage some switching between market segments, for example from beer to spirits, rather than to significantly increase total consumption. A number of studies carried out in Canada and the U.S.A. would tend to support this view. None of them demonstrated any change in consumption as a result of advertising restrictions (Ogborne & Smart 1980, Smart & Cutler 1980, Keller & Gurioli 1976). The U.S.S.R. has experienced a growth in alcohol consumption in the absence of advertising (Treml 1975).

Nevertheless advertising effects on elasticity of demand for alcohol do seem to vary from country to country and even from drink to drink. McGuinness (1980) concluded that spirit advertising particularly, did increase total U.K. consumption. He calculated that a 1% reduction of the advertising budget would be associated with a reduction in demand for spirits of 0.13%. On the basis of these figures a Lancet editorial (1980) argued that a complete ban on advertising would reduce spirit consumption by 13%. It is unwise however to extrapolate elasticity figures in this way. The probability is that the relationship between advertising and consumption is non linear at greater levels of expenditure reduction (Rix & Rix 1983). There is also the assumption that advertising expenditure is synonymous with penetration of the market and cost effectiveness of the campaign.

At best, advertising would seem to have a relatively minor effect on total consumption although it has been suggested that should restrictions continue over a generation some more substantial longer term impact may result (Maynard & Keenan 1981). It is also not inconsistent for advertising to reinforce social controls against alcohol misuse although this rarely occurs in practice.

## Conclusions

Prevention research in the area of drug and alcohol misuse has all too often focused on one particular approach without recourse to its place within the framework of a comprehensive policy. Much of the research has enabled workers to criticise what has been done in the name of prevention without providing novel or alternative ideas.

The efficacy of some of the more common preventive strategies reviewed above remains largely unevaluated and there are a considerable number of outstanding questions which have received scant attention. For example the evidence on the preventive significance of either voluntary or statutory prescribing controls on dangerous drugs has been in the main anecdotal. There has been little research on the specific effects of Customs surveillance or Drug Squad activity on the volume of drugs reaching the streets at times of heightened world-wide availability. The deterrent effect of custodial sentences or fines for users of different classes of drug has only begun to receive attention. While there is considerable evidence on the causal connection between alcohol consumption, income and price little is known about the contribution of substantial real price increases of alcohol to its illicit manufacture and distribution. The effect of a large reduction in advertising expenditure on alcohol demand is also far from clear. Much has been said but little is actually known about the contribution of wider social variables like unemployment, urban decay and social deprivation to the extent of substance misuse. What is clear is that a comprehensive prevention policy must operate in part at a community and individual level. Yates and Hebblethwaite (1983) argue with regard to alcohol that the 'distinctive character of any preventative work is the central place it must occupy in the ordinary life of the community'. They suggest that prevention is concerned with social problems in their natural state and more attention should be paid to specific community restrictions and self administered controls. Detailed knowledge of local drinking and drug taking practices would provide more information on naturally occurring preventive sanctions.

Prevention policy is also not immune from political and economic considerations. Western governments are aware that drug export can be a source of revenue for some Third World countries as is the production and distribution of alcohol in the West. The threat to an important source of income tends to create a less than favourable climate for radical political reform. In the U.K. a 'Think Tank' report of the central policy review staff advocated that tax on alcohol be linked to the RPI, that there should be licensing and advertising restrictions, that there should be a re-examination of the drink driving laws and that a new advisory council on alcohol policy should be established. The original report was left unpublished by the U.K. Government and none of the proposals implemented. Instead the Government view was expressed in the more innocuous DHSS document 'Drinking Sensibly' (1981). Thorley (1982) says of this that it advocates policies which side-step major statutory opportunities for prevention and health. He summarises the report by suggesting that 'drinking sensibly means politicking safely'. The central utilitarian assertion that the greatest happiness of the greatest number is the function of morals and legislation seems to have been a pervasive influence. When faced with the possibility of reduced tax revenue, increased unemployment and undoubted loss of popular support on the one hand and substantially reducing the level of alcohol related harm on the other the former takes precedence. A critique of this policy position (British Journal of Addiction Editorial 1982) suggests that health considerations are an 'optional extra'.

In the context of the wider political and social reality and with many questions remaining unresolved the prevention of drug and alcohol misuse is often the subject of controversy and ill informed debate. In the light of increasing problems produced by excessive use of alcohol and drugs a comprehensive and informed prevention policy remains a priority. Perhaps most important is an appreciation that ultimately it is the individual user who must respond to the prevention method. Like the move out of addiction becoming a user is not a single isolated event but a process which begins before the first use of alcohol or drugs. Edwards and Busch (1981) call for a clear understanding of the phasing and developmental nature of this process. When more is known about individual pathways into psycho-active substance misuse then we will be in a better position to divert people from these pathways.

REFERENCES

Ashton M 1981 Theory and practice in the British system. Druglink 16: 1–5
Bradshaw J 1983 Drug misuse in Ireland, 1982/83. The Medical Social Research Board, Dublin
Budd J, Gray P, McRon R 1983 The Tyne Tees alcohol education campaign: an evaluation. Health Education Council, London
Caetano P, Suzman R M, Rosen D H, Vorhees-Rosen D J 1983 The Shetland Islands: longitudinal changes in alcohol consumption in a changing environment. British Journal of Addiction 78: 21–36

Cartwright A K J, Shaw S J, Spratley T A 1975 Designing a comprehensive response to problems of alcohol abuse. Report to the DHSS by the Maudsley Alcohol Project

Cartwright A K J, Shaw S J, Spratley T A 1977 The validity of per capita alcohol consumption as an indicator of the prevalence of alcohol related problems. In: Madden J S, Walker R, Kenyon W H (eds) Alcoholism and drug dependence, Plenum Press, New York

Clayson C 1977 The role of licensing law in limiting the misuse of alcohol. In: Edwards G, Grant M (eds) Alcoholism: new knowledge and responses. Croom Helm, London, Ch 4

Colon I, Cutter H S G, Jones W C 1982 Prediction of alcoholism from alcohol availability, alcohol consumption and demographic data. Journal of Studies on Alcohol 43: 1199–1213

Cust G 1980 Health education about alcohol in the Tyne Tees area. In: Madden J S, Walker R, Kenyon W H (eds) Aspects of alcohol and drug dependence. Pitman, Melbourne

Delint J 1977 Alcohol control policy as a strategy of prevention. A critical examination of the evidence. In: Madden J S, Walker R, Kenyon W H (eds) Alcoholism and drug dependence, Plenum Press, New York

DHSS 1979 The pattern and range of services for problem drinkers. Report by the Advisory Committee on Alcoholism. HMSO, London

DHSS 1981 Drinking sensibly: a discussion document prepared by the Health Departments of Great Britain and Northern Ireland. HMSO, London

Dorn N 1981 Social analyses of drugs in health education and the media. In: Edwards G, Busch C (eds) Drug problems in Britain: a review of ten years. Academic Press, London, Ch 10

Duffy J C 1977 Estimating the proportion of heavy drinkers in the Ledermann curve. A. E. C. London

Duffy M 1980 Advertising taxation and the demand for beer, spirits and wine in the UK 1963/1978. Occasional Paper No 8009, Department of Management Science, University of Manchester, Institute of Science and Technology

Editorial 1980 Alcohol and advertising. Lancet ii: 1175

Editorial 1982 British Journal of Addiction 77: 1–2

Edwards G, Busch C 1981 The partnership between research and policy. In: Edwards G, Busch C (eds) Drug problems in Britain: a review of ten years. Academic Press, London, Ch 11

Edwards G, Chandler J, Hensman C 1972 Drinking in a London suburb 1: correlates of normal drinking. Quarterly Journal of Studies on Alcohol 6: 69–93

Hore B D 1980 Epidemiology, an overview. In: Madden J S, Walker R, Kenyon W H (eds) Aspects of alcohol and drug dependence. Pitman, Melbourne

Keller M, Gurioli C 1976 Statistics on consumption of alcohol and on alcoholism. Rutgers Centre of Alcohol Studies

Kendell R E 1979 Alcoholism: a medical or political problem? British Medical Journal. 1 367–371

Kendell R E, De Roumanie M, Ritson E B 1983 Influence of an increase in excise duty on alcohol consumption and its adverse effects. British Medical Journal 287: 809–811

Kinder W M, Pape L E, Walfish S 1980 Drug and alcohol education programmes: a review of outcome studies. International Journal of Addiction 15: 1035–1054

Kreitman N 1977 Three themes in the epidemiology of alcoholism. In: Edwards G, Grant M (eds) Alcoholism: new knowledge and responses. Croom Helm, London, Ch 1

Ledermann S 1956 Alcool, alcoolism. Presses Universitaires de France, Paris

Levy D, Sheflin N 1983 New evidence on controlling alcohol use through price. Journal of Studies on Alcohol 44: 929–933

McConville B 1983 Women under the influence: alcohol and its impact. Virago Press, London

McGuinness A J 1980 An econometric analyses of retail demand for alcoholic beverages in the UK 1956–1975. Journal of Industrial Economics 29: 85–109

McIntosh I D, Chir B 1981 Population consumption of alcohol and proportion drinking. British Journal of Addiction 76: 267–279

McKechnie R 1982 Prevention and drinking related problems. New Directions in the Study of Alcohol 3: 28–49

Madden J S 1979 A guide to alcohol and drug dependence. Wright, Bristol

Maynard A, Kennan P 1981 The economics of alcohol abuse. British Journal of Addiction 76: 339–345

Newton D 1984 Personal communication

Office of Population Consensi and Surveys 1980 General Household Survey 1978. Series GHS no 8, HMSO, London

Ogborne A C, Smart R G 1980 Will restrictions on alcohol advertising reduce alcohol consumption? British Journal of Addiction 75: 293–296

Ornstein S I 1980 Control of alcohol consumption through price increases. Journal of Studies on Alcohol 41: 807–818

Osterberg E 1979 Recorded consumption of alcohol in Finland 1950–75. Social Research Institute of Alcohol Studies. Helsinki

Paton A, Potter J F, Saunders J B 1982 A.B.C. of alcohol. Leagrave Press Ltd, Luton

Plant M A 1980 Drug taking and prevention: the implications of research for social policy. British Journal of Addiction 75: 245–254

Plant M A, Pirie F, Kreitman N 1979 Evaluation of the Scottish Health Education Unit 1976 campaign on alcoholism. Social Psychiatry 14: 11–24

Popham R E, Schmidt W, Delint L 1975 The prevention of alcoholism: epidemiological studies of the effects of Government control measures. British Journal of Addiction 70: 125–144

Prochaska J O, Di Clemente C C 1982 Transtheoretical therapy toward a more integrated model of change. Psychotherapy: Theory, Research and Practice 19: 276–288

Prochaska J O, Di Clemente C C 1983 Stages and processes of self-change of smoking: toward an integrated model of change. Journal of Consulting and Clinical Psychology 51: 390–395

Report of the Advisory Council on the Misuse of Drugs 1982 Treatment and rehabilitation HMSO, London

Report of the Departmental Committee on Liquor Licensing (Erroll Committee) 1972 HMSO, London

Report of the Departmental Committee on Morphine and Heroin Addiction (Rolleston Committee) 1926 HMSO, London

Report of the Departmental Committee on Scottish Licensing Law (Clayson Committee) 1973 HMSO, Edinburgh

Report of the Interdepartmental Committee on Drug Addiction (Brain Committee) 1965 HMSO, London

Report of the Royal Commission on the NHS 1979 HMSO, London

Rix J B, Rix E L 1983 Alcohol problems: a guide for nurses and other health professionals. Wright, Bristol

Roberts K 1983 Drinking: a sociology of leisure perspective. New Directions in the Study of Alcohol 6: 26–34

Royal College of Psychiatrists 1979 Report of a Special Committee on Alcohol and Alcoholism. Tavistock, London

Schaps E, Dibartolo R, Moskowitz J, Churgin S A 1981 Review of a 127 drug abuse prevention programme evaluations. Journal of Drug Issues 9: 17–43

190    *Alcoholism and drug addiction*

Schlegal R P, Norris J E 1980 Effects of attitude change on behaviour for highly involving issues: the case of marijuana smoking. Journal of Addictive Behaviours 5: 113–124

Senay E C 1983 Substance abuse disorders in clinical practice. Wright, Bristol

Shaw S 1982 What is problem drinking? In: Plant M A (ed) Drinking and problem drinking. Junction Books, London, Ch 1

Singh G 1979 Comment on the single distribution theory of alcohol consumption. Journal of Studies on Alcohol 40: 522–524

Skog O 1980 The single distribution theory of alcohol consumption: A rejoiner to Singh and a reply. Journal of Studies on Alcohol 41: 373–375

Smart R G 1977 The relationship of availability of alcoholic beverages to per capita consumption and alcoholism rates. Journal of Studies on Alcohol 38: 891–896

Smart R G, Cutler R E 1980 The alcohol advertising ban in British Columbia: problems and effects on beverage consumption. British Journal of Addiction 75: 293–296

Smart G S, Goodstadt M S 1977 Effects of reducing the legal alcohol-purchasing age on drinking and drinking problems. Journal of Studies on Alcohol 38: 1313–1323

Smith R 1982 Alcohol and alcoholism. Leagrave Press, London

Spellman W E, Jorgenson M R 1983 Liquor control and consumption. Journal of Studies on Alcohol 44: 194–197

Staulcup H, Kenward K, Frigo D 1979 A review of federal primary alcoholism efforts. Journal of Studies on Alcohol 40: 943–968

Stimson G V, Oppenheimer A 1982 Heroin addiction: treatment and control in Britain. Tavistock, London

Stuart R B 1974 Teaching facts about drugs: Pushing or preventing? Journal of Educational Psychology 66: 189–201

Sunday Times MORI poll on alcohol 1980

Taylor D 1981 Alcohol: reducing the harm. White Crescent Press, Luton

Thorley A 1982 Drinking sensibly means politicking safely. New Directions in the Study of Alcohol 3:5–14

Tomes B K 1977 Effectiveness and efficacy in health education. A review of theory and practice. Scottish Health Education Unit

Treml V G 1975 Production and consumption of alcoholic beverages in the USSR: A statistical study. Journal of Studies on Alcohol 36: 285–320

Trethowan W H 1977 Alcoholism: the possibility for prevention. Health Education Journal 36: 95–99

Weisheit R A 1983 The social contexts of alcohol and drug education: implication of programme evaluation. Journal of Alcohol and Drug Education 29: 72–81

Whitehead P C 1975 Effects of liberalising alcohol control measures. Addictive Behaviours: An International Journal 1: 3

Whitehead T P, Clarke C A, Whitfield A G W 1978 Biochemical and haematological markers of alcohol intake. Lancet i: 978–981

Wilson P 1980 Survey on drinking in England and Wales. HMSO, London

Yates F 1983 Institution: the cultural dimension in alcohol use. New directions in the study of alcohol 6: 35–52

Yates S, Hebblethwaite D 1983 A review of the problem prevention approach to drinking problems. British Journal of Addiction 78: 355–364

**Appendix 6.1** Annual per capita alcohol consumption in England

| Year | Spirits (litres of pure alcohol) | Beer (litres) | Wine (litres) |
|------|------|------|------|
| 1962 | 0.79 | 87.8 | 1.86 |
| 1963 | 0.84 | 87.5 | 2.07 |
| 1964 | 0.90 | 91.1 | 2.35 |
| 1965 | 0.84 | 91.2 | 2.19 |
| 1966 | 0.84 | 92.2 | 2.35 |
| 1967 | 0.84 | 93.8 | 2.64 |
| 1968 | 0.87 | 94.8 | 2.90 |
| 1969 | 0.82 | 98.4 | 2.76 |
| 1970 | 0.94 | 101.6 | 2.89 |
| 1971 | 0.99 | 105.4 | 3.46 |
| 1972 | 1.11 | 107.5 | 4.06 |
| 1973 | 1.40 | 112.1 | 5.18 |
| 1974 | 1.54 | 114.4 | 5.33 |
| 1975 | 1.47 | 117.6 | 5.21 |
| 1976 | 1.66 | 118.9 | 5.82 |
| 1977 | 1.42 | 118.0 | 5.41 |
| 1978 | 1.72 | 121.3 | 6.48 |
| 1979 | 1.89 | 122.1 | 7.09 |
| 1980 | 1.78 | 117.1 | 7.19 |
| 1981 | 1.69 | 111.5 | 7.75 |
| 1982 | 1.59 | 107.3 | 7.85 |

**Appendix 6.2**   Narcotic drug addicts notified to the Home Office during the year

| Year | 1973 | 1974 | 1975 | 1976 | 1977 | 1978 | 1979 | 1980 | 1981 | 1982 | 1983 |
|---|---|---|---|---|---|---|---|---|---|---|---|
| New addicts | 807 | 870 | 922 | 984 | 1109 | 1347 | 1597 | 1600 | 2248 | 2793 | 4186 |
| Former addicts | 599 | 566 | 536 | 541 | 622 | 753 | 788 | 841 | 1063 | 1325 | 1678 |
| Total | 1406 | 1436 | 1458 | 1525 | 1731 | 2100 | 2385 | 2441 | 3311 | 4118 | 5864 |

**Appendix 6.3**   Annual number of seizures of some controlled drugs in the U.K.

| Year | 1973 | 1974 | 1975 | 1976 | 1977 | 1978 | 1979 | 1980 | 1981 | 1982 | 1983 |
|---|---|---|---|---|---|---|---|---|---|---|---|
| Cocaine | 118 | 215 | 218 | 230 | 204 | 257 | 348 | 445 | 503 | 389 | 684 |
| Dipipanone | 110 | 150 | 192 | 158 | 241 | 283 | 344 | 259 | 370 | 428 | 292 |
| Heroin | 318 | 310 | 236 | 347 | 270 | 346 | 600 | 697 | 819 | 985 | 1946 |
| Methadone | 218 | 302 | 260 | 252 | 212 | 235 | 292 | 328 | 402 | 360 | 412 |
| L.S.D. | 857 | 601 | 626 | 434 | 202 | 289 | 216 | 268 | 384 | 464 | 518 |
| Cannabis | 2840 | 3893 | 3835 | 3912 | 3238 | 3986 | 5564 | 8830 | 8500 | 8775 | 8929 |
| Cannabis (resin) | 7094 | 5124 | 4969 | 6108 | 8080 | 8247 | 8826 | 6964 | 8911 | 10679 | 13976 |
| Amphetamines | 1419 | 857 | 915 | 1255 | 960 | 586 | 632 | 666 | 1076 | 1645 | 2329 |
| All controlled drugs | 12196 | 10817 | 10648 | 11800 | 13006 | 13454 | 16056 | 17617 | 19428 | 21636 | 26216 |

# Index

Acetaldehyde, alcohol metabolism and, 41–42, 45
Adulterants, see Injection, complications
Advisory Council on Misuse of Drugs, 173
Report (1982), 129, 143, 167, 170
Aetiology of misuse, 20–25
and the family, 23–24, 105
and genetics, 22
and learning, 22–23
and peers, 24, 105
and personality, 21–22
and sociocultural influences, 24–25
see also Prevention; Social theories of misuse
Affective states, 78–84
see also Anxiety; Depression; Mania
Age
clinic attenders, 107
and favourable treatment outcome, 135–137
legal drinking, 176
AIDS (Acquired Immune Deficiency Syndrome), 35
Alcohol (ethyl), 41–51
absorption and metabolism 41–43
acceptability, 5–6, 24–25
congeners, 35
consumption, 163–166
and advertising, 185
as prevalence indicator, 4–5
safe levels, 46
effects, 43
historical attitudes, 2–4, 102–104
medical complications, 45–51
pathoplasticity, 32
and personality, 7–8

pharmacokinetics, 41–43
and psychiatric disorders, 44–45, 75–76, 78–86, 88–89, 91–92, 92–94, 95–96
tolerance, 17, 43
withdrawal and management, 17, 44–45
see also Prevention; Social consequences of misuse; Treatment
Alcohol (methyl), 51
absorption and metabolism, 51
medical complications, 51
Alcohol dependence syndrome, 4–5, 7–8
core elements, 16–19
criticisms 18–19
longitudinal studies, 123–125
treatment methods, see Treatment
Alcoholics Anonymous (AA), 3–4, 134, 142, 143, 144–145
Alcoholism 7, 16, 18–19
disease model, 4–5
historical perspectives, 2–5
and temperance movements, 3–4
Amnesia, see Dysmnestic states
Amphetamines, 10, 36–38, 40
drugs similar to, 37
effects, 37
medical complications, 39–40
medical uses, 36
mode of action, 37
penalties for possession, 172
and psychiatric disorders, 37, 83, 89
tolerance, 37
withdrawal and management, 12, 38
Angel dust, see Phencyclidine
Antidepressants, 54

193

International Classification of Disease
(ICD-9), 16, 74
International Narcotics Control Board,
171
Intoxication
pathological drug, 77
and psychiatric assessment, 76–77
social consequences, *see* Social
consequences of misuse
*see also* Delirium
Irritants, *see* Injection, complications

Legislation
in preventative strategy, 170–176
Dangerous Drugs Act (1920, 1967),
172
historical, 102–104
Medicines Act (1968), 173
Mental Health Act (1983), 77
Misuse of Drugs Act (1971),
172–173
Liver
and alcohol, 41–42, 46–47
and barbiturates, 53
and codeine, 61
disease, psychiatric study of patients
with, 75
*see also* Hepatitis
Lothian Study, 177
LSD (Lysergic acid diethylamide), 10,
66–67
absorption and metabolism, 66
effects, 66–67
half-life, 67
and psychiatric disorders, 83, 89–90
*see also* Hallucinogenics

Mania, 82–83
Marijuana, *see* Cannabis
Meprobamate, *see* Sedatives and
hypnotics
Mescaline, *see* Hallucinogenics
Meta-analysis, 126–127
Methadone (Physeptone)
absorption and metabolism, 32, 62
half-life, 62
maintenance, 151
use in heroin withdrawal, 64, 122,
141
withdrawal, 64
*see also* Heroin; Opioids
Methaqualone, *see* Sedatives and
hypnotics
Methylphenidate (Ritalin), 10, 37

Misuse
causal influences, *see* Aetiology of
misuse
changing levels of, 1
consequences, *see* Social
consequences of misuse
definitions, 6–7
future study needs, 25–26
historical perspectives, 2–5
and physical harm, 30–69
and psychiatric disorders, 73–97
symptomatic, 75
*see also* specific substances; Social
theories of misuse
Misuse of Drugs Act, *see* Legislation
Models
of alcoholism, disease, 4–5
of drug use, 13–16
of change, transtheoretical, 117, 181
integration, 105
Morbid jealousy, 91
Mortality
among alcohol users, 124
among heroin users, 120, 121
Musculoskeletal disorders and alcohol,
48–49

Naloxone, *see* Opioid antagonists
Narcotics Anonymous, 134
Nervous system, disorders
and alcohol, 49, 93, 94, 95–96
and amphetamines, 94
and benzodiazepines, 94
and cannabis, 94
Neuroadaption, 11–13
*see also* Tolerance; Withdrawal
Nicotine, *see* Smoking
Nutrition, disorders
and alcohol, 95–96
and stimulants, 40
*see also* Vitamins

Opioid antagonists, 141
cyclazocine, 141–142
naloxone, 12, 60, 62, 63, 64, 142
naltrexone, 81, 142
Opioids, 9, 60–66
absorption and metabolism, 61–62
dipipanone (Diconal), 9, 34
effects, 63
equivalents, 61
heroin, *see* Heroin
medical complications, 65–66
medical uses, 60
methadone, *see* Methadone
mode of action, 62–63